L A T A

Blaine
Lenville
Middle Potlatch
Kendrick
Cameron
Southwick
Leland
Juliaetta
Genesee

Thorn Cr.

Dworshak
Reservoir

Clearwater River

Catholic Cr.

Myrtle
Cottonwood Cr.
Summit
Gifford
Jacks Cr.
Melrose
Orofino
Peck

Matwai Cr.

Spalding

LEWISTON

Clarkston

Lapwai
Sweetwater
Lapwai Cr.
Webb
Culdesac

N E Z   P E R C E

Asotin

Slickpoo
Reubens
Mohler

Nezperce

I N D I A N

N E Z   P E R C E   R E S E R V A T I O N

Snake River

Waha

W I S
Lawyer Cr.

Ferdinand

Grand Ronde River

WASH
= = = = =
ORE

Westlake

Waterville
Grave Cr.

Cottonwood

Fenn
Grangeville

Book Cr.

A H O

Imnaha River

Divide Cr.

Whitebird Cr.

Whitebird

Getta Cr.
White Bird Cr.
Rine Cr.
Canfield

Slate Cr.

shears

SALMON RIVER SAGA

Kenneth B. Platt
Born October 16, 1907

SALMON RIVER SAGA

Kenneth B. Platt

YE GALLEON PRESS

FAIRFIELD, WASHINGTON

1978

Library of Congress Cataloging in Publication Data

Platt, Kenneth B
  Salmon River saga.

  Includes index.
  1. Salmon Valley, Idaho—History—Addresses, essays, lectures. I. Title.
F752.S35P56   979.6'82   78-16159
ISBN 0-87770-207-1

SALMON RIVER SAGA

MY PRIVILEGE, TO INTRODUCE

Often when someone is presenting a speaker he will begin by saying: "Ladies and gentlemen, it is my privilege to introduce...," then say something about the speaker and his message. Out of more than 40 years' close acquaintance with Kenneth B. Platt, I am pleased to have the privilege now of introducing him and his book, *Salmon River Saga*.

A son of the wild and isolated area he writes about, Platt has undertaken to preserve the image he remembers from pioneer days. The land remains unchanged, but its erstwhile settlers are gone, the land again vacant. Though a labor of love, *Salmon River Saga* is intended mostly as a contribution to the history of Idaho's pioneer years. And though small in size, the recalled scene is the epitome of the final surge of Western settlement on many fronts.

Besides his own recollections, the author combines widely diverse contributory sources to produce the tapestry of scenes, events, people, social customs, action codes, living conditions and community life that comprised the pioneer picture. Three letters from homesteading ranch wives reveal the harsh facts behind the romantic haze that colors many of today's notions of frontier life. A ranch area teacher's autobiography presents many of the personalities that peopled the author's stage. Short stories and anecdotes provide further characters and action for the historic drama.

In a writing career reaching back to high school days at Genesee, Idaho, Platt has produced many popular and scientific articles on western range subjects, scores of professional reports, and three small volumes of published poetry. Agricultural science degrees from the University of Idaho (1930) and the University of Minnesota (1931) led him into a four-year stint of technical editing and radio script writing for the Idaho Extension Service from 1932 to 1935. His bent for writing found frequent employment in the 20 years he spent with the U.S. Bureau of Land Management before transferring to the State Department's foreign aid program in 1959. Retired after ten years in Iran and South Korea, where editing and writing activities were a major duty, he has focused since 1972 on collecting editing and writing local pioneer history for the Latah County Museum Society at Moscow, Idaho. *Salmon River Saga* was written as time permitted among these ongoing activities.

The book is in four parts, each distinctive in interest. Since the author has written his own introduction to each part, suffice it to say here that Part I is his own recollections; Part II is a documentary of the land settlement tide that swept over, then receded from, the story area; Part III combines second party experiences and fictionalized enlargement of actual persons and events; while Part IV is a collection of unrelated humorous anecdotes. The total work thus presents many different

5

insights and different writing styles, attaining its unity of interest in the author's central aim of painting the pioneer picture as it really was.

Although documentary in purpose, Part II holds special interest for its commentary on the human and economic forces that brought people to the lower Salmon River country, then took them away, to leave a "white space" on the map. The "why-what-who" of such spaces has been one of the impelling forces for adventure and exploration that have mapped the world, Platt believes. For him the now-vacant area of his boyhood home is such a white space, crying even more for explanation than if it never had been peopled. The fact that neither heroes nor villains, but only impersonal forces, are found responsible, somehow adds to the sense of loss felt in the closing stanza of "Requiem For An Empty Land," which introduces this section:

> "All silent now, the mighty canyons sleep,
> Uncomprehending of their gloried hour;
> And only memory returns to weep
> For shadows fleeting as a summer shower."

What *Salmon River Saga* lacks in geographic scope it more than makes up in reality and intimacy of subject and treatment. And though its area is small, the work well makes the point that the everyday lives of people of whatever time and place are the salt of history, without which the larger portion lacks savor.

"Forgotten Songs And Untold Tales" deals with scenes and experiences that can never be duplicated. For this very reason the author felt obliged to record them. He has done so in vivid language, aided by a liberal sprinkling of pen sketches by artist Duane Shears, himself sprung from Salmon River pioneer roots. Excellent photos of historic Salmon River scenes and citizens further authenticate the account.

Salmon River Saga is an entertaining new contribution to Idaho settlement history, that should find interested readers wherever Western frontier lore is enjoyed.

Dr. Clifford M. Drury
Pasadena, Calif.
November 25, 1977

SALMON RIVER SAGA

PREFACE

From the earliest western pioneer times Idaho was a name, a land, to be conjured with. Athwart the old Oregon emigrant trail, its canyon-cut and boulder-strewn Snake River Plains added new dimensions of hardship to those already endured by weary travelers. The few and impoverished "Snake" Indians along this part of the route, their name bespeaking their often miserable fare as well as the tortuous river course, reflected all too well the scarce food resources to be found there. The 250 thirsty desert miles between Fort Hall and Fort Boise usually were encountered by the toiling emigrants during the hottest, driest part of the year. Without doubt they were among the worst in the whole span from Council Bluffs to Oregon's Willamette Valley.

When Henry Harmon Spalding located his civilizing mission to the Nez Perce Indians on Lapwai Creek, a Clearwater River tributary, in 1836, the name Idaho was not yet born. But the station was set in the western lee of the Bitterroot Mountains, from which the name was to come. "E-da-ho," Spalding learned from his charges, meant "Behold the sun walking down the mountains." From Clark's Fork of the Columbia River, near the Canadian border, to the Snake River Plains on the south, only one east-west Indian trail crossed this massive barrier. Even this trail, the Lolo, was little more than a gleam in the eye, as Lewis and Clark had found while starving their westbound way along it in 1804. Nearly 150 years were to lapse from then until a modern highway would traverse this route, linking Idaho and Montana through the Lolo Pass.

The discovery of gold on west-flowing Orofino Creek some 75 miles northeast of Spalding's mission, by Captain Elias Pierce in 1861, brought a rush of treasure seekers, but not even this wave topped the Bitterroot barrier. Instead, the prospectors came around its northern and southern ends, and from British Columbia, Oregon and California, eddying eastward up the Clearwater and Salmon River drainages in their search for other gold strikes. Gold was there, aplenty, but where California's '49-ers had found theirs in relatively open country, Idaho miners found inaccessability and remoteness often their worst enemies. Central Idaho, where the treasure mostly lay, even yet is classified largely as wilderness, with only few and rugged roads penetrating the hinterlands.

Its continuing primeval character is conveyed in some degree by the following poem describing the upper reaches of the Salmon River.

KENNETH B. PLATT

River Of No Return*

Born of blue lakes that gem the rugged wild,
Where towering sawtooths notch the arching sky
In craggy grandeur, leaping range on range
To fling their circling strides across the miles,
And crown a State in mighty coronet:

Nourished by crystal springs and rivulets
Which know their pure existence from the snows
That winter heaps on myriad timbered hills,
Where warming suns, in season, send their bright
Commanding fingers to search out and bid
The icy stores of nature on their way
Again to seek the seas from which they sprang;

Gathering racing waters where they foam
From hidden canyons, ground through granite walls
By unknown centuries of roaring floods;
Gathering other rivers in your sweep —
Each in his own realm king, but swallowed up
By mightier than he — and surging on
In ever swelling current down the haunts
Laid for your course when still the world was young,
And even yet forbidden unto man;

River Of No Return, how well your name
Bespeaks the fastnesses inviolate
Through which your churning waters ever plunge.

As the gold fever began to wane, a new bonanza was found — the rich Palouse
Country prairies along the Idaho-Washington border from Lewiston to Spokane. The

*Name popularly given Idaho's Salmon River in its course across the wilderness area of central Idaho.

(Reprinted from *Underneath The Bough*, collected poems of Kenneth B. Platt, Meadowlark Press, Council, Idaho, 1976)

8

1870s and early 1880s saw nearly all tillable land in this area homesteaded. A similar area between the Salmon and Clearwater Rivers, within the original boundaries of the Nez Perce Indian Reservation, posed a continuing hope for other thousands of homestead seekers into the 1890s. When these Reservation lands were opened for settlement in 1895, the final claiming of the farmable prairie lands of northern Idaho quickly followed.

Not until after all such lands were gone did prospective settlers turn serious attention to less desirable lands. So it was that the grazing lands lying along and bordering the Salmon River canyon downstream from Whitebird became a pioneering area only after 1895. This area is the scene of my story.

From Riggins, where it turns north on emerging from its remote "River Of No Return" wilderness beginnings, to Whitebird, where it swings westward again, the Salmon River is familiar to travelers over Idaho's main north-south highway (U.S. 95) through a 30-mile stretch of relatively open country with numerous farms and ranches visible. Below this point the river disappears into a towering chasm that knows few breaks along the 60-mile remainder that brings it to rendezvous with the Snake River at the mouth of Hell's Canyon.

No through road follows the river below this point, and only one road crosses it in that reach. A hundred years ago its bars and side gulches felt the brief frenzy of the gold seekers; a few of their scars still remain. Sixty years ago its canyon slopes teemed with homesteaders seeking one last corner of the American West in which to realize the dream of an independent land holding. But the rough canyon lands, essentially untillable, would not support that dream. Within a decade of their coming, almost all the eager throng were gone. Unable to make a living there, they sold their grass or their lands to the few established stockmen who had preceded them, and who continued on after the tide of settlement had ebbed.

Today this area is virtually deserted. The fingers of one hand could tally nearly every yearlong home still remaining. The rough shacks that once housed the homesteaders have vanished almost without a trace. What few boards or logs remain are being fast consumed by the campfires of recreationists adventuring in 4-wheel-drive vehicles over recent access roads. Only a few of the former inhabitants remain who remember the land as it was in its pioneer heyday, and only they can preserve that era for future interest. The following account opens one small window upon that period and its people.

In offering this account, the author believes that most Americans are innately curious about what was gone before them in the history of whatever part of our country they chance to occupy. Especially, we want to know about the people who have preceded us in ownership and use of a house, a ranch, a town, an area:

Who made the welkin ring, and why,
Before the great centripetal "I"?

The eye witness account which makes up Part I, "Forgotten Songs and Untold Tales," was written several years ago. Part II, "Shadows On The Land," is a recent marshalling of the names and locations of all settlers of the area, as shown in the files of the General Land Office, U.S. Department of the Interior, which officially recorded all homestead claims. Part III, "Legends That Linger," combines fact and supposition, and recollections from other sources, to preserve related information of interest for its own sake, if not as history. Part IV, "Random Tales," is a collection of unrelated anecdotal pieces too small for separate publication, but supplying a lighter touch to an otherwise somber background.

The whole is offered here both as a legitimate contribution to history, and as what I hope most readers will find interesting and entertaining glimpses of people, events, and a way of life that cannot be relived.

The sketch illustrations gracing this volume are from the gifted pen of Duane Shears, a grandson of two of the pioneers appearing in Part I. Born and raised in the Craigmont area, he grew up in close touch with many of the characters, places and history of the story locale. His mother, Edna Weller Shears, still lives at Craigmont with his father, Carl Shears, whose family pioneered nearby. This dual pioneer heritage is reflected in the authenticity of line and setting with which he treats each subject.

The author hereby expresses his deep gratitude both for the livening effect of this artistry and for the generosity of the artist, who has donated his work purely for love of the story.

Mr. Shears now lives at Eugene, Ore., where he teaches high school biology.

Kenneth B. Platt
Moscow, Idaho
September, 1977

SALMON RIVER SAGA

TABLE OF CONTENTS

Part I   FORGOTTEN SONGS AND UNTOLD TALES   13

John A. Platt — Pioneer Cattleman   16
Emma Batdorf Platt — Pioneer Ranch Wife   18
The Deer Creek Irrigation System   19
Kootsie, The Intrepid   25
High Water on the Salmon   31
The Big House   34
Old Songs, and New Love   42
Of Horses and Riders   49
Coyotes, Mad and Sane   60
Up and Down Deer Creek   63
Up and Down the River   71
Going to the Mountain   79
Of Kings and Giants   88
The World at Ten   94

Part II   SHADOWS ON THE LAND   103

Requiem for an Empty Land   105
Where They Settled   107
Salmon River Settlers' Roster   119

Part III   LEGENDS THAT LINGER   139

"The Good Old Days"   139
Home, Sweet Home   140
Hands Across the Canyons   142
A Letter From Jennie   145
A Salmon River Homestead Teacher   160
Security No; Adventure, Yes!   162
Enter, Dashing Cowboys!   165
Homesteader Sociability   167
Blossom Time   168
Ranch Wife Days   170
First-child Joys and Problems   175
Salmon River Medicare   176
K Bar Ranch Life   177
"Just Mention My Name"   179
A Sojourn in the "City"   180
Real Life Teaching   181

Bigger School, Fringe Benefits 183
A Reluctant Goodby 186
Cold Nerve, Or Hot Lead? 190
A Case for the Inspector 206

Part IV RANDOM TALES 213
White Man with a Red Face 214
The Preacher and the Bear 215
Incident at Black Bear Inn 218
Charley and the Swede 223

I

FORGOTTEN SONGS AND UNTOLD TALES[1]

I hardly know how to begin this. The idea came to me with an early awakening when sleep would not return. Perhaps it was because the idea persisted that the sleep fled. At any rate, here I sit at 3:15 a.m. impelled to write at least the beginnings of a record of things past that only I can rescue from oblivion. Whether these things are worthy of the record, others must judge. But before such a judgment can be made the record must be set down. So, here am I, writing.

The idea which has gotten me out of bed at this hour is not new. It is simply that I hold in my mind memories of places, experiences and events that others can never know unless I take time to tell them. With us yet are my parents, past 90 but still carrying forward the memories of their vanished years which have so colored my own life. In the other direction I see my children, the youngest now 21 years of age and about to burst from college upon an unsuspecting world, who already have left behind them travels I never dreamed of at their age, who face even larger futures, and who in due time will arrive where I am now, wishing for some way to pass on to others their own accumulated memories out of fleeting time and changing place.

[1]As set down in 1967 while the author was serving as an agricultural economics advisor with the U.S. Agency For International Development, in South Korea.

13

Perhaps this idea has haunted all the generations of men since consciousness of purpose first dawned — the wish to be found significant by those who follow. We find it in Solomon's plaintive question:

> "Is there any thing whereof it may be said,
> See, this is new?
> It hath been already of old time,
> Which was before us.
> There is no remembrance of former things;
> Neither shall there be any remembrance of things that are to come
> With those that shall come after."

We find it less authoritatively but no less hauntingly phrased some 3,000 years later in the Whiffenpoof Song's lament for a graduating college generation: "Then we'll pass, and be forgotten like the rest."

But Solomon, even as the Whiffenpoof boys, undersold the staying power of the historic memory — whether written or traditional — abetted by man's unquenchable longing both to know what has gone before and to project himself into the consciousness of generations to come. Archeologists in our time have retrieved the past back to ages antedating Solomon much farther than he antedates us. It is a mistake to suppose that the fabric of our page in history, even to the trivia and the trite, will not be eagerly scanned in the distant future both for threads of continuity and for clues of things no longer known. And of those gleanings, by far the most prized will be the record of what once was common but now has become legend.

For so it is with men, that we value least those things which are in hand, and long most for those things which time and change have placed beyond recall.

Already much of what I have to tell has become legend. Though held in common with brothers, sisters and erstwhile companions who could tell much the same tale, it is of an era that never can be relived. Time has moved on to a new pattern of manners, of affairs, of occupations, and of living. The area of my recollection, once inhabited by hundreds, now is deserted. Though the places can be revisited, only faint traces now remain of the landmarks that once fixed their borders.

I speak of an area already made known by my father's book: *Whispers From Old Genesee And Echoes Of The Salmon River*. It is the Salmon River region of his account that holds my tale, for the most part. There I was born, on October 16, 1907, in a one-room log cabin that still stood in the summer of 1967. My recollections of the area are brief in span, for in the fall of 1917 my family moved from there to a ranch in the Genesee country. But the recollections are indelible. My brief visit last year, after 50 years of absence, confirmed their physical accuracy in almost every detail.

There stood the cabin of my birth, now weed-crowded and windowless, but still related to hill and trail as memory had painted. Past it on the east ran the waters of Deer Creek, still divided by the brushy, bouldered island across which we had gone from house to barn. To the south, beyond the Salmon River, towered Starveout Mountain, whose pyramid peak had speared the sun at noon on many a boyhood day. And there below Starveout flowed "The River" itself, swift and cold and powerful, coming from the vast Idaho wilderness to the east and hurrying on to its destiny in the even mightier Snake River below Hell's Canyon, deepest gorge on the North American continent.

"The River." To me and the generation of pioneers that spawned me and that now are bidding last farewells, those two words were a whole lexicon in themselves. The River always was just that, to those who lived by it. As a King in his time is King without need for a given name, so, The River. Its denizens commonly neglected the name Salmon, not out of dislike or disrespect, but because it was superfluous. When you were there you were "on The River." When you were anywhere else and heading home you were going "down to The River." In its 4,000-foot gorge, The River was absolute monarch, accepting the tribute of a thousand lesser streams rushing out of precipitous side canyons, and ruling in majesty.

And, as a King of England once could say, "I am England," so reference to The River bespoke not just the stream, but its domain as well.

And so, as my life began here, in this place begins my story. The title, *Fotgotten Songs And Untold Tales,* seems specially suited to this particular glimpse down one small corridor of the past.

Each element of the story has its own separate claim upon memory and interest. But I hope also to convey in their aggregate some broader reach that will engage a general audience and merit a more lasting appreciation than may be won by any or all as isolated episodes. To do this I shall bring to service some pioneer background which must be known to put The River and its people in credible perspective. Here will be snatches of songs which I doubt anyone but me any longer remembers. Some passages of purely personal memorabilia will be of interest to others only as part of the setting. You will meet more impressions of people than people themselves face to face, because often that is all I have to bring you. Many are only names I have heard, their owners barred from my boyhood sight by the interdiction of The River. They lived on the other side — a separate world to me.

My visible world, in fact, was rather literally limited to what I could see from our Deer Creek winter ranch, and from the few trails leading from it up or down river, or up the creek to our summer range at its source. It was a world tipped on edge, with its scattered inhabitants lodged in those sparse niches where The River and its tributaries,

15

with geologic ages at their disposal, had fashioned benches on the canyon walls large enough to hold a homesteader's cabin and garden patch, and maybe to permit some token of crop cultivation. Just how limited the crop land was you may judge from this: Our ranch, with 20-25 acres of alfalfa, had more hay than all the other lower Salmon River ranches put together. Tragedy lurked in that paucity of resource, but that story comes later. Suffice it here to say that the farthest radius of my Salmon River adventures was less than 25 miles, and even that reached only a quarter-pie wedge extending up Deer Creek and out onto the plateau lands of Craig Mountain.

Into this microcosm of recollection let me now introduce the men and women who brought it to life for that brief span between its maiden purity and its exploited abandonment. The time was the turn of the last Century. The lower Salmon River country was a last frontier. The people who came to it were as hardy a clan as any who took up the challenge of other frontiers before them. I will cite only two pedigrees in detail — those of my own father and mother — but they will be enough to typify the generation that settled The River.

John A. Platt—Pioneer Cattleman

My father was born in Iowa on April 5, 1877. His father, Edward T. Platt, was born in Wisconsin on November 1, 1852, of English immigrant parents. My grandfather Platt had a two-year Normal School education when he married my grandmother, Carrie Harris, at Mineral Point, Wisconsin, on November 6, 1875. He taught school for 2½ years near Lemars, Iowa, where my father was born. The pioneering period for that area was by no means closed then, even though most of the land was settled. The young couple went to Allentown, Dakota Territory, in 1877 to try their luck. It was not encouraging. I have heard my grandmother tell of stuffing twisted grass into a stove all night long to keep from freezing during a Dakota blizzard.

The richness of the Palouse Country soils out in Idaho Territory, and the comparative mildness of its climate, lured them to Genesee in 1881. They came via Southern Pacific emigrant train from Omaha to San Francisco, and by boat passage from there to Portland and up the Columbia and Snake rivers to the interior.

Genesee in 1881 still was a pioneer community in every sense. The town had been established just six years before. Roads were primitive. Houses were simple. Education was limited. Cultural touches were self-supplied. Money was scarce. Labor was hard. Much original prairie still was unbroken. The bounty of the land already in crop was so great, and markets so distant, that produce was almost unsaleable. The Nez Perce Indian War of 1877 still was fresh enough in memory to keep the stockade in use as a school.

The Nez Perce Indian Reservation boundary joined the Platt farm a bare mile south of Genesee. At that point the Reservation was a sea of mixed prairie grasses billowing away to the Clearwater River breaks, where the more drouth-resistant bunch grasses took over. The bunch grasses clothed the ridges and canyons of all the rough country along the Clearwater, Potlatch, Snake and Salmon River drainages, where they provided year-round feed for horses and cattle.

Much of this grass country still was untouched in those days. Stock raising offered opportunity for those hardy enough to take a few head to new ranges and live off the country while herds increased in size. The labor needed was small in relation to value of the enterprise, the expenses small, the grass virtually free. On the other hand, most of the valuable farmable land of the Genesee country already had been claimed before the Platt family arrived. These circumstances led my grandfather to send 18-year-old John Platt to the Salmon River country in the spring of 1895 to take up a range cattle venture. He located on the southeast side of the river, near its juncture with the Snake.

There were few there before him, and no settled stockmen. Some large outfits were operating cattle on the opposite side of the Salmon. A handful of venerable stragglers from the 1861-65 gold rush era still panned hopefully on the river sandbars, remembering the fabulous riches of Orofino Creek, Buffalo Hump and Florence, while eking a bare living by their daily toils. But their eyes already were dim, their dreams flickering to an end. The lingering golden ghost was finally done in by "sucker money" attempts to extract wealth from various well promoted but sterile gravel bars upriver from Deer Creek. Trestled flumes that brought water to the great hydraulic jet for one of these ventures passed near our ranch, and climbing on them provided one of the various hazardous pastimes of my early youth. This particular venture collapsed in 1912, and so far as I know it was the last of its kind in our area. Pop bought flume lumber from the departing miners and used it to build hay sheds at Deer Creek.

shears

A gleam in the pan puts a gleam in the eye."

17

KENNETH B. PLATT

In 1895 there were no homesteads on The River. A few aging miners lived in hillside dugouts, the nearest approach to houses. Food staples were flour, beans, lard, salt, coffee and sugar. Saddle horses were grazed in the open, the ones in use being hobbled or staked out to keep them within reach. There were no fences. No one, up to that time, had come expecting to stay.

My father and his contemporaries were the first permanent settlers. They built the first homes, established the first families. When he and my mother were married at Genesee on July 11, 1900, they had no house on Salmon River to go to. They lived in a dugout the first year, while he built a house of rough boards rafted from 25 miles upriver. Over the next 17 years they lived in similar rough shacks and log cabins along the river, and in the flanking mountains that provided summer range. Details of this period are told in the last half of this section.

Emma Batdorf Platt — Pioneer Ranch Wife

My mother was born Emma Caroline Batdorf at Lawrence, Kansas on February 2, 1878. In early May of 1889 my Grandfather Jesse Batdorf and Grandmother Mary Gaumer Batdorf loaded their family and possessions into two wagons and headed for Montana. Besides my mother there were her older sister, Jennie, two younger brothers, Charles and Sam, and a younger sister, Bertha. Long dusty months later they arrived at Beaver Creek in the Judith Basin, where Grandfather earned his living as a sawmill worker and carpenter until 1893. Extreme cold in the winter of 1892-93 convinced the family to head for a milder climate. The hardships of that season were recalled long after by Charles in a letter to a California-born nephew:

"---The last winter we were there it was extremely cold; somewhat below 50 degrees below zero, and at Judith Gap it was reported to be 65 below zero. We did not have a proper thermometer, but it was so cold that when we were out at night it felt as if a knife were cutting across our throats. Mr. LaFollett said it felt that way to him, too; and he was wearing a heavy beard. Our milk cows ran past our house, down the road, near milking time, so I jumped onto the saddle horse and went after them on the gallop. I went just about a quarter of a mile, and the late afternoon sun was shining, and I was wearing lined gloves, and had ear flaps on my cap. But by the time I got to the cows I felt my ears and fingers freezing, so I left them and started home as fast as the horse would carry me. When I got home my ears were frozen, and my fingers and thumbs were frozen stiff. I thawed my fingers out in cold water, slowly, but how they did hurt — all night, and for days they were very sore.

"Then Father had an attack of 'inflammatory rheumatism,' and almost died. For months the mill hands, two and two, came and stayed with him nights. He had to be turned in a sheet, too sore to be touched, and he was in such misery that he had to be turned often. Though he got the rheumatism in mid-winter, he did not get well enough to ride in a wagon until August . . . "

In August of 1893 the family again loaded their wagons and wheeled them to Boise, Idaho, by way of Yellowstone Park. Jennie had married Will Lewis at Beaver Creek, and stayed behind. Boise held the Batdorfs less than a year. In 1894 they trekked the long wagon route from there over the Blue Mountains of eastern Oregon to Pendleton, then on to Genesee. There the house party circuit that provided most of the community recreation brought together John Platt and Emma Batdorf in what was to become a life partnership.

One might suppose that the three 'removes' that had brought my mother from Kansas to Genesee would have satisfied the itchiest of feet, but not so. In the summer of 1897 the Batdorfs, and Jennie and Will Lewis who had joined them there, put teams to their wagons once more, and headed for California. They went past Harney Lake in the eastern Oregon high country so unforgettably pictured by Jackman and Long in *The Oregon Desert*. They traveled for weeks in sight of Mount Shasta. Hollister, south of San Fransisco, marked the end of this journey. There at last was climate mild enough to ease Grandpa Batdorf's rheumatic pains and induce him to settle more permanently. It was from there that Emma Batdorf returned to Genesee in the summer of 1900 to marry, this time traveling by river boat and train.

I have often wondered whether any Oregon Trail pioneer, or any other westward emigrant, traveled as far as she and her family did. The total of their four trips must have been not less than 3,000 miles. If prairie schooner months and miles be any index of pioneer qualification, then surely my mother arrived on Salmon River well qualified to take her place in that frontier environment.

A more direct index was the degree of self-reliance brought to the situation at hand. Spared the dangers of Indian conflicts, the Salmon River settlers nevertheless had their share of difficulties. Three of the seven children born into our family were delivered in ranch houses, with no help but that of neighbors. The first, a girl, died in infancy. Bringing the other six successfully through 15 years of unrelenting natural hazards and primitive living conditions was a demanding job. Where today's milk supplies come from contented cows in shiny milking parlors with background music, our first milk cow was an untamed range animal that had lost her calf. My mother was the milkmaid.

The Deer Creek Irrigation System

By the time I came on stage Pop and Muzzy, as we children called our parents, had moved from their original home at Skeleton Gulch on the southeast side of the river to the Deer Creek location, several miles upstream and on the opposite side. Uncle Will, Pop's younger brother, had taken over operations at the old location. By then or soon after, numerous other families had settled on that side. Among them the names that became familiar to me through family talk and occasional visits to our place include the McMahons, several Joneses, the Nash family; Boles, Aram, Brace, Jackson, Brown, Taylor and Van Pool. Bill McMahon was Pop's cousin, but my acquaintance with my cousins Jesse, Katherine and Willie McMahon was deferred by The River until both families later moved to Genesee for schooling purposes. Vivian Jones I saw briefly as Uncle Will's young wife during a short-lived marriage. Helen Brown came to our house for a school year as a teacher. Lena Jackson came as our hired girl for a few months. The others were only names in the background then, though some materialized as persons later on.

At Deer Creek, our quarters were first shared with my Aunt Laura, Pop's younger sister, her husband Wesley Dorchester, and cousins Leonard and Caroline. Soon afterward the Dorchesters moved to yet another frontier at Wetaskiwin, Alberta, where the Dorchester cousins still live.

The Deer Creek ranch was well located for a wintering place. It commanded several thousand acres of generally south-sloping and relatively "easy" country that favored winter grazing. More important, it included a large bench capable of being irrigated to raise alfalfa hay.

Increasing livestock numbers by now had put a heavy burden on the range, and winter areas had less and less carry-over feed each year. In earlier times occasional hard winter starvation losses had been considered part of the game. If very severe, you were "broke." If not so severe, you bought replacements or built up numbers again by natural increase. Now, however, the game was changing. The cattle had been improved with purebred beef bulls, and were too valuable to lose lightly. At the same time, risk of winter loss had been heightened by depletion of the old bunch grass stands. The country was becoming dangerously fed out.

When the alfalfa fields at Deer Creek were developed, their irrigation water came from the big ditch that supplied the up-river mining operation I have already mentioned. The water came out of Deer Creek about a mile above our place. It was carried on a gravity gradient around the ridge east of the creek to a point on the Salmon some two miles upstream from the mouth of the creek. The flow line crossed wide expanses of slide rock where ditching was impractical. Across these stretches the water was carried in wooden flumes supported by trestles. The flumes were two feet wide and two feet deep, built of 1-inch by 12-inch boards battened along the cracks, and with 2 by 4-inch framing to keep them from spreading. At full flow the system could carry more than 5,000 gallons of water per minute, or around 25 acre feet per day. A small fraction of this amount was enough to irrigate all our hay ground, and Pop bought water from the miners for this purpose.

When the mining company went out of business the fluming for their ditch line soon followed. The boards dried and cracked in winter when the water was cut off to prevent ice damage. Much repair work was required each spring, caulking cracks and replacing the worst boards. Although Pop had bought the abandoned line at small cost, its upkeep costs soon became prohibitive. At this point he built a new and smaller ditch line, starting nearer the ranch and on the opposite side of the creek.

For a small boy there were many fascinating aspects of the construction and operation of this irrigation system. Pop hired an engineer to stake out the flow line at proper gradient. Nevertheless, when dug to specifications the ditch would not carry water. By some small error of instrument reading or of calculation the water was being asked to run uphill at the point where it left the creek. To correct the error the ditch had to be dug deeper for some distance. When finished, a long stretch near the intake was much deeper than the top of my head, and for me it was an act of some daring to walk through it.

Determined not to be stuck with flume maintenance in the future, Pop in due time dug his ditch through solid rock where need be. This called for blasting where the rock was too hard to be dug with pick and crowbar. Nothing else in the line of firewords even approached witnessing the ditch blasting. Black powder was tried, but gave forth only with loud whooshes and great puffs of smoke, the rock remaining unmoved. Dynamite was required to get results.

After many hours of hand drilling inch-wide holes into the flinty stone, the dynamite shots were placed in these holes. Fuses were cut to suitable lengths. One end of each fuse was armed with a percussion cap, which then was poked into the dynamite 'set' several inches below the rock surface. Next, the holes were packed full of dirt. Now the shots were ready to set off.

All hands except the dynamite man retreated to a safe distance and took shelter under convenient rock ledges. Small fry were cautioned to keep heads down. Dogs were brought to heel. The dynamite man then lighted the fuses, longest first and shortest last, to give himself plenty of time to get away. Then he ran for cover with the rest of us, and all waited tensely for the shots to go off.

When the shots went, the hills seemed to rock, and echoes bounced from wall to wall of the surrounding canyons. Dogs yelped and howled at the painful onslaught of sound. Fragments of rock rained around. Dust from the blast area floated away as echoes died away in the distance. The shots were counted as they went off to make sure that all had fired, for fuses sometimes burned so slowly as to seem to have gone out. Art Keane, our dynamite man converted from cow hand, was cautiously respectful of the dangers of his work. Stories of men killed by late dynamite explosions where sets were inspected too soon were vividly in mind. When the count was complete a shout went up, and all trooped to see the results of the shots. With due caution and accompanying good fortune, this work was completed without mishap.

Exciting as was the blasting work, it was not in the same league with one other feature of the new irrigation line. This was a cable-slung pipeline across Deer Creek. To avoid the rock slide areas that had forced the miners to flume their water long stretches, Pop brought his ditch down the opposite side of the creek. This required putting the water across the creek to get it to the alfalfa fields. The point of crossing was flanked by a sheer cliff nearly 100 feet high on the field side, and almost as steep a rock slope opposite. The suspension was made at the top of this gorge, and was several hundred feet long.

A much longer pipe line had been strung across the Salmon several years earlier by miners working a large placer claim across from Wapshela Point, below us, so there was precedent to go by. Pop anchored his suspension cable to a 'deadman' concreted immovably into the cliff top on the field side of the creek. On the opposite side it was snubbed to two huge cottonwood posts set several feet into the ground. The 6-inch pipe was hung on iron straps that reached up to small pully wheels riding astride the cable.

The Deer Creek Ranch irrigation pipeline erected in 1915 by John A. Platt.
Photo 1976 by author

Length by length the pipe was extended across the gorge, the joints being held tightly in place by hooks riveted to the two adjoining section ends. In the middle portion of the span where the line hung lowest, there was enough leakage to permit the pipe to drain dry for winter.

To plug these holes for summer use, small quantities of fine sawdust were trickled into the pipe on a small flow of water. The sawdust lodged in the cracks and swelled enough to stop most of the leakage. The fine points of this technique were learned the hard way. On the first try too much sawdust was put in too rapidly, and completely blocked the pipe. Two days' hard work was needed to remove the pipe, unplug it, and replace it.

For reasons I do not remember, the pipe jointer could not do all his work safely situated on the ground. Periodically he was required to get into a sling seat hung from the cable, and be lowered out over the chasm to attend to some detail. These trips into space brought chills to my spine, but seemed not to bother Clyde Rencehausen, recruited from a neighboring homestead to do this job.

When completed, the pipeline was a wonder to behold and a joy to the owner: No more costly annual flume repairs. Just clean the ditch each spring and turn in the water. Two short sections of flume still remaining near the outlet were replaced by ditch the next year.

The system brought one entirely unforeseen and spectacular result. A run of large fish called suckers came down our ditch, through the pipe, and on out into the successively smaller irrigation channels until at last they flopped out onto the field and died. Over a period of weeks we could go to the outlet of the pipe and catch the emerging fish, 16 to 24 inches long, in our bare hands. It was a tame sport, though, for the fish were not wanted for food, and they did not resist strongly enough to make their capture much of a triumph. Accumulating on the field, their rotting bodies created a stench that fortunately was well removed from the house. Fortunately, too, they attracted a flock of vultures that in due time disposed of them.

The pipeline also had one serious unforeseen vulnerability. When a violent wind during a summer thunderstorm set the loaded pipe to swaying, the cottonwood posts, weakened by rot, broke and dropped much of the line into the gorge below.

It is the reconstruction after this disaster that I recall most clearly. Many lengths of the pipe were much mangled in the fall—some almost completely closed. To be salvaged, the damaged joints had to be separated, pounded out, and re-riveted. Finally the reclaimed joints had to be rejoined and restrung across the gorge. Many of the worst damaged sections were replaced with other pipe.

This time the cottonwood anchor posts for the cable were replaced with 16-inch iron pipe set six feet into the ground and filled with concrete. They still hold the pipeline today, although it has been out of use for many years.

With the irrigation system to keep the alfalfa growing all summer, we were able to harvest three cuttings a year, and in some years four cuttings, to a total of about 100 tons of hay. As long as the winters were mild and the old grass plentiful, this amount of hay brought the stock through in good shape. Other ranches operated on less hay by bringing feed grain up the Snake River by boat to landings near the mouth of the Salmon.

In the severe winter of 1914-15 our hay was not equal to the need. At the same time that deep snow covered the grass, intense cold made the animals' need for feed unusually high. Besides the cattle, we now had some 3,000 sheep. These animals were completely helpless to cope with the snow, which for a time was more than two feet deep. Most of the hay was fed to them. A dozen or more were buried and smothered by drifting snow in the corral. As the winter dragged on and the hay dwindled, rations were cut to the barest minimum. Cows that had been fat in the fall shrank to walking skeletons. They became so weak they could not fight off the magpies, which perched on their backs and pecked holes in the living flesh. On a walk to the Upper Barn one day I saw a cow with a hole in her back clear into the paunch cavity, that I could have put my hand through. It was common for magpies to peck at the small open sores in cows' backs caused by warble grubs, but this time the birds didn't stop with the grub, but went right on eating the cow.

When winter finally broke and the grass began to grow, the watery new feed acted as a laxative that weakened the animals still further. Many cows became too weak to get up from lying down through the night. Among these the riders made daily rounds with gunnysacks full of the last remnants of the hay, doling out the least amounts they thought would give a chance of survival. Each day the weakened and disheartened creatures were 'tailed up' to their feet if possible, in the hope that they would have enough strength to find food for themselves. Cows in this condition become perverse, and many spent their final energies trying to chase their helpers, only to fall again. Many died in spite of all that could be done for them.

The sheep were in worse straits than the cattle. Nearly all were ewes heavy with lamb, and should have been on good feed. The best we could do for them after the hay was exhausted was to herd them on the south slopes where the snow was melting off soonest, exposing some old grass. Though this was not good sheep feed, it enabled most of them to survive. Those that died of starvation, or in the snow smothering incident, were dragged out onto the ridge just above the hayfield. When warm weather came at last, the men skinned as many as they could, to save the pelts and wool. Before they could finish, the wool loosened on the decaying carcasses, so that skinning no longer was practical. At that stage I drew the unhappy job of pulling the wool from the stinking remains and stuffing it into gunny sacks to be packed to the barn. I remember doing it, but doubt that I lasted long at the task.

SALMON RIVER SAGA

Kootsie, The Intrepid

Adventure always is at its best when shared with an enthusiastic and daring accomplice. Accomplice is the right word here, for most of the adventures I undertook on The River which still remain memorable were at least frowned upon, and many were proscribed. Only a well utilized combination of collusive silence, evasive answers and occasional flat lies, combined with considerable parental tolerance, brought us through various escapades with untanned hides.

With six children in our family, the adventure combinations varied from day to day. By far the most common one, however, paired me with my sister Frances, a year and a half older. Mary, our older sister, was not the adventurous type, though we sometimes persuaded her to join us. Lorene and Jack were too young. Tom, nearly six years older than I, already was assigned a man's role in ranch affairs by the time I became venturesome, so was both too busy and too responsible to be involved.

Frances was not known to me by that name then. In the family her everyday name was "Kootsie." Where this nickname came from no one now knows. It has no known derivation, no aptness, no significance. By contrast, Tom got his name logically. Christened Edward Jesse in honor of his two grandfathers, he became "Tom" in deference to the paternal side, where Grandfather Edward Thomas Platt went by the name of Tom. Kootsie was Kootsie for no reason any longer remembered. But in the family the name still stands.

The accident of being born a girl had little effect on Kootsie's outlook or actions during our years on The River. She was born to adventure, nothing daunted her, and few opportunities escaped her. Whether we were daring known dangers or probing some new unknown, no hint of hesitation on her part showed through to weaken my own less hardy resolve. The question with her seldom was "shall we?" but rather, "how?"

This was a bold spirit's response to a demanding environment. Hazards lay in every direction, and coping with them was a matter of daily living. There were cactus beds, thornbrush and bent nails to be avoided with bare feet—and I never owned a pair of summer shoes until I was 13 years old. There were loose rocks poised on every steep slope, ready to roll if clutched in climbing or stepped on in descending. Rattlesnakes lurked in rocks and brush, ready to strike the unwary. Spring snowmelt and summer cloudbursts transformed Deer Creek into a roaring, grinding torrent that rolled hundred-pound boulders along its bed. The river at any stage was capable of pulling down the most powerful swimmer. Of all the dangers that surrounded us, I think the danger of falling into one of those streams and being swept away awed us most.

Given these conditions, two facts from that era now stand out as most remarkable: First, parental restrictions were minimal; and second, none of us ever was seriously hurt. But there were some close calls, and I will now mention a few that involved Kootsie.

Deer Creek empties into the Salmon River through a gap in a 50-foot high rock ledge. Jutting out into the river on the downstream side stands a rock mass as big as a house, separated from the main ledge. When the river is in flood it rushes past this rock in a swirling, surging, sucking power that fascinates the beholder. The creek, having finished its spring runoff earlier, is clear at this season, and fish by thousands take refuge in the great pool formed there by the 20-foot rise in the river level. Shiners, suckers, chubs and squaw fish were its most numerous visitors when I was a boy, but there was always the possibility of hooking a passing salmon.

Fishing in the mouth of the creek was one of our annual special times. We caught the ordinary kinds almost at will. That was fun, but the big dream was of some day catching a salmon. The best I ever did was three 30-inch suckers, which I caught in rapid succession one fine day and carried home in high elation. Their record size was my only reward, for these fish were too bony to eat, and they made so little resistance that catching them was not unlike towing in three sticks of wood. To fish for salmon you had to go out on the Big Rock and cast into the river itself. I don't recall that anyone, child or adult, ever caught one there, but each year got its share of trying.

It was out on the Big Rock that Kootsie experienced a brush with death that was to leave her permanently marked. She and Mary were playing there, Kootsie five or six years old and Mary two years older. She fell and cut a deep gash in her scalp. In the fall she narrowly missed tumbling into the powerful current, from which there would have been no possible rescue. The scar from that gash served as a reminder long afterward of the dangers we grew up with. It still shows today if you know where to look for it.

In the winter of 1914-15 the Salmon River froze over and remained frozen for a long period. Only the rapids remained open. Great blocks of ice breaking off above came charging down to pile up on top of the massive barrier below. These piles became several feet high. The ice became so thick that men rode their horses across it without hesitation. One man even crossed a herd of cattle.

Although no one had skates, we children did a lot of sliding on our shoe soles. A fast run from the bank would slide you 30 feet on the glassy surface.

Despite its thickness of 16 inches or more, the ice was continually cracking under the tremendous pressures of expansion against the river banks. Some times a crack would start right under you, and in a fraction of a second run a hundred yards or more, with accompanying popping sounds as loud as pistol shots. It took quite a bit of self-possession and nerve to convince yourself that the ice was not about to open wide and drop you through.

26

Actually, there was danger of just that, though not from pressure cracks. Certain points where great currents swelled up from deep parts of the river froze over only after the ice was a foot thick elsewhere. At such places the ice remained thin enough to see through, and it was truly spine chilling to suddenly encounter one of these spots and see the dark water rushing by beneath your feet. We soon learned where these spots were, and gave them wide berth.

Pop and Muzzy, when told of these places, rightly forbade us to go out on the river ice again. But as weeks came and went with the cold unabated and the horsemen continuing to cross the river on the ice, we chafed under the seemingly unwarranted restriction. On a fateful day Mary, Kootsie and I decided to disobey, and go slide at the Big Eddy, opposite Starveout Mountain.

Starveout Mountain sticks its foot into the Salmon River in the form of a cliff some 300 feet high, just above and across from the mouth of Deer Creek. How deep is the river bed at the foot of this cliff no one knows, but it may well be a full hundred feet. Coming down from the long rapids above, the river surges against this cliff, then away from it in a great circling current that turns back upstream against the opposite bank. There over the centuries the slow backwash has deposited thousands of tons of sand. This current to us was the Big Eddy; this bar, the Big Sandbar.

On this day we had left home headed for the comparative safety of the creek, then at low flow. Once out of sight from the house, however, we struck toward the river. There we headed up toward the Big Eddy, where the ice was the smoothest of all. We ran and slid on the shining surface with special delight after the long absence from this pleasure, working our way gradually upstream. Finally we were satisfied and decided to go up the hill and play in the hay at the Upper Barn, which stood on the high bench above the Big Sandbar.

I headed off the ice first, perhaps 50 feet ahead of the girls. As I neared the bank I was puzzled to see that the ice was full of sand grains, and that it was surprisingly thin. How could this be? I wondered, as I stepped ashore and turned to watch Kootsie and Mary, approaching together. Then, to my horror, the ice broke beneath them and they were thrashing among its brittle fragments ten feet from shore in water that might as well have been bottomless. The next few seconds were an age of desperation that comes back to me yet. Neither of them could swim, and I can only suppose it was the air held under their dresses and coats that kept them afloat while their frantic reaching efforts gradually brought them close enough for me to help them out.

Too young to realize the depths of the tragedy we had just escaped, we were nonetheless badly frightened. But now the worst part was that we dared not go home and admit our wrongdoing. The wintry sun that had seemed warm as long as we were dry now seemed to give no heat at all as the girls' soaked garments clung icily to them.

It was Kootsie who thought of a way out, though a spartan one: They would go to the barn, spread their clothes in the sun on the hay, and cover themselves with hay to keep warm while the clothes dried. And so it was done, with more misplaced fortitude than success. The clothes did not dry, and the girls did not keep warm. After an hour or so of this misery they gave up the attempt in favor of a new scheme, again from Kootsie's fertile brain. They redressed and we all ran across the hayfield to a point on the creek above the house. From there we went quickly home, with a tale of having broken through the creek ice. This was classed as a misfortune but not a misdeed.

Only years later did we dare divulge the truth. And only long after did I realize that the sand-filled ice had been formed only shortly before Kootsie and Mary broke through it. A huge chunk of the steep sandbank, undermined by the eddy, had broken off and carried the old thick ice down with it, swirling the water full of sand which was then caught in the newly formed ice.

I have mentioned that Deer Creek sometimes became a roaring torrent. This was characteristic of all creeks emptying into the Salmon River in our area. All flow out of the high timbered country of either Craig Mountain to the north or west, or out of Joseph Plain to the south and east, where several feet of snow produces a heavy spring runoff. Their courses are generally short and steep. In its precipitous plunge from the rim of Craig Mountain, Deer Creek drops 2,000 feet or more in the first two miles. Even in its gentler lower reaches the rate of fall must approach 200 feet to the mile. Early summer thunderstorms striking along its course can turn this usually peaceful stream quickly into a mad turmoil of rolling rocks and floating debris.

Between our house and barn, Deer Creek divided around a three-acre island. Over each branch we went back and forth on log bridges constructed by simply felling a bankside tree across the channel and trimming off its branches. To us, these were "footlogs," a term not listed in my present *Webster's New World Dictionary of the American Language*. They were not always graced with handrails, and to use them called for a degree of self confidence and sure-footedness.

The creek banks were low, and the footlogs lay close to the water surface when the stream ran high. Exceptionally high floods sometimes swept away the logs. Over the years this process gradually used up most of the trees located along the banks that were both tall enough to reach across and big enough to walk on. Also, one fork of the creek became so wide that no tree located by it would reach across. There Pop built rock cribs high enough to place the footlog well above the highest flows. Before this improvement was installed, however, there was a year when a log was laid across the creek above the island, so as to bridge it all at one place. This, of course, was called the Upper Footlog.

In using the footlogs, we children learned that by standing still and looking intently at the passing water we got the illusion that it was the water that was standing still, and that we were racing upstream. It was a scary sort of 'ride' at first, but grew to be a favorite pastime when more promising activities did not occur to us. Today's generation can get the same sensation, if not the same thrill, in a parked bus by watching another bus, parked alongside, move ahead. So strong is the illusion that you must shift your glance to some fixed object to bring yourself to a 'halt.'

Kootsie and I had been enjoying this sort of horseless ride on the Upper Footlog one day when Deer Creek was in spring flood. In time we tired of the sport and sought a more exciting activity. Our seeking took the form of racing across the footlog. We made several round trips. Then, whether by accident or intent, we were at opposite ends of the log, running across and passing each other at midstream. Only two small, nimble, barefooted, willow-bodied, and utterly self-confident sprites could have performed this miracle on a 10-inch log! And even *we* couldn't do it every time.

I was about three steps from shore and headed out when the inevitable finally foreclosed: Kootsie bumped me as she came by, and into the creek I plunged.

Kootsie near where she pulled the author from flooding creek a month earlier.

Luckily she was not even slowed by the collision, and was onto the creek bank almost as soon as I hit the water. She sprinted downstream ahead of me, looking for some piece of pole or board to reach out to me. Before she could find one, fate intervened—the current carried me into some half-submerged willow shoots extending from shore. I seized these and was immediately whipped toward the shore itself. There Kootsie pulled me out.

29

Although that day was more than 50 years ago, I can still see the lifesaving willows bent under the racing water as I floated helplessly toward them. I still feel their slippery withes in my desperate clutch. I still see Kootsie wading hip-deep to reach out to me while she clung to a larger willow on the bank. But it is not a harrowing memory, and it never stood in the way of my making many a cheerily ear-splitting willow whistle in later years.

The "final edition" footlog with hewn plank and handrail, that even grandmothers could cross. Platt children: Mary, Jack, Lorene, Frances. Behind, Emma C. Platt and Carrie Harris Platt.

Not all our joint adventures were either daring or heroic. Most, in fact, had no saving bravura, but charitable readers may find in them some common ground with youthful pranks of their own, even though in different realms of experience. There was the time, for example, when we tied together the hair on the tails of a gentle cow and a small bull, thinking only to amuse ourselves momentarily with their antics until the hair on one tail or the other should break. Our initial glee at seeing them determinedly pulling against each other soon vanished when we realized that the hair would not break. Rather, the popping joints of the tails brought visions of tails being pulled out by the roots! When the two befuddled beasts walked on opposite sides of a tree and stood side by side straining with all their strength, we so feared the certainty of Pop's wrath when he should find them thus that neither of us had the presence of mind to run get a knife and cut them apart. Luckily no harm was done, and our punishment was only a rough scolding.

Other occasions had to do with filching dried fruits or sugar lumps out of the storehouse to eat surreptitiously behind some convenient rock or bush. Sometimes we were caught and had to surrender our illicit treasures, sometimes not. On one such occasion Kootsie and I made off with a hard lump of sugar as big as a small cabbage. I think we involved Mary in this, too. We took the lump to a spot near the milking corral, where we placed it on the ground like a block of cattle salt. Then, pretending to be cattle, we licked it to our hearts' content, meantime making suitable bellowing noises, pawing dirt, switching flies, etc. When this posturing became tiresome we shifted to our real selves and began an honest assault on the sugar lump.

Having confidently expected to eat it all, we were aghast to find ourselves sated before any great dent had been made in it. Now we were trapped in our own mischief. To cache the lump was impractical—the ants would get it or rain would spoil it. To throw it away was unthinkable. The only course open was to return it to the storehouse. Despite our best efforts, we did not succeed in doing this undetected, and the lump brought us some well deserved thumps.

High Water On The Salmon

The Salmon River in full flood was and is an awesome spectacle. Draining the main mountain heartland of Idaho, where winter snows pile to the eaves of the few cabins located there, this is the fabled "River Of No Return." By the time it reaches Deer Creek it has gathered all but the last few trickles of tributary waters. Here it rises 20 feet in an ordinary year, and as much as 30 feet in exceptional years. Confined between canyon walls that sometimes converge to a scant 50 yards apart, the river forms a crest at mid-stream that seems to rise feet higher than its shore level.

Driftwood of every size rides the flood. Hundred-foot firs, cast into its upper reaches by avalanche or old age, are tossed along like corks on a millrace. Day in, day out, through the weeks of late May and early June the show of rampant power swirls past the bank-bound beholder.

It was a sight that held me for hours on end. Not even a small boy's imagination could picture whence this wild stream might come, nor what immensity below possibly could swallow up its boundless waters. But the main fascination was the sense of sheer power that the crested flood gave—a sense that drew you to put foot in the very edge and follow along as if somehow to catch and hold some of it for yourself. It was for this, I think, that we waded the icy shore waters till our legs grew numb; certainly there was no physical pleasure in the wading.

There were incidental rewards, though. One was to find occasional brightly colored Indian beads and other trinkets exposed along the river's edge. These were prizes in themselves, but their main value was in how they opened the gates of fancy about their original owners. How long ago had the Indians been there? What had they been doing? How were they dressed? Were they men or women, boys or girls? What had they eaten? Where had they camped? Where were they now? The questions and answering speculations were endless and, underneath, more than a little fearful. Though Indians seldom came this way any more, we had an uneasy respect for these original Americans, about whom tales of terrors scarce a generation old still floated among our elders. What it they should suddenly come back? What if they should "get" us?

Nezperce on his Appaloosa

Another reward was the excitement of anticipation for what the river might bring. A floating board signified some other human habitation, far upstream. But did it also speak of disaster? Had the river seized some building—maybe even a house—and this was the only remnant? An unusually large log was both a prize spectacle and a challenge to watch for one still larger. Odd shaped pieces of root or limb sparked a search for the still more bizarre. Water-worn pieces spoke of unmeasured years enroute, of waterfalls and eddies and hidden crevices that caught and prisoned the few while the many swept endlessly by.

Still another reward was the occasional appearance on the opposite side of some denizen of that other world beyond the river. He might ride by on the high trail that passed above Starveout Mountain's craggy foot, with only a wave of the hat to answer to our yells of greeting. Or he might ride to the water's edge and try to shout some message across the roar of the great rapids that broke away shortly below the mouth of Deer Creek. Sometimes the words came through, sometimes not. Sometimes the visitor was someone we knew, sometimes a stranger. Any cross-river encounter was an event for excited reporting back to grown-ups.

The ultimate reward would be to see some daring soul riding the tiger that was the river in flood. It was a reward that never really came in full form. No man put boat from shore to cross or follow the Salmon at its mightiest, save in desperation or ignorance. The chances of getting across without being swept downstream were too slim, the chances of being rammed or capsized by some careening log too great. When the flood had subsided to where the larger driftwood stopped running, hazards were reduced, and might be dared.

Twice we found partial fulfillment of our hope for the ultimate. Once was when a group of miners somewhere above us loaded their effects onto a raft and started to ride back to civilization on the stream whose canyon fastnesses had disappointed their dreams of riches. We did not witness the ride, but reconstructed it with somber imagination when Pop retrieved from the wreck of this effort a few items they succeeded in beaching a mile below the ranch. One of those that still sticks in hazy memory was a large keg of blackstrap molasses, whose bitter-sweet contents I came to detest long before the keg was emptied.

The other occasion was a happy one. It was when Pop brought the lumber from Cottonwood to build our new house at Deer Creek. This lumber was hauled to the river at a point some 20 miles upstream and floated down in rafts. The safe arrival of the rafts at our landing, triumphant over the storied dangers of China Rapids and unknown other threats of the river above us, was a time for rejoicing. In contrast to the browned, weatherbeaten rough finish of our old house, the planed new pine boards were things of golden beauty. The River could bless as well as destroy.

KENNETH B. PLATT

The Big House

The house that Pop fashioned in the summer of 1912 from the rafted lumber was a landmark not only of my young memory but of the whole River community as well. It was unique in many ways. It was the only two-story house in the area, and the only one with a brick chimney instead of the usual stovepipe. It was of mansion proportions, compared with the homestead cabins on other places, with four rooms upstairs and five down, counting the large pantry. The living-dining room, running the full length of one side, boasted a bay window overlooking the old house and the log cabin where I was born—now the bunkhouse. New with the house was a telephone, our share in a marvellous enterprise that connected us with eleven other ranches and with the town of Forest, a half-day's ride away.

The brick chimney was a precaution against fire danger, which was multiplied in a house of this size. We had three stoves instead of the usual lone cookstove, and the two stories gave much added height in which a pipe might overheat. Like the lumber, the bricks came from afar. Made at one of the towns on Craig Mountain, they were hauled to the end of the road six miles above us and brought down from there on pack horses.

Another distinctive feature of this house, for me, was that there I started to school. In one of the downstairs rooms Tom, Mary, Kootsie and I sat to the teaching of "Winnie" Spurbeck, daughter of Genesee neighbors of the Platt family, and fresh from Lewiston Normal. Tom and Mary had started school at Genesee, staying with Grandma Platt. For Kootsie and me, the school at home was our first introduction to the A-B-Cs and the 1 plus 1's. Winnie got us well started that year, then graduated to a home of her own by marrying Billy Freeburn, a homesteader on Eagle Creek. Next year we moved the school to an upstairs room, where Helen Brown, sister of homesteaders Paul and Frank Brown from across the river, was our teacher. Third grade brought Alice Nelson, whose crystal beads magically produced rainbow colors in winter when struck by sunlight from the window. Alice was a younger sister of Mrs. Ben Reeves, from the Reeves ranch downriver some 10 miles. Lorene joined the school that year.

With only five of us in the school, and only three grades, our teachers spent much time reading aloud to us. Here my horizons were extended to far Arizona, where Zane Gray's blazing red mustang stallion, "Wildfire," pranced and fled across the pages of successive issues of *Country Gentleman,* relentlessly pursued by a cowboy hero whose name now eludes me but who I now suspect may have been the interest that kept Miss Nelson reading. Here, too, I learned to love the impressionist magic of poetic expression, saying so much that was not in the words themselves, but in the way they made you feel. The music of *Hiawatha* sank deep, and still lingers.

The "Big House" at Deer Creek Ranch, built in 1912, as it looked in 1914. End of original 1890's log cabin at left, stone cellar beyond. Man by porch unidentified.

Dear Creek Ranch site in 1974, showing house built after Big House burned in 1915.

Original Deer Creek Ranch cabin, as seen in 1967. Birthplace of the author in 1907.

Close view of log wall showing axe marks from the squaring process. Detail of corner morticing shown on near corner of cabin above.

First (right, 1890s) and last (left, 1915) houses built at Deer Creek Ranch, as seen in 1974. Lorene Platt (Mrs. Stanley) Gilson at left, and Marge Nebelseik (Mrs. Dale) Gilson.

1974 condition of original Deer Creek Ranch cabin, with east side fallen out. Note size of hackberry trees not present in 1914 photo.

KENNETH B. PLATT

It was in the Big House that we marked the winter of dried codfish. Pop loved fish of all kinds, and in all forms. In summer we kids never caught too many trout to suit him. Winter was a long lean season on fish, with streams frozen over and the season closed anyway. Canned salmon was on the expensive side when you were feeding a family of eight plus two or three cow hands, and it was heavy to pack in on the horses in much quantity. Dried codfish seemed the perfect answer—comparatively cheap, light to pack, easy to store, no damage from freezing. Pop bought a lot of it.

At the table it turned out that he was the only one who liked the codfish. Under stern insistence we choked it down for more weeks than I would care to remember if I could. It came to our plates in many forms, none of which I relished above any other. The final blow was when it appeared as codfish gravy. Now I couldn't even enjoy my boiled potatoes, ruined by that gravy! That was a long winter.

Another adventure in eating which I suspect might turn Duncan Hines pale around the gills had to do with weiners. To supply the lambing crew one spring, Pop bought two 50-lb kegs of brined weiners. Like the codfish, this seemed a good plan, as the lambing camp was located several miles from the ranch, and supplying it with food was somewhat difficult. In particular, there was no way to supply it with fresh meat. Although the lambers were numerous and ate with gusto, they wore out their taste for brined weiners before the first keg was emptied. When they decamped, the remaining weiners came back to the ranch to be consumed. For us there was no escape—we ate weiners until there were no more, and that was far too long a time. Tom avoided weiners for the next 20 years or so. My aversion vanished by the time I got to college and hot dog sandwiches.

On the lighter side was our musical life. Muzzy and our teachers taught us many pleasant little ditties, but it was Pop who led off the family sings, who brought home "Tipperary" and other new hits from the outside world, and who played the harmonica with a zest that did full justice to "Redwing," "Arawana," "Over the Waves Waltz," "The Irish Washerman," and other classics of the time. Some of his songs that intrigued me most were ones of which he sang only tantalizing snatches that left you dangling and wondering. One such that has stuck with me through the years, nameless and without beginning or end, was as shown on the following page.

Another form of live music was what we got at the house dances. A dance meant Dan Critchfield and his fiddle, any other musical instrument available, and a square dance caller. The square dances were of some circus interest, but beyond my understanding. Waltzes, one-steps and two-steps were the "in" shuffles of that period, until the turkey trot came along. Too small to participate, I was more often a sleepy than an enthusiastic observer. After many years of indifferent success at dancing since then, I have concluded that I was born with two left feet, and this may explain why it

38

I was roaming a — long, Sim — ply roam-ing a — long,

Soft-ly hum-ming a song. Think-ing no — thing was wrong:

Roam-ing here, roam-ing there, And I did-n't know where.

And I did-n't much care — I was roam-ing a — long.

did not attract me then.

But there were side benefits of the occasions for dances which I could appreciate, not the least of which were the exciting new foods brought together by the in-gatherings. The incidental excitement sometimes was rewarding, too. There was the time, for example, when Uncle Will, attending an affair at the Big House, and quite the most eligible bachelor present, stepped off the porch into the kitchen slop bucket up to his knee, in the dark having mistaken it for a big rock. This brought a flurry of hilarity and activity connected with washing the pants leg, drying and re-pressing it, while he hid out. When the housewarming for Elmer Taylor's homestead cabin was held, Muzzy honored it with a large cake with gained distinction by arriving soaked with kerosene that leaked from the lamp which also was taken along.

Then there was the phonograph. It was an Edison of about 1910 vintage, that played cylinder records. Each record started off with an announcement that went: "E-D-I-S-O-N R-E-C-O-R-D, Number 1457" or whatever else its serial number was, and then the title. By the time it got that far the machine would be up to full speed, and the musical rendition at its best. One winding of the machine with the hand crank on the side was good for two, but not three, records. It was better to crank up after each record so as not to forget. In our limited record treasury such artists as John McCormack, Ada Jones and Len Spencer vied with Uncle Josh, and "Whistling Rufus" might be played next to "The Holy City." The music could be heard all through the house if there was not too much competition, being amplified by a great horn some two feet long and 18 inches across the outer end.

Today's home recording buffs may marvel that our Edison, too, was equipped for home recordings. You simply reversed the playing process. Replace the playing needle with a recording needle. Put a blank record on the machine, having first washed it with coal oil to de-wax the surface. Gather in front of the horn, ready to sing down its throat. Drape a sheet over horn and singers, start the phonograph, and all sing your loudest. Then the play-back. Listen carefully now. Yes, it had recorded, all right—you could hear it a good ten feet away!

"Fiddling Dan Critchfield"

SALMON RIVER SAGA

No piano found its way to The River in my time, but during our latter years Pop bought a pedal organ of respectable size, which was not more than a horse could carry. This regal instrument was a sort of community contribution, since no one in our family could play it. I don't recall who did play it, but talent equal to the opportunity came from somewhere to swell the musical output at dances and house warmings thereafter.

The Big House stood on a bench about a hundred yards from the creek and fifty feet above it. Water for the house was carried from the creek. The supply at the house seldom was more than a bucketful or two, except on washday or bathday. It was neither of those days the evening that Kootsie, soon after school, saw smoke rolling from under the eaves of the school room as she returned from the creek with a bucket of water, and gave the alarm.

Muzzy seized the bucket from her, ran upstairs, and flung the water against the blazing walls of the school room, but it was not enough. The contents of the teakettle and the reservoir in the kitchen range also were used. Tom came racing back from the barn and went for more water. Together he and Muzzy filled a 15-gallon washtub and lugged it from the frozen creek to the school room door. But by the time they got there the inferno in the room was so hot they could not throw the water effectively on the fire.

Then came the frantic efforts to save what could be saved. Little was saved from the top floor, for the schoolroom door opened on the head of the stairs. With no men at home, nothing heavy could be moved. Helen Brown helped Muzzy and Tom, while Grandma herded the rest of us into the yard and kept us out of the way. Pop's business papers and the bedding from the one downstairs bed; the phonograph and a few other small items from the living room; pantry contents and part of the kitchen utensils, were hustled or flung out. In the incredibly short space of 20 minutes from the time the fire was discovered, the roof caved in. Soon after, the futile chimney crashed through the gutted interior.

We stood in the winter twilight among the scattered salvage, six stunned children and three exhausted, disconsolate women. Muzzy stamped on a smoking spot in one of the bed quilts. Pistol and rifle ammunition exploded one shell at a time as the fire ate into the last of the downstairs. The flames reached out toward us and consumed porch and pantry, the last parts to go.

As night fell, two horsemen passing on the far side of the river rode across on the ice to confirm what their unbelieving eyes had told them. While they talked, Pop and the other men of the ranch came in from a hard day's ride among the cattle upriver to see, instead of the lights of home, only a heap of glowing embers.

The Big House was no more. We were left with the clothes we had on, and little else.

41

Drastic family readjustments followed. Mary and Kootsie went to stay with the George Vallem family on Eagle Creek, a few miles away. Lorene, Jack and I were taken by Grandma, then living in her homestead cabin half a mile up Deer Creek. Pop, muzzy and Tom moved into the bunkhouse. Helen Brown went across the river to the Nash ranch.

Work to build another house started at once. It was built on the site of the old Dorchester house, close to the bunkhouse. The lumber came from the Ralph Ross homestead, a mile up the creek, which Pop had bought two years before. The Ross house was dismantled with care to save every board and every nail. The boards were tied into bunches and dragged to our place by riders, drag ropes snubbed to saddle horns. Men came from neighboring ranches to help with the carpentry. Frank and Tom Aytch, Frank Grounds and Art Keane, and doubtless others.

I don't remember how long the job took—perhaps as little as a week or two. But I remember the occasion well because I was recruited to straighten the bent nails brought from the Ross house. The work had to be done bare-handed, and my freezing fingers ached each time a held nail flipped out of them as I hammered at the bent places. The hard old lumber caused many nails to bend again when the men tried to drive them, and back to me these came for more straightening, for none could be wasted. My closing recollection of the episode is the shout of joy that went up when a neighbor who had been dispatched to Forest for supplies came in view on the trail. One man threw down his hammer and ran up the trail to reach for the precious bag of new nails, even before the pack string came to a stop!

I agreed heartily in his sentiments.

Old Songs, And New Love

After the Big House burned, its replacement, with only four modest rooms, had less space for holding school. We finished the school year there in the dining room, but next year we walked to school at Grandma's house. Grandma moved back to Genesee, and Mrs. Cora Ashenfelter came down from the Deer Creek Mine, five miles above us, to live in Grandma's house and be our teacher. With her came her black haired 5-year-old daughter, Carmen.

Mrs. Ashenfelter was a divorcee, a rare thing in our area. Her father, as owner of the Deer Creek Mine, maintained connections in the East and spent a fair amount of time there promoting funds for his venture. As a girl, Mrs. Ashenfelter attended finishing schools in the East. When her marriage there did not succeed she came with her small daughter to join her parents at The Mine. Thus she was available to fill our need for a teacher.

Considering her background, I suspect Mrs. Ashenfelter may have been a lonely and frustrated woman in that isolated homestead cabin. Her schooling had included voice training that enabled her to do the high trills and other vocal gymnastics of various renowned arias, but this kind of singing fell on generally unappreciative ears in our less cultured surroundings. There it tended to be regarded as "screeching" rather than as musical accomplishment.

For my part, I give her better than 'passing' marks. She introduced us to the world of the concert stage, to the extent that we were able to grasp it at our years and in our setting. Out of that world I retained the word "encore," and a cherished memory of several songs I have never heard since, save when I have sung them myself. Perhaps none of them ever graced a concert program, but for old time's sake—which is what this backward looking rendezvous is all about anyway—I record them here as witness of a gift still dear to memory.

The Shady Nook song did not appeal much to me at the age of nine. In particular, those girls yacking while they were fishing was strictly against the code—you just didn't talk when you were fishing for trout. Beginning about ten years later, I came to appreciate its sentiments for their true worth, and not to be too concerned about the trout. The song stood me in good stead, for it was a lot of years after that before I found the one who was "waiting for me."

The Jungle Moon song is imaginative, to say the least, and the only one I have ever heard on the subject. I used to wonder how it had escaped into print. To what public could its publisher appeal? What enamoured youth would feel the urge to sing it to his sweetheart? After hearing the common run of songs on the disc jockey and TV programs today, however, I make no apologies for resurrecting it here.

The encore song, Three Little Chestnuts, has a simple charm that needs no apologies. One more song that I have never heard sung since then is in the patriotic class. Whatever public acclaim it may have had up to then was submerged by the more fervent products of World War I. If it ever surfaced after then, it was only to fall prey to the "debunking" binge that destroyed so many of our earlier patriotic images during the late 1920s and the 1930s. But I give it this revival, however brief, because its sentiments have been appropriate to many moments in my overseas work in more recent years. It is called The Good Old U.S.A.

Among the romantic and genteel influences of Mrs. Ashenfelter's tutelage I made my first conquest of the fair sex. The fact that it was altogether unsought did not deter my sisters from bringing it to public attention at inopportune moments for years afterward. Because they would not let me forget it then, I remember still little Carmen's unabashed declaration: "I love Kenneth because he has golden hair and golden eyelashes." Fate separated us shortly after, and I never saw her again. I still have the eyelashes she admired, but the hair is gone.

SOMEBODY'S WAITING FOR YOU

In a cool sha-dy nook, by the side of a brook, Two sweet
Then a youth passing by hear the maid-en's re-ply, and he

maid — ens wer fish-ing a — lone. They talked as they fished and the
joined in their chat half in fun. He said: "It is true, some-one's

young-er girl wished For a sweet-heart she nev-er had known. The
wait-ing for you. And I wish you thought I were the one. She

old — er girl said, with a toss of her head, "Cheer up, dear, you've no cause to be
paused for a while, and then said with a smile: "I don't know, but perhaps you are

blue: Your love you've not met, but he'll come to you yet, For there's
right: But if you are wrong, you will not wor-ry long, For there's

somebody waiting for you. Some-where, some-body's waiting for you, just you;

Some-where, some-bo-dy's wait-ing for you, just you.

JUNGLE LOVE SONG

When the jung-le breeze is play-ing. Gent-ly through the branch-es sway-ing.

Af — ter the sun goes down, Lit-tle monk-ey eyes are gleam-ing.

Lit-tle monk-ey hearts are dream-ing, Down in jungle town.

Ev-ery eye is turned toward the eastern sky: They're watching for the jungle

moon. Watch-ing for its beams of yel-low; When the jungle moon is mel-low,

That's the time when monk-eys like to spoon. By the light of the

jungle moon, in the tree-tops a-bove, Monkey boy sings a lov-ing tune to his

own tur-tle dove. And he whis-pers: "Sweet monk-ey maid, oh won't you

come out and spoon. Here's where your bliss is, come get your

kiss-es, By the light of the jung-le moon."

IN THE GOOD OLD U.S.A.

"Oh, Fath-er won't you tell me Why in that great big crowd, Oh,

Fath-er won't you tell me Why each one act so proud?"

List-en my lad and I'll tell you: 'Twas the tune the brass band played — The

tune: My Coun-try 'Tis of Thee, On the land and on the sea.

"Makes no dif-fer-ence where you wand-er, Makes no dif-fer-ence where you roam;

You don't have to stop and pon-der For a place to call your home.

When they ask you where you're born, lad, Speak right up and proud-ly

say That your home's the land of Un-cle Sam, In the good old U.S.A."

THREE LITTLE CHESTNUTS

Three lit-tle chest-nuts in from the coun!try. Dressed up ev-er so bold:
Three lit-tle chest-nuts rol'd on the roaster. Over a big i-ron pot:
One lit-tle news-boy dropt down a penny and gobbled them down like a shark:

One said, "Oo," and one said, 'Boo," And one said, "Gee ain't it cold."
One said, "Oo," and one said, "Boo," And one said, "Gee ain't it hot."
One said, "Oo," and one said, "Boo," And one said, "Gee ain't it dark."

SALMON RIVER SAGA

Of Horses and Riders

The Salmon River country of my recollections was roadless. All incoming roads stopped at the edges of the bordering mountain plateaus. Drag trails wide enough for skidding heavy loads along the ground followed down a few of the broadest ridges. Dragging on these trails was strictly a one-way passage, down but never up. So far as human locomotion was concerned, you were either afoot or a-horseback once you entered the domain of The River. The same limitation applied to the transport of nearly all supplies and equipment, for drag trails could only be used to go down a slope, not along the sides of the precipitous ridges and canyons.

Lower Salmon River Country

Horses carried in the great majority of all materials brought to the ranches. Items too large for one horse to carry were dismantled and packed in pieces. The mowing machine, hayrake and wagon at Deer Creek ranch came that way. The steel cable that supported the irrigation pipeline across Deer Creek came in one piece, but on two horses in tandem, each carrying half, with the uncut cable running between them. The much longer, larger cable that spanned the river at Wapshela was packed by several horses in one continuous string.

Wheels of a hayrake enroute to Deer Creek Ranch on a pack horse.

A pack string carrying summer supplies into the high country from unidentified outpost, about 1910.

Pack saddles were specially designed for tying on the loads, and various special equipment was developed to be used with them. The alforja, two connected pouches hanging on opposite sides of the horse, came up from Mexico, and was pronounced "alforka" in our area. It was introduced into Mexico by the Spanish, who got it from the Arabs, who got it from the Persians, who have been using it for more than a thousand years and still use it on everything from bicycles to camels, with or without packsaddles. The alforja was well suited for bagged materials, like flour, sugar, beans, and stock salt, and for small items that could be packed so as not to dig into the sides of the horse. Rigid heavy items, unless they could be loaded to lie flat against the horse, required packing in wooden boxes or balancing on top of the pack.

"sheep camp packer"

Balance was the key to successful packing. If the load was not well balanced it was likely to slip to one side and require reloading enroute. A badly balanced load also might cause the horse to lose his footing and fall from the steep trails, with possible loss of both load and horse.

51

Next to balance, the most important skill of the packer was the system he used for fastening the load in place. The diamond hitch was a favorite, but not suited to all kinds of loads. You needed to know the alternatives. Lash ropes of various lengths and sizes were used for different stages of the loading, with special knots at special points to expedite the process and to prevent possible later slippage. The final step was to cover the load with a heavy canvas and lash this firmly in place, both to fend off damage from brush along the trails and to put a lid of sorts on open pouches or boxes whose contents otherwise might jostle out in the rough journey.

Once loaded, the pack horses usually were led. The narrow trails required that they walk in single file. The packer rode in front, leading the first pack-horse by a rope looped around his saddle horn but ready to be cast off if necessary. The second packhorse was led by a short rope tied to the tail of the first—short because it must never sag low enough for either horse to step on or over it. The third packhorse was led in the same way by the second, and so on back to the last horse. The total group constituted a "packstring." The maximum number of horses in a packstring usually was 5 or 6, because that was all one man could pack, unpack, take care of, and still get in enough hours of travel time. The dangers of mishaps along the hazardous trails if more horses were tied together were further reason for limiting the packstring. Because of these dangers, a packstring sometimes was separated into two groups, with a well trained and wise old horse leading the second group. Well trained horses occasionally were allowed to follow independently, without being led.

The ideal packhorse was gentle and plodding. Unfortunately for packers, not many horses reached this ideal temperament while they were still young and strong and sure-footed enough to carry a heavy pack over the Salmon River trails. To get high load-carrying ability required a compromise with the hazards of using younger, less sedate animals. These younger horses tended to be on the fractious side. Often they were those weeded out of riding strings by the cowboys because they were too tough-mouthed or intractable to be good saddle ponies. The likelihood of such a horse bucking with a pack, kicking his packer, or fouling up the string along the trail had to be balanced against the need for his agility and strength.

The distinction between horses for packing and those for riding was not sharp. Most of the packing was done in the fall, when winter supplies were being stockpiled at the ranches for the four or five months when snow on the mountain and ice on the trails made packing difficult and extra hazardous. The younger pack animals were likely to be pressed into riding duty during the summer and put out on the range to fend for themselves in winter.

As a result of this regimen, the horses on which Kootsie and I learned to ride were old and gentle ones in more or less retired status. We learned to ride bareback, as all saddles were in use by grownups. This posed two problems: How to get onto a horse so tall you couldn't reach its mane for a starter, and how to stay on after you got there. The first one to mount could be boosted up by his partner, but the last one up had to have a high point to stand on. If we were both riding the same horse this was no great difficulty, for the rider could maneuver the horse to the right spot. But if each had a horse, the second mounting could have difficulties from the antics of the horse. Our wise old steeds knew just how much to move away from a rock or stump to be out of reach for a stubby-legged boy or girl, just how much to shift after the mounting was started to cause you to slip off and have to start over again.

The mounting problem was largely one of strategy, and in this we soon learned how to outsmart the horses. Staying on was a skill of degree, and came gradually. There was no problem as long as the horse walked, but who wanted to ride no faster than you could go on your own two legs? Speed was what we craved, even as today's hotrodder.

New problems attached to speed, the first of which was how to get it. Our small bare feet carried no such authority as the spurred heels of a cowboy, and the horses paid scant attention to our puny kicks. A nice limber switch was the answer, but one not easy to come by. If you got the switch beforehand, the horse would not let you mount. If you rode him up to a tree or bush that might yield such a persuader, he would not stand there long enough for you to break it off. When riding anywhere but along the creek, our choice of switch sources was serviceberry, thornbrush or hackberry. Each of these was so tough that breaking off the desired limb took much twisting and jerking. Usually we had to settle for one so small that it was not very persuasive.

This is turn posed another problem: The horses could be persuaded to trot but not to gallop. About all there is to be said for a trot is that it is faster than a walk. Anyone who has learned to ride a horse knows that the trot is the roughest of all gaits in the equine repertoire. For small bareback riders it is especially jolting, and on an old stiff-jointed horse it is at its worst. Our real concern, however, was not for the discomfort of the jolting, but for the fact that it bounced you so high you were in danger of falling off. And fall off we did, many a time.

A fall from a trotting horse always was a bruising affair, but it was an occupational risk we were willing to take. Just to be able to ride was the obvious first desideratum in a horseback society. All of us traveled many miles by horse before we learned to walk, and many more miles standing in deep boxes tied in packsaddles before we launched into independent riding. For us, learning to ride was akin to young birds learning to fly.

At Deer Creek ranch a special hazard went with falling off your horse, and that was that you might land in some cactus. Beds of prickly pear were common. The spines of this cactus ranged from two inches long down to almost too small to see with the naked eye. All sizes were barbed to resist coming out, and the small ones were so brittle that they broke easily when you tried to pull them. The pain of one sticking into you was exceeded only by the pain of having it tweezered out of your flinching hide. The smallest ones simply could not be pulled, but had to be left until they festered and could be squeezed out. I once fell from a horse into this misery-dealing stuff, and had my share of encounters with it on foot.

Occasionally a grown rider would have the misfortune to be thrown into cactus from a bucking or falling horse. When this happened the luckless victim had to be stripped naked and plucked like a chicken to get the needles out. His clothes could only be thrown away, for there was no way to get the small needles out of them.

For us who were younger, Tom was the ideal and envy of our horsemanship ambitions. Already a confident rider at 10, he rode a wild bull for the 4th of July celebration in Winchester at 12, and competed with grown men in summer roundup bucking contests when he was 15. This competence was hard earned, and came only after a multitude of spills in a long succession of well-manured branding corrals. There Pop would snub up some half grown bull calf and Tom would cinch on his saddle, mount, and ride for a mad few seconds until the agile, twisting, whirling, bucking, bawling creature unseated him, or his saddle turned and dumped him. Then he would pick himself up, dust or scrape off the manure, retrieve his saddle, and be ready for the next contest when another break in work permitted it.

This was an arena I never had the nerve to enter, though Kootsie well might have, had she been allowed to do so.

Horses had names, personalities, idiosyncracies, reputations; and this was as it should be. One aspect of horse talk that I have never figured out, though, was that any and every horse, as soon as he had worked a year or two, became "old" this or "old" that. Geldings commonly were named for their colors, their brands, or some other sight characteristic. Ours included Satan, Pop's coal black cutting horse; Kay Bar, for his brand ($\underline{K}$); Buck and Sorrel and Blue and Brownie, for their colors; Hatrack for his ever-bony frame. Mares usually had feminine names such as Maud or Belle, but did not escape being "old" before their time. Stallions were likely to be "Duke," or "King," or some other title of rank.

shears

"2-year-old"

54

With horses and riding so central in everyday affairs, our humor frequently was built around them. So many stories have been told of sleepy-looking buckers being foisted on unsuspecting greenhorn riders that I add one here only because it has the distinction of being set to music. I know not its source, whether original or parody. Nor do I know the whole ditty, but for the record, here it is as we adapted it in our own special setting:

They sad—dled me up old gray Hat—rack, With three big blisters on his back;
I went up in the air and turned around, And busted the earth when I came down;

They pad—ded him down with gunny-sack: They used my bed - ding all.
I picked my-self up from the ground: "You're do-ing well," says Brown.

The Hollywood model cowboy so familiar to present generations bears little resemblance to the men who rode the Salmon River country. The big hats, flaming shirts, buckskin jackets, tailored riding pants and colored boots, so far as I know have all evolved out of moviedom's yen for spectacles. A typical Salmon River cowpuncher wore ordinary blue jeans and a blue, gray or black cotton shirt. In spring he wore a blue denim jacket and carried a slicker on his saddle in case of rain. In winter he wore a heavy dark colored wool mackinaw and angora chaps, usually plain black, brown or white. His hat, in a serviceable color, was of modest dimensions for riding through brush and trees, where an outsize hat would have been a nuisance. His boots were plain black or brown, with a minimum of stitching, and were covered to the ankles by his pants legs.

Not everyone wore boots. Pop tried them but didn't like them, and quit. They were strange to many of the men who first went to The River, and were far from being thought indispensible to the range cattle business. Nevertheless cowboy boots were and are a specialized footgear developed just for this business, and since I have never seen a written explanation of them I take the liberty of saying a few words about them here.

Genuine cowboy boots have six distinct basic features. They have 1) pointed toes, 2) tightly rounded insteps, 3) extra strong arch construction, 4) high heels, 5) heels rounded forward from top to bottom at the back, and 6) heels set farther forward than the heels of walking shoes. This design makes the boots awkward to walk in, and their

Typical "cowboys" of the Salmon River Country who lived or worked in the Deer Creek community, L to R standing, Chauncy Emerich, Carson Moffett, Herschel Emerich Seated, Elmer Taylor, Fred "Boots" Merrill, Walter Lemons, Harry Weller, Walter Patton. Most of these men ran cattle of their own.

Two typical homesteader-cowman of Eagle Creek community, Leonard Ringer(L) and Robert Vallem. Dogs were a necessity for working cattle in the steep and often brushy country.

56

high heels and customary tight fit give an impression of vanity. Despite these appearances there is good reason for each feature.

The total purpose of the cowboy boot is to give its wearer maximum utility and safety in an often strenuous and hazardous occupation. The heels are high to give them an extra 'hook' on the stirrup and to lessen the chance that the wearer's foot may slip forward through it in a moment of violent action. They are rounded forward from the back so as to slip easily out of the stirrup in case a foot does get thrust through it. This probably is the most important single feature, for a foot hung in a stirrup when a rider loses his seat for any reason easily can be a fatal predicament. The heels are set forward to hold the rider's shins back out of contact with the stirrup, for protection from rubbing or bruising. The toes of the boots are pointed to facilitate getting the foot quickly back into the stirrup in case it slips out. The arch is extra strong so as to take the full weight of the rider here where the boot thrusts against the stirrup, and to distribute it over the whole foot. The tightly rounded instep supplements this function.

Close-fitting boots have the same utility as close-fitted gloves, giving maximum position awareness with minimum interfering structure. Like tight gloves, they are hard to take off. No cowboy, however, ever had the services of a footman to help him take them off Hollywood style, by straddling the leg, holding the boot, and being shoved ignobly in the behind with the other foot. In lieu of this ceremony the puncher had recourse to a bootjack, placed near the ranch house or bunkhouse door. The usual bootjack was an 18-inch length of 8-inch board with a notch sawed in one end. This end of the board was raised six to eight inches by a vertical piece. The boot was removed by hooking the heel of it in the notch and pulling the foot out while standing on the jack board with the other foot.

The River had its share of riders in the bronc buster class, and they were no less glamorous there than elsewhere. To be at or near the top of this class was to be a man of distinction in your own right, without respect to social or financial standing. To stay there very long usually involved accumulating such incidentals as sprained joints, broken bones, twisted backs, floating kidneys, and multiple bruises and scars commemorating violent contacts with corral poles, rocks on the ground, or the vindictive hooves of ornery cayuses. The fact that these occupational hazards deterred practically no one testifies to the prestige attached to high attainment in the ranks.

A solid degree of proficiency in horsemanship was a minimum requirement for even routine work in that steep country. Most men broke and trained their own horses. Some, like Pop and Ben Reeves, preferred to do it by easy degrees, gentling their animals in ways that seldom involved pitched battles. Those who aspired to reputation must be prepared to conquer their mounts by direct assault, pitting strength and skill against the wildest efforts of the untamed horse. It was a hard school. As in other highly demanding activities, many aspired but few attained.

The riding skill built up in day-to-day ranch work was put to competitive test at the roundups. These, I should explain, were what are called rodeos in many parts of the West, rather than occasions for working cattle on the range. A roundup was the common mode of celebrating the 4th of July, then by far the most important public event of the year. There the entrants drew lots for order of appearance and horses to be ridden. Among the lower ranks these were matters of small concern, as each rider got a fixed amount of "day money," usually $5.00 to $10.00 for each horse ridden into the arena, irrespective of the success of the ride or the cheers of the multitude. For those in the top competition, the luck of the draw could be important, for each rider was scored not only on how well he rode but, more importantly, on how difficult a horse he rode. No matter how good the rider, he could not score high on a poor bucker.

"sitting a fresh one!"

My recollections of the "Who's Who" of riders at that time are very sketchy. Certain names drift back in uncertain rank, and I mention most of them only as having been among those present. Jackson Sundown, Indian rider of Pendleton Roundup fame, was of championship caliber. I regret that I never got to see him ride. "Red" Pruitt, "Red" Patton, Len Ringer, Frank Woods and Gilbert Wayne enjoyed at least local reputation. Herschel Emerick, Ernest Lemon, Heman Vanpool, Frank Miller, Martin Bottorf - - - the list trails off.

Martin Bottorf was a hard luck rider. Some would say he crowded his luck in entering this strenuous occupation at all, for he was handicapped by a crippled foot on not too good a leg. A less gritty man certainly would have opted out, as did many more physically fit than he. But not Martin. Perhaps because of his handicap he felt a need to

Working "cowboys" of the Forest community dressed up for a picture—note white shirts and neckties. The angora chaps were standard gear for brushy riding and rope work in summer, and for warmth in winter. L to R Willie Wilkes, Harry Clovis, Billy Freeburn, Harry Weller, Paul Wohlen, Eddie Nelson, Walter "Red" Patton.

"Red Patton scratching out a rough one at the Forest roundup, 1910.

prove himself in the fraternity. Or perhaps he was determined to master horses because he had been crippled by one. For whatever reason, he dared with the hardiest.

As a boy, Martin told me, he had the chore of tending his father's stallion. The animal was high strung and contrary, and caused him much trouble when led to water, by jerking the halter rope out of his hands and then running about. After several such occurrences, Martin decided to use a longer rope, wrapping it around himself so that the horse could not jerk away. This worked for a time, but led to his downfall. For one day the stallion reared and pulled Martin off his feet, then began to run. The coiled rope slipped down around the boy's legs and dragged him feet first. His feet caught on the barn sill as the frightened horse charged into his stall, breaking both Martin's legs. One foot was crooked from then on.

While he was riding for Pop one spring, Martin was breaking a young mare. Raymond, his younger brother, was riding with him the day this untamed animal bolted and threw him, causing an inguinal rupture. Recovered from this injury, he entered the bucking contest at the Forest Roundup of that summer. The first horse he mounted threw him and stepped on his foot. This put him out of action for a day or two only. My last memory of Martin in that affair is of his later riding another horse in the contest, his injured foot still bandaged and the bandage end loosened and flying in the fray.

This was one case in which a white flag certainly was no token of surrender!

Coyotes, Mad And Sane

The threat of rabies stalked the Salmon River country throughout our stay there. It was endemic among the coyote population, and coyotes were numerous. In the late stages of rabies the afflicted animals become deranged, lose their normal fears, and are likely to snap at any other animal that comes within reach. Some cattle were lost to the disease.

Humans are susceptible to this dread scourge, along with most other mammals. Small children are especially likely to be infected because of their trust of pets which may carry rabies to an advanced stage without being suspected until the fateful bite has been delivered. One such case involved a small Genesee boy who came crying to his mother, saying he had been bitten by a big dog. No dog was found that the boy could identify as the one that bit him. When he later developed rabies and died it was surmised that he had been bitten by a mad coyote passing by.

Although treatment to prevent development of rabies in a bite victim was known then, it was not locally available. The treatment was prolonged and costly, and the disease was deservedly feared. Coyotes had the misfortune to become its symbol, and their extermination was earnestly sought. Guns, poison, traps and hounds were employed. Bounty hunters and government trappers added their efforts to those of the ranchers. The wily coyote survived them all. In later years it has been learned that he took all the blame for a disease that is carried over in many other small animals relatively immune to it, such as skunks and coons, which serve as reservoirs of infection for its periodic outbreaks. But this was not known then, and we kids were closely schooled in precautions about mad coyotes, and in anti-coyote doctrine in general.

My first recollection in this field is of Pop's hound, chained to a stake on the island between our house and barn. He had shown signs of rabies, and was tied there for observation until the diagnosis could be confirmed by further development of the disease, or dismissed as unfounded. In a short time his symptoms became unmistakeable and he was killed to end his suffering. He was the last of a pack of hounds Pop had used to run down and kill the coyotes. His fate illustrated the limitations of this approach to the coyote problem.

No one who has not felt the primeval chill that a coyote's howl at night sends along the human spine can appreciate the effect these animals had on us as children. For one thing, you always felt outnumbered. The coyote's howl is mixed with bursts of staccato yaps so rapid they sound like the product of a pack. When one coyote howls it is almost invariably answered by a brother in some other direction. If there are more within earshot, all take up the cry, and in a matter of seconds the wild sound may be coming from all quarters. Three or four coyotes orchestrating in this manner can give the impression of a small army.

One frosty moonlit night Kootsie and I had taken a horse to the Upper Barn to stable him. To get there we went up the wagon road from the Lower Barn, where Pop was busy. This road was cut at a slope into the side of the 50-foot high bench that rose above Deer Creek. On top of the bench was the alfalfa field, and across the field some two hundred yards was the Upper Barn. As we approached the barn a coyote howled at the upper edge of the field, a short eighth of a mile away. He was immediately joined by others. They sounded like a dozen.

We left the horse in the barn with unspoken but great reluctance. Had either of us been alone I am sure his nerve would have failed, and he would have ridden back to the other barn. Without admitting aloud that we were afraid, we started walking back. No sooner were we out of the shadow of the barn than the eerie coyote chorus broke out again, this time from well inside the field. We broke into a run, fear lending wings as only fear can. The coyotes gave chase, their sharp yaps coming closer at a terrifying rate. With a desperate burst of speed we hit the cutbank road and headed down toward the safety of the Lower Barn. As we did so I glanced up to the edge of the field to see five coyotes silhouetted against the moon, watching our flight.

It was one spring after the Big House burned that I had my only close brush with a mad coyote.

Pop, Muzzy and Tom were away somewhere, and Mrs. Ralph Ross was keeping house for us. She had three small children, the youngest of whom was Tommy, about three years old. I was at the woodshed, some 50 yards from the house, splitting wood to cook the noon meal. Tommy was playing nearby. The other Ross children were indoors, along with Mrs. Ross, Mary, Kootsie, Lorene and Jack.

I glanced up from my work just in time to see a pack of coyotes come over the hill 200 yards away, chasing another coyote along the trail. As I looked up they headed straight toward the house. Though no specific warning about mad coyotes had prepared me for this moment, I sensed instantly that the coyote being chased must be mad. With a shout of warning that sent the chickens squawking and brought everyone inside running to the doors, I grabbed up Tommy and dashed for the house. I was scarcely inside when the emaciated fugitive loped through the yard, seemingly near exhaustion, his tongue hanging out, his wild eyes staring. His pursuers stopped a short way off and went back the way they had come.

By the time we had caught our breaths from the tense moments of excitement, two men working on the ranch rode up, seized guns, and raced off after the fleeing coyote. They disappeared into the brush up the creek and reappeared on the far side, riding up through the steep rocks. Coyote and riders were in sight only briefly before passing from view over a ridge. Twenty minutes later the riders returned to report that their quarry had eluded and outdistanced them, making good his escape. Despite his deathly sickness and the ordeal already dealt him by his own kind, he was still the victor over man in this last dramatic contest before the fatal end soon to come from his disease.

It was one of the instinctive group defenses of nature, I learned later, for coyotes to turn upon a sick member of the pack and kill him. Presumably it was such a case that we witnessed that day. The group defense mechanism actually worked against them in the case of rabies, for more coyotes were infected in the fighting with the already diseased member.

No one knows how many coyotes died in the rabies epidemic that appeared at that time. It ran its course in a few seasons and dropped back to its endemic balance in the manner decreed by nature over countless centuries.

The coyote population was thinned more drastically by a new enemy introduced by man. This was the mange mite, brought into the country by infested livestock. Against this pest the coyote had no defense. Among the domestic stock the parasite was soon controlled by strict quarantine and dipping the animals in strong insecticide, but not before it got established among the wild Indian ponies that roamed the rough range country by the thousands, and among the coyotes. No respecter of species, the mange mite burrows into the skin of its victims to consume its hosts alive. Its activities cause intolerable itching, hair or wool falls out, the skin becomes raw and thickened from rubbing and scratching until the luckless victim dies from these multiplied miseries. Both ponies and coyotes were decimated, the ponies virtually exterminated.

Up And Down Deer Creek

Deer Creek is one of the largest on the north side of the Salmon River for a long distance. Upriver as far as Riggins it is exceeded only by Whitebird and Slate Creeks. Downriver the creeks get rapidly smaller with their successively smaller drainage basins as the western end of Craig Mountain tapers to a mere dividing ridge between the Salmon and Snake Rivers. Deer Creek has more drainage area on top of the mountain than all the creeks below it combined.

These facts had much to do with the flow characteristics of the creek as I knew it. Because most of its discharge came from the top of the mountain, it got a bigger surge of runoff during spring snowmelt than did the other creeks. But because there were very few springs on top of the mountain or elsewhere along its course, the summer flow of Deer Creek was small, and the lower end of the creek dwindled to a trickle by fall. The rapid drop of the creek course after it left the mountain top did not permit it to form many large deep pools. Hence, although the lower reaches of the creek teemed with small trout in the spring, there were few large ones in it.

For a small boy this was the ideal situation. You could depend on a bountiful catch of 6- to 9-inchers, with the chance of one as much as 12 inches long always a possiblity but not common enough to dull the edge of anticipation. Each of us first fished with a bent pin on a cotton or linen string, hung from a willow pole. Later we graduated to real store-boughten hooks and line, but never beyond the willow pole, except for Tom. I spent many happy hours along the creek, either alone or with Kootsie or Tom. Tom became a master angler for the wary trout, and set the record for that stream with a 14-inch whopper. He could always let me go first along the creek fishing the best holes, and take two trout to my one, coming along behind. He can still do it today on any stream we fish together.

On one occasion Tom and I had fished some three miles up Deer Creek, arriving at the Vincent Lorang place toward noon. We had brought no lunch and were famished. Finding the Lorangs were gone dashed our expectations of a free meal there in the custom of the country. Houses were never locked, so we could have fed ourselves, but the family had moved away and left neither food nor utensils behind. Knowing this could have happened only a few days before, we trusted the three eggs we found in the chicken

Deer Creek Falls going off the rim of Craig Mountain. Dropping 60 feet, this falls prevented downstream fish species from reaching the headwaters.

Bottom of Deer Creek falls, where deep pools held large trout such as the 12-inch rainbow displayed here by Tom Platt on a 1947 visit.

Emma C. (Mrs. John) Platt crossing Deer Creek in spring flood season, 1910. Note loose bridle reins. Because of uncertain footing among the rolling rocks of the creek bed, the horse was allowed to pick its own way.

John A. Platt with children Kenneth, Frances and Mary seated, Lorene standing. Preparing garden for planting, spring of 1910, Deer Creek Ranch.

Deer Creek Ranch home, spring of 1908. Standing, Emma C. Platt (L) and Elizabeth Steltz McMahon. On teeter-totter, Catherine McMahon, Frances Platt, Mary Platt, Tom Platt, Jesse McMahon.

house. We then looked for something to boil them in, but found no receptacle that would hold water. There were empty tin cans aplenty, but in those days the ends of tin cans were soldered on, and promptly fell off if the cans were heated.

Never mind, said Tom—we would roast the eggs. Soon we had fire going by the creek. After a fair bed of coals had developed Tom raked them aside, placed the eggs, and covered them over with ashes and hot embers. Our mouths watered for the feast soon to come, as we settled back to wait a while for the eggs to cook. Neither of us had ever eaten roasted eggs, but in our condition they loomed as a gourmet's delight.

But this delight was not to be. Our technique was faulty. When a small pop among the coals raised a puff of ash dust, we first thought a burning stick had snapped, as they do sometimes. But even as the thought came and went, two more muffled pops signaled the bad news: All three eggs had exploded from the heat because we had not thought to make a small hole in each of them for the expanding internal vapor to escape!

Our hunger now doubled by this rude disappointment, we faced the long walk home. Tom reached for his last resource. Out came a well secreted—and wholly forbidden—sack of Bull Durham cigarette tobacco, complete with attached papers. "Ne plus ultra" said the sign on the packet of papers—nothing finer. He set about rolling two cigarettes, the firm consolation of all true cowboys. We were not licked yet, not by a darned sight! Soon we were puffing the illicit products.

Up to this time I would have regarded myself as an accomplished smoker. At the seasoned age of 9 I had smoked every variety of grass and hollow-stemmed weed I could find. I had tested pine pollen cigarettes done in old newspaper. I had even ventured one purloined cigar, turning off several respectable puffs before a certain giddiness overtook me. Though most of these ventures had proved downright unpleasant, and none had given the satisfaction I imagined they should, I considered myself fully ready for the real thing. Now I was to learn a new respect for the one forbidden weed. The first few drags on the nicotinous "coffin nail" Tom had fashioned for me were my last. With violent retching my empty, protesting stomach rebelled.

As it turned out, this was my last serious attempt at smoking. Tom, already well inured, did not get sick, and went on to greater heights in this realm, culminating in the ability to roll a cigarette with one hand. I seem to recall that at one stage he aspired to the more demanding accomplishment of rolling a cigarette while riding at full gallop. If he never reached this goal I am sure it was because his limited supplies of "the makings" could not cover the wastage of the training period, and not for lack of determination or ultimate skill.

I have already mentioned the hazards of cactus for the unlucky rider or the unwary foot traveler. An even more prevalent and more dreaded threat for barefoot walking was the wild hawthorn brush that lined Deer Creek and extended up every side canyon.

The thorns on this tree grow in all directions from the twig, so that when a branch is broken off and drops to the ground some of the thorns are sure to be sticking up. As we made our barefoot way along the creek fishing, intent on evading the clawing branches above, it was all too easy to set foot on an upturned thorn. These barbs were from half an inch to an inch and a half long, needle sharp at the tip, thick as a bridge pencil at the base, and capable of running clear through your foot forward of the instep. If you felt the thorn in time you might be able to draw back or turn your foot so as to avoid the worst. But sometimes your stride was already past changing before the thorn struck home, and then you were out of luck.

The pain was always excruciating. To look down and see the wicked point of the thorn showing under the skin on the top of your foot, or actually sticking out through it, magnified the torture. At this stage you were lucky if the thorn was strong enough to be still attached to the branch, so that it could be pulled out. The old, brittle ones would break off and have to be dug for. It was a good thing that these seldom penetrated deeply before breaking.

Punctures clear through the foot were rare, I am glad to report. I remember only one of my own and one of Kootsie's. But we each had many lesser punctures to our credit. Anyone who has read the story of Androcles and the lion will recall that a thorn in the foot can disable even the king of beasts. We, too, were disabled, but not for long, and never so severely as to keep us from daring the thorny places once again. With the buoyancy of untaught youth, we were always confident that we could do better the next time.

A more dangerous, though less pervasive, threat to bare feet was upturned nails in old bits of board. No doubt we all had our turns, but I remember only the time that Kootsie stepped on one in the milking corral. It was old and rusty, and fouled with manure—a certain carrier of lockjaw germs by every criterion. It went clear through her foot. At her scream of pain, "Shorty," the hired man who was helping Muzzy at the moment, picked her up and yanked the nail out by standing on the board from which it protruded.

But now, how to disinfect this dangerous wound? The nearest doctor was a day's ride away; the ranch medicine supply offered nothing better than linament and hydrogen peroxide. "Shorty" had the answer: Put the foot immediately into warm cow dung, which would serve as a poultice to "draw the poison out." No more promising idea being thought of, the treatment was applied on the spot for the next 20 minutes. Whether because of this or in spite of it, the foot recovered in a few days, and without infection.

One of our prime spring pastimes took us directly to the thorn trees. These were the favorite nesting place of the detested magpie. There this cunning bird built a veritable castle for his family, and to rob or destory it took time and determination.

To keep a whole skin in the process required painstaking removal of thorns and limbs guarding the chosen approach. Once within reach of the nest you might find your main work still before you. Built of dead thorn twigs and branches up to half an inch thick, the nest was a tangled mass a foot or more across and up to two feet high. Entry into the hollow center was through an irregular hole in one side. This hole was usually too small for the hand, and often out of reach anyway. The crown of the structure must be dismantled stick by thorny stick until an opening big enough to reach through had been made.

Our objective was the eggs inside, or the young birds, as the case might be. The eggs were a speckled pale brown, prized as trophies rather than for their beauty. We pierced both ends with a thorn point, blew out the contents, and strung the shells on a thread brought along for the purpose. Young birds we destroyed without compunction, thinking of how the mature birds would peck out the eyes of a starving cow too weak to fight them off, or perch on its back and eat holes between its ribs. Robbing magpie nests could fill whole days, but the nesting season was short and did not afford many excursions. Our depredations afflicted a negligible portion of the total magpie population even within our immediate territory.

Another pest that led us to adventure was the much maligned skunk. Skunks were regular inhabitants along Deer Creek, though not in large numbers. They were unwelcome when close to the ranch because they were a threat to the chickens. In a way the threat was not great, since a skunk will take only one hen at a time, whereas a weasel will slaughter a whole flock just for the fun of it. On the other hand, with chicken feed having to be packed in on horses, to have chickens at all was something of a luxury, and one usually limited to a dozen or so hens. We were not inclined to share this luxury with visiting skunks.

One thing about a skunk, he is no secret agent. His comings and goings are well advertised by his strong, far reaching, long lasting, unmistakeable, and singularly offensive odor. If it were not for this odor I think skunks might even be welcome at many tea parties. They are dainty creatures, beautifully marked with a broad white stripe from nose to plume-like tail contrasting with jet black fur everywere else. They are easily tamed, make cuddly pets, and catch mice as well as cats do. But all these virtues are as naught when set over against smelling like a skunk and having a taste for poultry.

So it was that when Mary and I one day sighted a skunk ambling across an open grassy area a quarter mile up the creek, we seized sticks and stones and went in hot pursuit with all the zeal of our elders' prejudices.

69

The skunk is not built for speed, relying for defense on his strong offense. This is more than just the odor. As the enemy closes in, the skunk hoists his tail and fires a fine spray of eye-burning, blinding liquid from a special gland. This is enough to turn back most of his natural enemies such as dogs, coyotes, badgers and bobcats. It is not adequate against humans, who can stand out of range of the skunk's gun and throw rocks and clubs. Mary and I pursued our quarry relentlessly. When he dashed for cover we cut him off. When he survived direct hits with the small rocks we were able to find, we dashed rashly in and beat him to the ground with sticks.

The unequal struggle was finished in a matter of minutes. Triumphantly I grabbed the lifeless form and flung it into the creek to quench its reeking odor. Then, flushed with victory and virtue, we ran for home to receive the accolades we had earned.

Alas for the idealism of youth! The rest of the family, plus the usual two or three hired men, were at dinner when we arrived. We scarcely got inside the door. As one voice came the chorus: "Get out of here! You smell like skunks."

How quickly can joy turn to bitterness! We stood condemned for an incidental aspect of a basically noble deed. Had not all those who condemned us benefitted from our action? Indeed they had! Had not we taken upon ourselves the entire disagreeable job of disposing of the enemy? Indeed we had! Yet all our virtue was as naught when set over against smelling like a skunk. The judgment of society gave us short shrift. We were no more welcome than the skunk himself.

Well, almost. We were first sent back to the scene of our late triumph to retrieve the dead skunk from the creek and bury him. It seems I had failed to consider the effect his carcass would have on the flavor of our drinking water, dipped from the creek below. When we returned from this ignominious chore, Muzzy tossed us each a change of clothes and told us to go shuck our contaminated gear. Then, after prolonged washing of hands and faces, we were at last admitted—though not really welcomed—back into the house.

There were other encounters with skunks. Kootsie and I found a den of kits one spring, which we thought would make good pets. The young skunk does not have the stink gland of the adult developed to usable size, so does not give off its evil odor. Having no way to carry them home, we tied them by their tails to a nearby hackberry limb so they could not get out of reach while we went for a gunnysack. But adult judgment vetoed our idea as impractical, and adult executioners dispatched both the helpless kits and their mother.

This particular cluster of natural gems would be incomplete should I fail to pay my respects to the joys and pains of going barefoot in a country setting. Cactus and thorns were hazards implicit in our otherwise superior way of life. But that these weighed less in the balance than the joys of winged feet is attested by the fact that the shoe season was always too long and barefoot summer too short. At this date I no longer recall why our shoes became unbearable as spring edged away from winter. I only remember that we teased and complained and lamented each new season until Muzzy yielded against her better judgment, risking the colds we might catch rather than longer endure our importuning.

Those who have gone barefoot only on city sidewalks and grassy lawns have tasted neither the highs nor the lows of this most primitive and ancient mode of ambulation. They have not known either the velvet caress of soft cool dust along a morning trail, or the numbing, stabbing, hobbling pain of a toe stubbed at full speed against an unnoted rock. They have not felt the primordial thrill of untrammeled contact with natural earth and water. They have not learned the gladdening way of the foot in gradually toughening to withstand rough going. They have missed the sense of awareness that flows from feet relaying to the control centers of poise and locomotion the shape and size, the texture and temperature, the wetness or dryness or slickness, the slope and stability, of all that they press upon.

I cannot explain all this. I cannot even describe it well any more. I only let the fact speak for itself, that each summer until my 13th the joys of going barefoot outweighed all the woes of cuts and thorn punctures, heat blisters and stone bruises, cracked and stubbed toes, chapping, compulsory washing, horsefly bites and hornet stings. Perhaps this periodic return to nature answered an instinctive urge of the child, as falling in love answers the instinctive need of approaching maturity. I can only speculate.

Finally, let me say we were not barefoot because Pop and Muzzy begrudged us shoes. They would much rather have had us shod, I am sure, than to bear with the summerlong round of washing and medicating and bandaging the five pairs of feet from Mary's on down. One memorable year Pop outfitted us in the spring with what should have been the ultimate answer to our rocky trails and hills—copper-toed shoes! In our stony realm, toe-caps always were the first part of the shoe to go. The copper caps were designed to end that vulnerability. We gave them a good testing, no doubt, but they must have been less than a perfect solution for we never got more of them.

Up And Down The River

The Salmon River canyon, from its beginning 250 miles upstream to its mouth at the Snake River, is a land of precipitious slopes, precarious rockslides, jutting rimrocks, plunging depths, impassable gorges. Cutting from east to west across the central mountain mass of Idaho, it divides the state into two sections which, for the first 75 years from territorial beginnings, hardly knew each other. Because of this division, the idea of forming two states was a lively poltical subject throughout pioneer times. Even as late as

1930 it was a truth-in-jest saying that Idaho had three capitals, none of them in the state: Salt Lake City for the southeast, Portland for the southwest, and Spokane for the area north of the Salmon. Portland no longer exerts the pull it once did, but the north-south split dividing at the southern end of Idaho county still holds to an unfortunate degree.

Among the ideas explored for tying north and south more firmly together was that of building a north-south railroad within Idaho to join the two sections. One prospective route for it lay along the Salmon River from Riggins on down. Earliest transcontinental railway surveys had seen a Northern Pacific survey in 1872 along the full length of the Salmon. In 1886 Union Pacific surveyors ran a line up the Weiser River and down the Little Salmon and main Salmon Rivers. A railroad later was built up the Weiser to New Meadows, but was not extended down the Salmon. For occupants along the river the dream died hard, and talk of it was revived when land survey crews came along 20 years later. The spring of 1911 saw a land survey crew encamped for some weeks at the mouth of Deer Creek, within sight of our house, putting final touches on original surveys done in 1906. From then until we left The River in 1917 our young imaginations were spurred from time to time as we came across the survey stakes they left behind. To us the stakes attested the possibility of passage through our world, and the existence of larger worlds beyond. They beckoned to wider peregrinations.

The main lure was upriver. Downriver we could see several miles along the canyon, and in that direction we knew the names of all of the inhabitants. Most of them rode to or by our ranch enroute to Forest; there was no mystery about them. Upstream a massive ridge reached down from Craig Mountain to block the view less than two miles away. Behind that barrier Elmer Taylor had a homestead, we knew, and somewhere up there also lived Jim Kennedy. These solid figures occasionally rode our way, lending reality to their habitat, but beyond them was only the unknown. At some vast distance it contained Whitebird, site of a storied moment in the Nez Perce Indian war of 1877. And even beyond Whitebird, we dimly understood, lay the Buffalo Hump country where our band of sheep were swallowed up in summer, and where hardy herders like Clyde Rencehausen and "Scotty" Hollingsworth defended them against bear and cougar.

As long as we were afoot the trail upriver, climbing high over the ridge to get above its towering terminal cliffs, was too arduous to tempt us. Midway between trail and river, though, ran the flume line leading to the placer mine I have already mentioned. We were introduced to its possibilities as a walk-way when it went out of service and Pop bought lumber from it for the ranch. The first major section of the flume, in fact, stood not far from the upper end of our alfalfa field. There it bridged a sharp canyon, supported by a trestle of awesome height, perhaps 50 feet or more. I remember

72

"helping" to dismantle this flume, with a tendency to keep one foot on solid ground as much as possible. The trestle was left standing, as the work of salvaging it was greater than the value of its lumber.

When Kootsie and I finally ventured beyond this point the remaining flume already was going to pieces. Some sections had collapsed where earth or rock slips below had broken the trestling. Other sections were beginning to sag from general deterioration. These conditions added spice to the adventure of following it as far as we could. Without mishap we went to where a large and high section had broken away and tumbled down the cliff it once had skirted. Maybe it was as much as a mile from our field. There prudence, or perhaps the growing distance from home and the next meal, turned us back.

That day we saw a sight of the once-in-a-lifetime category. A large hawk from among the many soaring above suddenly dived to a nearby ledge and lofted away with a three-foot rattlesnake hung from its talons. As we watched, the hawk dropped his writhing captive and we thought it had wriggled free. But not so. Swooping close behind, the hawk again snatched the snake from the ground and carried it up. From a height of 300 feet or so the drop was repeated. Again the swooping retrieval, followed by another drop. After still another drop or two the hapless rattler dangled lifeless as the hawk sailed off with it for a grisly feast.

A year later we dared the unknown with a horseback venture beyond this point to the Taylor homestead cabin. There we found Elmer Taylor and Roy Murdick and their respective sisters, in a setting that many Western story writers have turned to good account over the years. In real life, Elmer, a great grandson of Zachary Taylor, married Eva Murdick, and a 1967 Lewiston newspaper story recounted their 50th wedding anniversary, celebrated on their Salmon River ranch. On the occasion of our visit, Elmer's phonograph was rendering a popular tune of the day which contained the lines:

"Where there are wild men there must be wild women —
So where did Robinson Crusoe go.
With Friday on Saturday night?"

Elmer and Eva evidently found the right answer.

Few excursions up the ridges of our surrounding area were complete without a stint of rock rolling. Many climbs were made for this sport alone. There was a special fascination in watching the loosened boulders gather speed down the steep inclines, leaping ever wider spaces, to send up clouds of dust and electrifying rumbles from the final shattering crash at the bottom. The greater the height from which the dislodgement started, the longer the sight lasted. The larger the size of the boulder, the greater the thrill of watching its devastating descent.

There were strict admonitions from Pop never to roll rocks where there might be people or livestock below, or across trails, or into places where we could not see what was there. We found abundant opportunity within these limitations, and rarely transgressed them.

The rocks at hand were ideal for our purpose. The ancient lava flows that had formed the ledges and rimrocks were crystallized into vertical hexagonal columns from one to two feet across. The columns were packed together like the cells in a honeycomb. Sometimes they were only a few feet high; sometimes 50 feet or more, usually in vertical position. Where exposed, through the ages these columns had weathered into horizontal sections, often about the same length as their diameters. Turned up on one of its hexagonal sides, such a section rolled readily. The dense, hard basalt rarely broke in rolling, even when it hit more of its own kind, but bounded from one strike to the next with ever greater force and seeming indestructability. If there were other loose boulders along its path, some of these might be struck and set rolling, in turn setting off still others, so that in the end a score or more of assorted sizes would be racing pell mell toward the bottom.

No particular episode comes back to me from these rock rollings. But there was something about them—the setting in motion of immeasurable latent powers, to create spectacles of speed and force—that answered a deep seated urge. In them we triggered displays of natural violence without retributive consequences. It was at once an exciting and a primitively satisfying experience, giving the sense of daring to use fragments of a power vastly greater than our own.

In all our walking of the hills we kept a sharp eye out for Indian relics. The most common of these were arrowheads. They varied in color from pure white quartz to pitch black obsidian, with many shades of red and brown flints in between. Sizes ran from half an inch to an inch long. In this stony land, few had come to our time without some breakage. Finding one that was both complete in all details and superior in workmanship was its own reward. When those qualities were combined in an arrowhead of especially attractive color, it merited mounting as a tiepin or brooch. Over the years our collection grew to a shoe box full. When the Big House burned, the heat shattered most of these, and we did not stay long enough on The River afterward to recoup our loss.

Apparently the predecessor people whose artifacts we found had been far along in the stone-age advance in weaponry. The arrowheads we collected were mostly of the type with two barb points at the back to keep the arrow from coming out, once well embedded in its victim. Such points could not move backward, but would work on inward as long as the animal continued to move. Occasionally we found parts of mortars and pestles. These grinding implements were fashioned of granite, for the basalt was so hard it could only be sized and shaped with much labor. Our one fully perfect and matched set, found by Kootsie, also was destroyed in the Big House fire.

Rattlesnakes, bullsnakes, blacksnakes, watersnakes, blue racers, and lizards of several sizes and colors engaged our interest in the warm spring months. The harmless bullsnakes we handled at will and did not harm. The quick darting lizards were a challenge to catch and hard to hold, as their tails broke off easily. We had the notion that their tails grew back on, but never had the chance to prove it.

Rattlesnakes outnumbered all the rest. They were always an object of sharp lookout as we wandered the hills. This poisonous reptile was rightly feared and duly respected. By the same token, he was inexorably destroyed whenever encountered, if his escape could be prevented.

I am not sure that this treatment was warranted. The rattler always warned of his presence, and seldom initiated combat. When attacked, he usually retreated if possible. I only knew of one person being bitten by a rattlesnake, and that case was not fatal. Like other snakes, the rattler doubtless had his place in the scheme of nature, helping to keep in check the small rodents and other creatures whose over abundance could destroy the necessary food supplies of yet other species.

These finer points of nature's equity, however, were unknown to either our elders or ourselves at that time. The rattler led our "most wanted" list, and suffered the consequences. How many we killed I could not guess, other than to suppose it was in the scores. Whenever we did kill one, the rattles on his tail were taken for a trophy and proof of the kill. The rattles are made up of a succession of loosely jointed hollow sections of thin horny material. The widest section is joined to the living flesh of the tail, which somehow produces it as a finger produces a fingernail. If complete, the set tapers to a point. The piece joining the tail of the snake is called a "button".

As big rattlesnakes were considered more dangerous than small ones, so the rattle trophies were prized for size and length. It was unusual to find a set of more than 10 sections. A new section was formed each time the snake cast its skin. We used to count the snake's age by the number of its rattles, but in a good food year more than one skin cast might occur and more than one new rattle be formed. I have killed many large rattlers with only seven or eight rattles attached, but with the smallest section wider than the biggest one on a complete string of 12 or more. I have supposed that these larger snakes were as old as 20 years or more.

The most dangerous time to encounter a rattlesnake is right after it has cast its skin. At that time it is temporarily blind, very irritable and suspicious, and likely to strike defensively with little or no warning. In most cases this period occurs in late summer or early fall.

There is something about the buzz of a rattlesnake "sounding off" that is like no other sound, and that carries an instinctive warning to man. Many kinds of plants produce vaguely similar sounds when ripened seed pods are brushed against. These may startle the rattler-tuned ear momentarily, but only so. On the other hand, I have never known the real thing to be mistaken for a harmless sound. I have seen men who had never heard it before leap quickly out of the way at their first true encounter. The sound seems to carry a note of urgency that is recognized by dogs and horses also, for both will quickly take their distance when they hear it. No doubt other animals likewise know and respect this sound.

Various aspects of our ranch life not of episodic or adventure caliber nevertheless call for a place in this account. Though the reader may find similar items chronicled elsewhere, they are included here as part of the era being recalled. One of these was a household institution known as the kitchen range.

Housewives today enjoy its successors—immaculate white enameled symbols of efficiency, convenience and cleanliness. The modern versions have automatic ovens, pushbutton heat controls, limitless supplies of electricity or gas to fuel them at a flick of the finger. Believe me, ladies, the kitchen range was not ever thus. Today's proud beauty queen grew from Cinderella beginnings. Readers living even yet beyond the reach of electricity or gas will please bear with me on this subject.

One evolutionary step back of the kitchen range of 50-60 years ago was the ordinary "cook stove." This was a wood burning 4-lid model with an 18 x 24-inch top and an oven big enough for a 12 x 15-inch pan of biscuits or three 5 x 12-inch loaves. Heat for the entire stove came from the firebox at the left side. There the fire was kindled with wood shavings or pitch splinters or newspaper, and some fast-burning small sticks. Distribution of heat to the rest of the stove was accomplished by leading the smoke and flames through various courses to reach the exit pipe. Until the initial smoke had cleared out and a brisk fire was established, the shortest course to the stove pipe was left open, and maximum draft openings were used. Once the fire was burning hot and clear you could set the damper system to force the heat stream to pass around the oven on its way to the pipe. Greatest heat was directly over the firebox, and that was where the frying and other fast cooking was done. Pots needing less heat were placed farther to the right; those that needed only to simmer were placed on the back corner.

The range was of this same basic design, but a more elaborate model. It had a bigger firebox, six lids instead of four, and a 24 x 40-inch top. On the right hand side it had a reservoir holding up to four gallons, where water could be heated to scalding temperature in the course of a day's cooking. Rising from the back across the full length of the cooking surface was a heavy iron sheet supporting, at eye level, a large warming oven. The warming oven stuck forward a foot or so over the top of the stove and provided space to set steaks, biscuits, hotcakes, gravy, or other items that needed to be stockpiled or kept warm while other cooking proceeded. Under the warming oven at each end was a small iron shelf for the salt box, the grease can, and other items frequently needed.

Plain ranges were all black iron. All models had heat guard bars across the front and the left end to prevent burning yourself or your clothes if you leaned against the stove. On the fancier models these guard bars and the warming oven trim would be of shiny nickel steel. The curved pull-down covers of the warming oven might even be white enamel. The main body of the stove was black, and was refurbished from time to time with a brisk rubdown with stove blacking, which usually left its mark on your hands until about time for the next rubbing.

The oven had no thermometer, the cook's face serving as a register when the oven door was opened for checking. Fuel injection was through the firebox door at the left front—always too hot to open or close with the bare hand—or through the front lid opening on top. The skillful cook was, by definition, a skillful fireman as well. Ashes fell through the firebox grate into an ashbox at floor level, and were removed whenever this receptacle got full. This was one detail which the designers never perfected, for a good share of the ashes always fell behind and beside the pull-out box, and had to be pulled out with an ash rake. Invariably the ashes were so light and fine that this process raised clouds of dust which settled on every exposed surface in the kitchen, and simultaneously raised the ire of the cook, no matter who. Soot and fly ash also accumulated under the rest of the cooking surface and inside the stovepipe, and had to be removed once or twice a year with great caution to minimize the dust.

By the time I was eight years old I had become inseparably associated with our kitchen range. It was my job to keep the woodbox beside it filled and the kindling supply replenished, and to carry out the ashes weekly or oftener. I kept these jobs until I went off to college. The wood stocking turned out to be an education in itself. I learned how to split the toughest knots long before I developed enough strength to master them by brute force. That skill saved me a lot of sweat over the years, but it is a skill almost as much abandoned now as the region where I learned it.

The woodpile from which the stove supplies came was an institution in its own right. Let me note a few highlights of the Deer Creek woodpile unique to the time and place.

When Pop and Muzzy first moved to Deer Creek from their earlier home at

Skeleton Gulch on the other side of the Salmon, with Tom, Mary and Kootsie in tow, the Dorchester family still lived there. They included Uncle Wes, Aunt Laura, and their children Leonard and Caroline. The men, busy with their daily rounds on the ranch, neglected the woodpile. Despite repeated wifely reminders it dwindled to nothing. The women scrounged up dead brush from along the creek to keep the home fires going, but warned that this could not go on indefinitely.

All urgings and pleadings having failed, Aunt Laura and Muzzy at last resolved on a stratagem of counter attack against this indifference, at its most vulnerable point. On a day when no manly strokes of the ax were struck, they prepared all the makings of a feast for bear-hungry men—and set them on rocks in the yard for the sun to cook! When Pop and Uncle Wes rode in that evening from a lunchless ten hours of cowpunching, there the meal still stood, as raw as ever. There were brief fireworks of temper before the men saw that they were properly licked, and hastened to get the kitchen fire going and the woodbox filled.

A new era in wood supplying was ushered in that night. Thereafter annual supplies were laid in each spring. Whether cut from green trees or obtained by pulling passing logs out of the river during flood, it was well dried and seasoned for the following winter. By the time I inherited the work of the wood pile there was at least an assured stock of wood to work on.

One year of this era stands apart. That year we got our wood from Eagle Creek. It was cut several miles up the creek by Martin and Raymond Bottorf on the homestead from which they were eking out a thin living. During the winter they cut big fir and pine trees into stovewood lengths, split the round blocks into sizeable wedges, and ricked them alongside the creek to dry. When spring runoff came, they threw the wood into the creek to be floated down. Eagle Creek was one of the brushiest creeks on earth, and the wood lodged in a thousand places. Long pike poles armed at one end with a combination iron spike point and hook were used to push or pull the blocks loose and keep them moving.

Meanwhile, Pop had laid a sturdy log across the creek on the downstream side of the wagon crossing at the Mike Rudolph place, just above where Eagle Creek empties into the Salmon. On the upstream side of the log he thrust stout poles against the creek bed, slanting them away from the log and nailing them to it at 6-inch intervals to form a grill through which the floating wood blocks could not pass. As the blocks arrived, Pop and the other men dipped them out with pitchforks, tossing them onto a heap on our side of the creek. There a wagon was kept busy hauling the wood to our place, a mile away.

All this was too heavy work for my 8-year-old frame, but I was an interested spectator. The wood drive lasted a week or so. Each day the men would work till dark, and next morning a new supply that had come down during the night would be floating against the boom. The creek rose each day as the sun melted more snow on the headwaters, and fell each night when the melting stopped. Thus the floating blocks tended to lodge along the creek at night, and the "night delivery" usually was light.

This regimen was just what was needed to fit the main arrivals of wood to the daylight hours. It worked well until a rain in the high country raised the creek during the night. When we went to pitch out wood next morning the hundreds of blocks carried down that night had broken the boom and escaped into the river. The boom was quickly repaired and the pitching out process resumed. Luckily a big eddy at the mouth of Eagle Creek had trapped most of the lost blocks, and there Pop retrieved them with our rowboat, which he brought down through the rapids. But some went on, I suppose, to the Pacific Ocean, for there were no dams to stop them at that time.

Going To the Mountain

As the lower Salmon River canyon was The River to all its denizens, so Craig Mountain bordering its north and west sides was The Mountain to us. It is a region rather than a peak. Beginning at Cottonwood Butte on the east, it fills most of the 40-mile space between the Salmon and Clearwater Rivers from there westward to the Snake River, a distance of 40 to 60 miles according to where you measure. The region is named for its first recorded white occupant, William Craig, who settled there with an Indian wife soon after Presbyterian missionary Henry Harmon Spalding established his mission station in 1836 at the present site of the town of Lapwai ("Butterfly Valley" in the Nez Perce language) 12 miles above present day Lewiston.

Craig Mountain may best be described as a massive plateau. Cotto__ ood Butte at its eastern end and Mason Butte 15 miles to the west are the only points of any consequence rising above the general level of 4,500 to 5,000 feet. The many creeks draining off to north and south have cut their respective canyons into its flanks. The larger ones all start as gently flowing streams in flat basins on top of the plateau. Deer Creek takes its rise in such a setting.

In the years that we lived at Deer Creek Ranch, our summer cattle range was on the headwaters of Deer Creek. The creek then flowed through several miles of meadows. There its sodded banks overhung deep, smoke-blue, dark, still, mysterious pools in which lay concealed shy eastern brook trout so beautiful with their red-dotted sides that I almost regretted catching them. They were an introduced species in a part of the creek that had no other fish. Deer Creek falls, leaping a sheer 60 feet off the rim of the mountain, barred all downstream fishes.

The undulating ridges reaching back from the meadows were clothed with majestic yellow pine, red fir and tamarack trees. White fir shared the shady, damp north and east slopes, and blue spruce claimed certain boggy spots. Lodgepole pine occupied sites not well suited to the larger trees. Occasional small groves of aspen found place where soil depth and moisture favored them. Alder thickets followed down the small streams flowing from upland springs to the main creek, carpeted underneath with ferns and sedges.

Except for the small clearings left by the former timber claim holders who had built their cabins, proved up their claims, sold out and moved on, the whole was virgin forest untouched by ax or saw. A small sawmill formerly operated at Forest was defunct, its last slab piles rotting and crumbling away. The only mill operating west of Cottonwood was at Winchester, near the center of the Mountain. The old pines were three to five feet in diameter and up to 100 feet tall. The tamaracks were just as big, and sometimes 120 feet tall. The firs were similarly lordly, the spruce and lodgepole smaller. Beneath the canopy of the mature trees were either open grassy forest floor or thickets of young pine or fir. There was no brush save the ankle-high kinnikinic, scattered wild rose and snowberry, and occasional patches of huckleberries. Despite a few stretches of sagging rail or pole fence and some primitive roads, I remember it as forest primeval, with all the lure of the unknown, and with limitless scope for adventure.

Our annual pilgrimage to The Mountain usually fell on or about July 1, right after the first cutting of alfalfa hay had been put into the barns at Deer Creek Ranch. By that time the cattle had grazed their way gradually up the long ridges to the mountain top, and the sheep had been herded to their summer range at distant Buffalo Hump. The Salmon River canyon bottom by then was a place where even the lizards and rattlesnakes sought shade at midday, and where smooth rocks on the trails were blistering hot to bare feet. We were glad to head for the cool region of the tall timber.

Going to The Mountain marked annual entry into a different realm, enlarging every year as we grew in knowledge and understanding. But it was more than just the door to another area — it was an event in itself. Preceded by much parental thought and preparation, the day nevertheless always was a crowded one, especially for Muzzy. Hers was the job of sorting and packing the family clothing, bedding, cooking utensils, food supplies, and other necessities to equip our summer camp. Even though years of experience brought a pattern to this task, and the limit of available pack horses precluded the non-essential, moving day seemed to precipitate upon her an irreducible, indivisible, time-demanding quota of tedious work.

First, family and ranch crew must be fed, and the breakfast dishes washed. Next, small fry too young to look after themselves must be seen to and gotten out from under foot. Then Pop would bring the pack boxes to be filled. Into them went every household item that would be needed over the next four months. Groceries would be replenished during that time, but not many other things. Few breakables or perishables were included. Everything was fitted into something else. The teakettle would hold table cutlery, spice cans, salt and pepper shakers; all properly bedded in dishtowels to prevent rattling noises that might "spook" the packhorse. Skillets were layered with back issues of *The Genesee News* or *The Toledo Blade* and nested into one another by size. Tin or granite cups went into cooking kettles, along with more dishtowels. Food supplies to be packed were minimal, for it was easier to bring these from Forest than to take them from the ranch.

In our earlier years we children were a special packing problem. One could be carried, though with great inconvenience, by an adult rider, but what to do with the rest? The answer—put them in boxes! Boxes well suited for the purpose were at hand. In those days before the automobile age had ushered in bulk deliveries, kerosene for lamps and lanterns came in rectangular 5-gallon cans, and the cans came two in a box. Kerosene was not "kerosene" then, but "coal oil," a byproduct of the coking industry. Coal oil boxes were stoutly made of first-grade pine lumber to hold the heavy oil cans. They were the universal packing box of the Salmon River country, and the natural recourse used for solving the "children packing" problem. One box on each side of a gentle packhorse. A large child in one box, two small ones in the other, for balance. The passengers could stand up or squat, view the scenery or duck into the box to escape raking brush along the trail, or even sleep in safety.

This mode of travel was outgrown at five or six years of age. By then you could ride behind a grownup and hold on. At eight you rode independently if there were enough horses.

The trail we usually used to go to The Mountain was a scenic route. It climbed some 4,000 feet in about six miles. Beginning with a short steep rise to get above the gorge where the irrigation pipeline crossed Deer Creek, it joined the main trail coming from ranches downriver. From there the course ran nearly level as far as the Ross homestead, then angled steeply up and along the canyon side. Just above the Lorang place it went into a series of switch-backs which we called the zigzag. The zigzag went up nearly a thousand feet in the next mile. It brought the trail to the top of a large bench area that extended horizontally along the canyon some two miles, ending at Deer Creek Mine. At the mine the trail crossed to the east side of Deer Creek and went up a hogback ridge as steep as a cow's face, or up the steep gulch that flanked it. The gulch trail, by winding around a lot, took a somewhat easier grade, but it was brushy and disagreeable to ride. The two came together again at the Weller place, just at timberline and not far from the top. A wagon road came to the Weller place from Forest. Branches of it went to the Aytch place at the lower end of Deer Creek meadows, and various other places nearer town. The Aytch family, and, some miles upstream, the Starrs, Wyeths, Worhans and Bedwells, were the only families then living on that part of The

81

"from Craig Mountain to the Salmon — down, down, down

Mountain. Our summer camps, in the years of my recollection, were three different cabins left by departed timber claim settlers.

The first of these was the Burton place. It was a log cabin located on the west side of Deer Creek, and was reached by a different trail than the one I have described. I remember little of this trail, but I remember well the occasion of my last trip over it. Tom and I were sent up a day ahead of the rest of the family, to take the milk cow. The cow had a young calf that tired out by mid-afternoon of the long, hot climb. The calf had the full sympathy of its mother, and at every opportunity one or both would turn off the trail into bordering brush. As an extra rider sitting behind Tom on our one horse, I was a hindrance to him in the frequent job of getting the reluctant beasts out of the brush and on their way again. Toward the end of the day the trail became steeper and progress slower. Darkness overtook us when we were still far below the cabin. No longer able to see the cow and calf when they slipped off into the brush, we had to go on without them. Fortunately they were too tired to have any notion of going back down during the night, and Tom easily found them next day and brought them on up.

We had left the ranch in hot-weather clothes, coatless and, in my case, barefoot. With darkness the high mountain air soon became cold. By the time we got to the cabin my teeth were chattering. When Tom draped a quilt around me while he started the fire, my discomfort was compounded at first, for the quilt itself was cold. But in a short time I learned a lesson that has been useful to me many times since, for even my shivering body gave off enough heat to warm the quilt, and the quilt held the heat against me. I was comfortable from my own body heat well before the fire had warmed the room.

Another experience of that night still stays with me. After the fire had done its work and the open grate across the front of the stove was glowing with the heat, a piece of unburned limb sticking through it seemed to me in need of being pushed inside. I pushed, the limb slipped in more easily than I expected, and I touched a bar of the grate. The scar from that contact still slants the length of the second joint of my left index finger.

The chill of that night was a foretaste of the next few days. We woke on the morning of the 4th of July to half an inch of fresh snow! Our few firecrackers, hoarded from the year before, were slender 2-inch "lady-fingers" with little authority even at their best. They failed miserably to meet our expectations that they would shatter the small snowballs in which we packed them. That was the all-round least successful 4th of July of my experience.

In the summer of 1917, when I was 9½ years old, Mary, Kootsie, Lorene and I were sent up the trail ahead of the packstring. We rode double, on two horses. On the back of each saddle Muzzy had tied fried egg sandwiches, slung in the small cotton bags

Packed for leaving Craig Mountain summer camp, 1908
Emma C. Platt mounted.

"Children's special" for riding the Salmon River trails. The "Continental Safety Oil" was household lamp oil, two 5-gallon cans to the box. The boxes were reused as seats, cupboards, and sawhorses, as well as for packing. L to R Platt children Mary (4½), Frances (2½), and Kenneth (1) under the black hat.

Riding from Craig Mountain summer camp to Deer Creek Ranch in December, 1910. Art Keane in the lead with Mary Platt holding on behind him, Frances and Kenneth in boxes on middle horse, Emma C. Platt at rear carrying baby Lorene.

1916-1917 Platt summer camp on Craig Mountain. Size and density of trees were typical of most of the mountain then.

in which table salt then was dispensed in 10-pound lots. The day was bright and hot. As we climbed above the Ross place we soon reached an elevation where the countless splashings of the creek below filled the canyon with a subdued roar. At first it was hardly noticeable. But its persistent buffeting sound finally demanded conscious attention. Presently we covered our ears with our hands, wagging them to produce all manner of on-and-off sound patterns. When this amusement wore thin we could only bear the now monotonous and oppressive sound with impatience as our heaving horses toiled up the trail.

The zigzag that day seemed endless, and I do not doubt that we urged our steeds on to get away from the creek noise as soon as possible. At any rate, by the time we topped out onto the bench at the Ernest Verzanni place their flanks were dripping sweat and small patches of lather bordered the saddle skirts. Horses and riders both were glad to take a lunch stop and cool off in the shade of nearby thornbrush. Off came the salt sacks, and down we sat to eat the sandwiches.

But then what dismay! Dangling behind the saddles on the steep climb, the bags had slid out onto the sweating hides of the horses, and the bottom half of each sandwich was soggy with their brine! Famished though we were, we could not stomach this fare. Only the top slice of bread on each sandwich was edible, and that was far from enough. We made up the deficit with cold baking powder biscuits and syrup at the Carson Moffet ranch, next along the trail.

Like so many other families soon to follow, the Verzannis already had vacated their canyonside homestead. Like others, they had fulfilled the minimum requirements of the homestead law by living there at least six months each year for three consecutive years, fencing their land, and plowing and planting a token acreage. But such a place could not possibly make a living for a family. With no good hayland, it could not even serve as a home base for grazing livestock on open lands of the surrounding area. As soon as the homestead was "proved up" it was sold to someone with a hayland base. I have mentioned already that the Lorang family had left that spring; they never returned. Although we did not know it that day, we also were going up from The River for the last time.

From the Verzanni place, when coming up the trail, we always looked back down Deer Creek canyon, across the Salmon River canyon, over the timber-blue mountains beyond, to search the distant horizon for a glimpse of the Seven Devils peaks. On this day we were not disappointed. Glistening with snow, their sharp caps pierced the sky a full 60 airline miles away, where they towered above the Idaho side of Hells Canyon. Both name and appearance took added grandeur from the distance, and the multiple barriers between clothed them with an aura of unattainability. Who could say what mysteries they might hold?

Mining at Deer Creek, 1916

I do not know to this day, though I have passed over them on plane trips between Lewiston and Boise. One does not savor the mysteries nor sense the challenges of mountains the easy way. For that you must meet them head-on, climb and explore. Perhaps I will do that yet, for the challenge has not diminished with the years. Towering some 7,000 feet in their craggy isolation, The Devils still rank among the least visited parts of Idaho.

On that day in 1917 we had finer and grander views of the Seven Devils, and of all the pitched and chasmed landscape between them and us, as we went on up the trail. The ridge that knifed nearly 2,000 feet up from Deer Creek Mine to the old Weller homestead gave an unrestricted view whenever we cared to stop and look. Our laboring horses willingly gave us many opportunities.

But even the sublime has limits of appreciation, and especially when one is too young to realize its rarity. Sated with grandeur, we pushed on at last with the business of the day, which was to get to the summer cabin in time to have wood and water supplies ready when the others arrived.

Of Kings and Giants

As I have said, The Mountain was a realm of limitless adventure. The River dwarfed you with power and spectacle and barrier. The Mountain engulfed you with boundless expanse. For our limited means of travel, and within the scope of childhood need for returning home every night, it was essentially a land without borders. The great trees stretched away in every direction, tunneled here and there by probing roads, interspersed by occasional natural openings, but always closing ranks beyond. Kingly sentinel trees, thrusting above the rest, spurred endless speculation on, and searches for, the tallest, the biggest.

This was a game at which, as the directions often say, "any number can play," and almost everyone did. "The Biggest Tree On Craig Mountain" was a contest which never was clearly won, so far as I know. Various yellow pines in the 6 to 7 foot diameter class were locally recognized rulers, but none was regionally crowned. Riders passing anywhere near one of these automatically paid homage by bending their courses to its foot, to wonder and admire.

I had my share of fun of the search. The biggest trees took on added interest because they were so often scarred by lightning. The bolt would run spirally around the tree on its way to the ground, ripping out a strip of bark and living wood an inch or more thick and up to six inches wide. The strike might start a fire either in the top of the tree or among dry limbs and needles at its foot, and thus create a forest fire. Fire scars on many ancient veterans showed that they had survived such burns repeatedly over the centuries. In our time all fires were quickly controlled.

One of the kingly qualities of the biggest trees was that they could not be climbed. The great pines and tamaracks often were limbless for the first 60 to 80 feet above the ground, and their smooth, perpendicular cylindrical boles offered no possible means of ascent. They could only be conquered by destroying them.

The firs were less inviolate. White firs, particularly, often retained limbs within reach from the ground, no matter how big the tree. They could be climbed, but the rewards seldom justified the effort. The limbs were so many and so close that you had to hunt and squeeze your way up among them, usually losing some skin in the process. As you got above the old dead limbs near the ground you encountered soft pitch on the live ones. Your hands and clothes were sure to be gummed with it, and your hair took its share—no hats in this sport. When you arrived at the top you seldom could see much, no matter how tall the tree, for white firs never occupied high ground.

Red firs were more difficult but more rewarding. With an assist from a small pole leaned against the trunk you could shinny up the 12 to 15 feet to the first limb of some sizeable specimens. If you could reach the next limb from there, you had it made. The red firs gave no trouble with pitch. Adapted to drier sites than white fir, they often stood on high ground or on the edges of open places in the forest. From the top of one of these you vied with the very birds in your view of things away and below. Today only dire necessity could drive me to make such a climb, but then it was a challenge and a sport. And besides, it was one of the few things at which I could outdo Kootsie!

Singly or together, I think we climbed every kind and size of tree that our prowess could master. One favorite pastime was to climb small jackpines to the top, then fling our bodies out and go dipping down to the ground, supported by a grip on the springy tree top. This was a progressive sport. It started with trees of a size that let you down almost with a thud, and went on up the scale to sizes that bent only part way, so that you had to let go and drop the last few feet. Finally you came to trees too stiff and strong to bow down with your weight. Then you were left dangling too high to drop, and had to climb back to where you could retreat down the trunk.

A variation on this sport was to climb larger trees and cling to the tops while the wind swept them back and forth. This reached its ultimate, at least as far as we were concerned, in a stand of 50-foot lodgepole at the edge of the clearing at one of our camps. There on a breezy day Kootsie and I dared each other to the tops of a pair of these slender stalks, then froze to them as they swept in dizzying arcs. With each extra-strong puff of wind the trees bent as if they would never stop, only to sweep back as far in the other direction. It was a sport that chilled more than it thrilled. We gave it up by mutual consent.

Ground level, too, had its quota of diversions. There were always ground squirrels to be dug for, assisted by one or more excited dogs. Chipmunks, tempted in by kitchen scraps, could be trapped by jerking the stick from under a box propped up over the food. Of course, the 'munk invariably evaded capture when you lifted the box to grab him, but that was part of the game. The raucus camp robber bird could be caught in the same way, but only with much more patience and a long enough string to pull the prop from behind a log or stump a goodly distance away.

A campaign to catch a flying squirrel required combined aerial and ground forces. Having located our quarry near a clearing, I climbed trees between him and the main forest area, to shoo him closer to the edge. The strategy was to maneuver the squirrel to successive refuge trees farther and farther apart, until you isolated him where he could retreat no more. Then he would be driven to earth, where the waiting ground forces would pounce for the capture. Sometimes the strategy almost worked. It came near enough to keep us trying. But the fleeing squirrel always managed to break back at the last moment and make good his chattering escape into dense timber.

Horse wrangling had attractions of a different sort. It combined the opportunity to ride with some of the challenge of the "whodunit." One never knew just where, within a mile or so from camp, the horses might be found. Hidden in the timber, they could be passed unseen at close range. For this reason one of them had a large bell strapped to its neck. The first stop in the search was to listen for the bell, which could be heard as much as half a mile down wind. But seldom was the bell heard at the outset. Next came some scouting of the main trails to find the most promising tracks. A known hoof shape or shoe mark might be the clue, or perhaps the freshness of the sign. Tracks made yesterday, tracks made since last night's dew...tracks in the direction of some favored feeding place, tracks in another direction...

At each new indication came a stop for intent listening. To hear the possible faintest sound of the bell you held your breath, and the horse you were riding learned to hold his, too. If you were lucky enough to hear the bell at a distance you could go toward it, but that did not mean that the horses were found. The trees spread and bounced the sound around, so that as you approached it seemed to come first from one quarter, then from another. the hunted band also might become crafty. If they heard you coming they sometimes would all stand perfectly still, especially the bell horse. You could pass close by them, and only know it from hearing the bell from a new direction. Then it might become a waiting game—standing stock still until flies or mosquitoes or impatience caused the bell horse to move his head and disclose his location. Following the ears of your horse when closing in was another good device.

Once found, the horses knew the game was up for this time, and a yell or a whistle would set them frisking and galloping toward camp.

The cattle in summer were scattered over a wide area, usually not including the near vicinity of camp. Pop and Tom and the hired cowboys rode out daily to look after them, but we only saw them on special occasions. One such occasion was when they were called for salting.

Grazing cattle like and need salt in their diet, especially when on green forage, and are easily trained to come for it when called, no matter how wild they may be otherwise. I suppose any call would do, once the animals learned it. The principal qualifications are that it be different from the sounds made for driving, that it be easy to make, and that it have a penetrating carrying quality. Pop's call was a long "coo-o-ooh," rising and falling on a musical range at about the pitch of Middle C on a piano, repeated at intervals of one or two breaths. If there were cattle within earshot they bawled immediate answer. Other cattle farther away hearing them would join in. Soon the surrounding timber and meadows would be resounding to a chorus of bawling as they trooped toward the salt caller.

Stock salt was in coarse crystals as big as peas. It came in 50-pound bags, and was dispensed in handfuls tossed out around the salt gorund by a rider with a bag of it in front of him on the saddle. There the cattle stood and licked it out of the dust, fighting one another for the choicer piles. The beasts ate a lot of dirt for what salt they got, but the method at least assured that no one animal would get more than it needed, at the expense of the rest.

Nowadays salt is more commonly put out in hard blocks that yield only small amounts at a time as the animals lick them. Such blocks are left out all summer long, so the stock can get salt whenever they want it. Instead of being put at natural gathering places, the block salt is used to lure cattle to parts of the range they otherwise might neglect, thus getting more uniform use of all available feed.

On our range the riders usually salted near water in open places where the cattle could be easily counted when called in. The herd was divided around over the range among the different salting places at the beginning of the season, then moved a few at a time from one area to another during the summer in keeping with how the feed held out. Around each salt ground every animal was known on sight. When more than a few were missed at salting, riders searched out the missing and restationed the strays.

Just to see a hundred or more cattle gathered at a salt call held no special treat for us, but there was almost sure to be a bullfight or two. Each lord of the range had his own territory, and one of the jobs of the riders was to keep them in place. A salt ground, however, might serve the domains of three of four bulls, and the salt call brought them together. The contests that ensued were preceded by fierce challenges, pawing of earth, and thunderous bawls. Then with heads together the great brutes went at their trial of strength, pushing and snorting and trying to get the opponent off balance long enough to get at his ribs with the horns. In this aspect agility sometimes offset size. The biggest bull was no cinch to win with his weight advantage. To even things up, some of the larger bulls had been dehorned. Few fights drew blood from the thick-hided adversaries. Fights were let go until a winner was established, to reduce the likelihood of future fights between these two bulls. Sometimes a fight would last half an hour or so, and it was pretty sure to be exciting even if brief.

A modicum of household chores went with our summer camp life. There was water to carry and wood to cut, as always. At the Burton place the spring was a long stone's throw from the cabin, down a steep hill. Sharing the work of carrying the daily supplies up that hill taught an early respect for the virtue of careful use of this most indispensable of all earth's minerals. I think of that hill now and then when I see a city boy or girl, for whom water originates in a faucet, stand at a wash basin and run off 20 gallons to wet a comb.

Wood gathering at the Burton place, on the other hand, was about as much fun as work. Within a short distance from the cabin, fallen pines and firs seasoned for many years furnished a good supply of dry limbs of suitable sizes for stovewood. Brittle with age, these limbs broke easily when struck smartly across a solid log. In a matter of minutes we could snap off an armload of sticks the right length for the stove.

In front of the Burton cabin stood a 20-foot remnant of a fire-killed pine, long dead. The lower part of this venerable snag was rich with pitch, and served as a convenient source of chips and splinters for starting the cooking fire each morning. Half way up to the top a pair of redheaded woodpeckers had their nest. Their flashing comings and goings through the 3-inch entry hole were a feature attraction. When one of these noble birds chose to drill for wood grubs in dead trees near by, the neighborhood rang with the drumming sound. They brooked no threat to their home, as Tom learned one day when he put a hand over the hole. He got an instant drill job on it!

The Burton cabin was located near the breaks where The Mountain dropped away to The River. It was an area favored by big blue grouse. When the season opened, Pop's shotgun kept the table frequently supplied with the delicious young birds. I was privileged to go with him on one hunting expedition that brought down all the birds we could carry. Muzzy canned them, but our canning equipment and methods were not adequate, and the fine meat all spoiled. I have since seen grouse home canned with complete success by covering it with hot bacon grease, which forms a seal that excludes air from the top of the jar. Too bad we didn't know that then, for lard was plentiful and cheap.

At the Burton place Tom got his first gun, a Winchester, .22 Special rifle that bagged enough ground squirrels to bring treats of squirrel pie to our table.

At our next camp the water came from a boxed hole at the bottom of a swale below the cabin. Early in the season the water stood near ground level in this box, then lowered as the season advanced. By midsummer the water was down several feet. Mosquitoes hatched in it, requiring each bucketful of water to have its quota of "wrigglers" strained out. By the end of the season the quality was poor. It was just as well that the late season supply was only hip-deep to 3-year-old brother Jack when he fell into this 8-foot pit, and Muzzy had to run from the cabin to rescue him.

The shortcomings of this water source may have been the reason we located the next year at still another cabin. This last place had a fine spring that flowed from under a huge live tamarack tree. The water was cold and sparkling clear. I don't recall that I ever begrudged carrying this excellent drink the hundred yards or so to the cabin in the 10-pound lard buckets that were the measure of my load capacity then.

A job that came at the beginning of each summer was to gather fir boughs for our beds. No bed springs or mattresses made the pack journey to summer camp. Instead, beds were made by spreading fir boughs on the floor several inches deep. Beginning with branches half an inch thick and grading off to smaller and smaller ones, the pad was tested and retested to find and fill any low spots and to pad over the hard places. When finished it made a springy, aromatic bed that was a pleasure to sleep on.

Once installed in camp, we were too immersed in our fresh surroundings and daily doings to think much about affairs back at the ranch. A work crew left behind continued irrigating the alfalfa, and harvested two or three more crops. Fruit ripened and was canned for winter. Potatoes and other garden things were tended and used or stored. In our forest fastness, these matters were out of mind. It was a rare case, then, when Kootsie was dispatched back down to the ranch one summer for a packload of fresh apricots, tomatoes, early peaches, peach plums and garden stuff. With never a doubt of her 11-year-old competence to handle this assignment, she set off riding Kay Bar and leading Hatrack as her packhorse.

Due back the third day, she did not arrive until toward evening. When at last she rode into camp she was bedraggled and tear-stained. Old Hatrack had slipped off the zigzag trail and rolled with his pack, scattering the soft fruits among the rocks and dirt, and barely managing to save himself from tumbling on down the steep slope to his death. Kootsie had gathered up the spilled load as best she could, but most of it was unsalvageable. Although unhurt, she was badly shaken by the frightening event, angered at the loss of the prized and irreplaceable fruit, and deeply chagrined at having failed to carry through without mishap, even though by no fault of her own. It was enough to upset anyone, but it was one of the few times I ever saw Kootsie overwhelmed by adversity.

"No man is a hero to his valet," someone has said. Few Jeeveses, on the other hand, ever emerge plainly enough from the background to be recognized as the true source of all that starch holding up the stuffed shirt. With no intention of image building in either direction, I thus introduce an unsung character from behind the scenes of my youthful "on stage."

Harry Weller was no Jeeves, but he was a competent, hard working, trusted, loyal, patient and understanding employee and friend of the family, whose helping hand was felt at every level. It was Harry who knew exactly how to sugar a small boy's oatmeal so that delicious beads of syrup would form on it, and who understood that the milk should be poured carefully around the edge of the bowl so as not to wash them away. It was Harry who could untie the hardest knot in a boy's or girl's muddy shoelace at bedtime, and who knew how to jolly you up after a fall from a horse, a hornet sting, or some other misfortune. Always ready to hand his coat to someone less warmly dressed and to laugh the cold off his own back, he looked at the world with a warm and cheerful eye that bred optimism in all around.

As a son of the homesteader at the edge of The Mountain, whose place I have mentioned, Harry was not born to the saddle. He never developed a strong urge for it. Rather, it was he who took charge of the Deer Creek Ranch in summer, irrigated the fields, put up the hay, and tended the garden while we were gone. When the Big House was built he brought his bride, nee Theodosia Freeburn, there to live for a while. Later they homesteaded on China Creek, some five miles below us, but Harry still worked at Deer Creek much of the time.

I am sure none of us kids was any hero to Harry, for he knew our every mean streak and childish weakness. What makes him something special for this story is that he could know us that well and still make us feel somehow special to himself. And what higher specialness is there, than this?

The World At Ten

Our summer camps were six to eight miles from Forest, the postoffice town listed as my birthplace. There we got supplies and mail throughout the year, and there we sojourned for some two months in the fall for a prelude of public school before heading back to Deer Creek. That broadening experience deserves mention in this chronicle.

Forest when I knew it was already past its prime, which must have come with the peak of the timber claim period just after the turn of the Century. Along its single business street were several empty buildings testifying to former glories. At the western end the deserted sawmill rusted among stacks of rotting slab cuts. There Chris Holly shod countless cow ponies, fixed farm machinery, and did the other iron work of the community at his blacksmith shop. Surviving at the city center were the Spence Clovis livery stable on one side of the street, and across from it the general store, postoffice, and a two-story 8-room hotel. These three enterprises changed hands at least three times in the brief span of my contacts. Thad Maynard, Harry Clovis, and the Stevens Brothers

A representative group of Forest community citizens in 1900. L to R Jimmy Reed on horse, Kemmie Jacobson at horse's nose. Back row: John Miller, Billy Wolf, next 7 unidentified, Jim Sands. Front: Ed Holly seated, Tom Holden, next 2 unidentified, Billie Freeburn, Jim Reed (store owner) seated, Jacob Freeburn behind Reed, store clerk, . . . Powell, Mrs. Powell, Mrs. Reed, Mrs. Jacob Freeburn, Cora Freeburn, far right, Della Freeburn (smallest girl), Theodosia Freeburn.

Packstring loaded with dry cowhides in front of Maynard's store, Forest, 1910. John A. Platt in dark shirt standing by open door; Harry Weller mounted at center. Others unidentified.

In front of Forest Hotel, Dec. 1910, ready to drive to Salmon River breaks for horseback trip down Deer Creek trail to the Platt ranch. Emma (Mrs. John) Platt holding baby Lorene. L to R in back of sled, Kenneth, Frances and Mary Platt. Spence Clovis driving, Art Keane standing.

are names I associate with them. Mrs. Doug Radley ran the hotel for a while. A short length of board sidewalk dignified the store frontage, and afforded a treasure of lost nickels and dimes that Donald Radley and I discovered and retrieved one happy day.

Along the one side street, leading out toward Winchester 12 miles away, were a house or two, the Oddfellows Lodge, and the school. The city water supply was a dug well near the eastern end of town, where you let down the bucket on 30-odd feet of rope and hoped for the best, for it sometimes scraped bottom. There may have been more than a dozen families living there then; I am no longer sure. The school drew students from outlying farms, but the total enrollment was accommodated in one room, under one teacher. I can recall the following: Beatrice, Ellen, Jack and Kenneth Bedwell; Nettie Clovis; Aaron and Margaret Currier; Dorothy and Wilder Guthrie; Eva, Harvey, Ralph and Timothy Hosley; Agnes and Jack Kenyon; Julia, Olivia and Ray Lorang; Dewitt, Donald, Lillian and Lionel Radley; May and Ted Woods; Beulah Wyeth. There may have been others.

In my brief association with these fellow travelers on life's road, I learned various lessons one does not learn in isolation. I learned that approaches to people outside the family must be made with more caution and less trust than I had been accustomed to. Donald Radley and Teddy Woods could be my pals one day and punch me in the face the next, according to unpredictable moods. At the same time I learned that, while I was not cut out to be a fighter, I could hold my own in most of the noncombative competitions. I learned that the natural orneriness of small boys, including myself, had a remarkable multiplier effect when any two of them got together. They could perpetrate more deviltry in a day than either of them alone would undertake in a year. And I swore off liquor for life after Ray Lorang tricked me into swallowing a big swig of kerosene out of a whiskey bottle he had sneaked from home and pretended to drink from.

In addition to our urban exposure at Forest, glimpses and hints of still wider realms multiplied with the years. Peddlers traveling by hack to sell fresh salmon, new potatoes and summer fruits from the Clearwater Valley proved that the distance to that scarce-heard-of place was not insuperable. An automobile made its way to our summer camp as early as 1915, bringing the marvel of a vehicle that could go fast enough to outrun its own dust, which a wagon could not do, and introducing the exciting new smell of gasoline.

Bob Hosley put a Model T. Ford into service on his Forest-Winchester mail route that year. In 1916 Harry Clovis added a Model T to the Forest transportation complex. That summer Vince Lorang bought an Oakland that defied the hills by trailing a heavy iron peg from a rear axle so that it stuck into the ground and stopped the car from backing down when the motor died on a steep pull.

Forest Saloon & Hotel — early 1900s

In that summer, too, we went by wagon to Winchester, a town several times as big as Forest, for a week of camping out at the 4th of July celebration. New experiences there ushered in a still bigger world, and showed how to cope with it. "All you can drink for a nickel," cried the lemonade vendor by his barrel at the gate of the roundup grounds. Having proved his drink several times through the week, I went with my last nickel and a thirsty friend to bargain for one glass apiece. When the vendor short-sightedly refused this reasonable proposition I drank six glasses by myself.

In the summer of 1917 Uncle Will Hickman, Aunt Susie, and cousins Carrie Mae, Esther, Marvin, Harriet, John and Ormond came all the way from Genesee in their big Reo touring car for a long visit. They brought Genesee into focus as a real place even bigger than Winchester, with electric lights and piped water. Shortly thereafter Pop bought a used Model T and brought it to camp, where we spent forbidden hours behind the wheel pretending to drive.

Unannounced and unrecognized, a new age had arrived.

"Cabin on the mountain"

That fall we moved to an entirely different life on a big wheat and cattle ranch near Genesee. Tom and I were the first to go, taking several horses as far as Spalding the first day. Next morning we crossed the Clearwater River on a ferry, there being no bridge at that time, and rode up Coyote Grade and on to the old Platt ranch at Genesee. The rest of the family followed a few days later in the Model T. From then on, our Salmon River and Craig Mountain days were to be only memories.

The mighty trees I knew on Craig Mountain now are gone, and no new generation shall see their like there again. Today's utilitarian pace does not allow centuries for trees to grow.

Tomorrow's human population will demand that food be grown on all suitable lands, and this will deny the best soils of The Mountain to forest uses as well as to grazing.

With deforestation, The Mountain lost its capacity to slow the spring snow melt and to temper the impact of summer rains. Torrential runoffs since have gutted the channels of Deer Creek and Eagle Creek, ripping out the protective brush that shaded them, destroying the pools that once nurtured countless pan size trout, and leaving habitats fit only for fingerlings. Where cattle once grazed in thousands, now they number in hundreds.

Steelhead anglers and grouse hunters now drive Jeeps and pickups to the Salmon River and along it on a road following down Eagle Creek. Powerful motorboats course the river almost at will. Plane passengers looking down see momentary glimpses of the canyons and their streams, but no people.

All these present day viewers see only an empty land. How can they visualize the land as it once was, or sense the lives and purposes that once centered there?

They cannot, fully. Yet perhaps this brief note will help.

And so I have thought it worth while to set down this firsthand view of "how it was" in one last microcosm of the American frontier, as seen through the eyes of a boy coming ten in the fall of 1917.

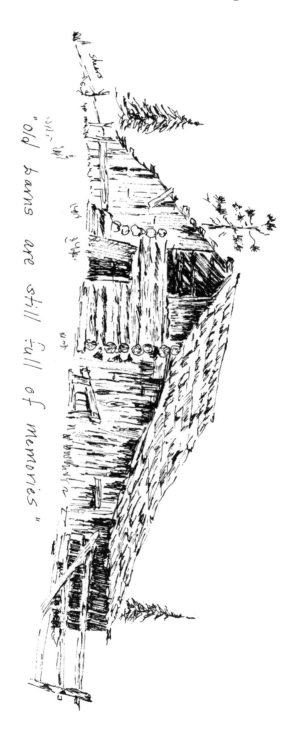

"Old barns are still full of memories"

KENNETH B. PLATT

II

SHADOWS ON THE LAND

I once read of a man whose greatest urge was "to fill in the white spaces on the map." Those vacant areas, without towns or landmark names, fascinated him. What were they like? Who had seen them? Why were they unknown? How could you get into them? Were they really uninhabited? If not, who lived there, and what did they do?

The surge of European exploration activity that "discovered" America in 1492 and swept on to map the main outlines of all the then unknown—to them—principal land and sea areas of the world, had its final echo in the polar explorations that became possible only with modern flight and motorized ground transport. Today there are no large "unknowns" left on the world's surface, such as challenged Columbus, Vespucius, Magellan, Cortez, Balboa, Drake, Cook, De Soto, De Leon, Hudson, Lewis & Clark, Von Humboldt, Peary, Amundson, Byrd, and the host of the other bold souls who put rivers, lakes, seas, ice fields, mountains, forests, plains, animals and peoples onto the great blank spaces their maps showed up to 50 years ago. Today all has been seen, at least from the air. All has been recorded by the magic of modern satellite photography. And almost all has been traversed once or more on the surface by men with enough training to record and evaluate what they saw.

But now a new "white space" phenomenon has arisen in areas once known and settled, but now vacant and forgotten. One that has long intrigued me is the northern half of Maine, where thousands of square miles show townless and roadless on today's road maps. Some day I must go there. But for now I want to focus on a smaller area nearer home—the lower Salmon River area of my boyhood, west of Whitebird to the mouth of the river.

In 1895 this area contained just 12 settlers, according to the recollections of my father, who went there that year to settle. By 1920 almost every habitable acre of the area had been claimed and lived on. By 1935 the land again was essentially vacant, and it remains so today, swept clean by one of the many tides of U.S. economic development and fortune that have moved populations here and there throughout the country and throughout our history.

In historic perspective, the people who once populated this isolated Salmon River segment, then moved on, were mere shadows on the land. They were drawn to other areas, and they went away leaving little more visible trace than a passing cloud. We might dismiss them as inconsequential to our day were it not for one thing: Their going has left a white space on the map that cries out for answers. Who were they? What brought them there? What did they do? How did they live? Why did they leave? Where did they go?

Part II of *Salmon River Saga* attempts to repeople this white space with the figures who gave it life and substance in that turn of the Century period that marked the final surge of Western pioneering as seen in Idaho. The series of maps and charts which follow show the progress of settlement as reflected in Land Office patents issued to final claimants on the land. Many more names could be shown if we listed all those who filed claims they later relinquished to others. These names would be no less valid and interesting than those of the final land title recipients, but to get them would require more digging into old records than seems justified.

"Deer Creek Breaks"

SALMON RIVER SAGA

With enough work one could learn where most of the settlers came from, and where they went. But time does not permit this indulgence, interesting as their individual histories might be. Instead, we must let the detailed account of the characters in Part I typify the rest. The photo section will help lend reality to the way of life described, while bringing many actual persons back to view as they looked in the years of their pioneering.

The purpose here is both to salute them and to perserve their memory for those who can only meet them on the printed page. Most have gone to their reward. Those who remain will soon join them. The following lament addresses both the people and the land they once gave meaning, and now have left as only a white space on the map.

Requiem For An Empty Land

Where eagles soared above the craggy steeps —
    Proud freedom's symbol lifted to the sky —
Where sped the deer; where still the torrent leaps;
    Where coyotes keened their wild, primordial cry;

Where came the hardy clan of yesteryore,
    Defying precipice and river wide
To spread their herds and harvest nature's store
    From rearing ridge and plunging canyon side;

There now the eagle lofts in lonely grace,
    With none to mark his course against the sun.
Gone is the voice of man, and gone his trace —
    Tilled field, crude cabin, other works begun.

No longer curls the smoke of purposed morn;
    No longer spurs the rider o'er the land.
No canyon echoes; on no breeze is borne
    The sounds of human industry at hand.

All empty now, the mighty canyons sleep
    Uncomprehending of their gloried hour,
And only memory returns to weep
    For shadows fleeting as a summer shower.

Moscow, Idaho

July, 1976

shears

The rectangular land ownership pattern shown on the following township sheets illustrates the survey system that was applied to all U.S. continental territory outside the 13 original states. The township pattern was six miles square, the land being surveyed and marked into 36 sections each one mile square. Each section was subdivided and marked into quarters one-half mile square, containing 160 acres. Quarter sections were platted into quarter-mile squares of 40 acres each, but these subdivisions were not marked on the ground. In rough country few townships were perfectly square. The imperfections were accommodated in odd-size lots along the northern and western sides.

Settlers were required to conform their claims to the lines of the surveys, in 40-acre blocks or the nearest approximation in irregular lots. Selections usually were in contiguous blocks, to facilitate use, but separated tracts could be claimed. The total claim need not lie all in the same township. Selections took all manner of shapes within these guidelines.

The 160-acre homestead law of 1862, under which the earlier homesteads of the

Standard Layout Of A Township
Under The U.S. Government Land Survey System

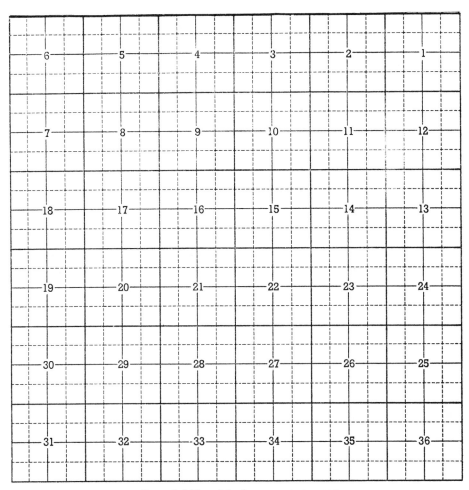

Record Of Land Settlement, 1910 - 1939

[ ]	Occupied but not patented	▤	Patented 1921 - 1925
⊠	Patented through 1910	▥	Patented 1926 - 1939
◩	Patented 1911 - 1915	S	State land
▨	Patented 1916 - 1920	▢	Vacant U.S.G.

Salmon River country were filed, put primary emphasis on agricultural settlement. It was designed for the Mississippi Valley, and had to be modified as settlement moved into the drier lands of the West. In due time supplemental claims were allowed up to 320 acres, and finally in 1916 a new law permitted grazing homesteads of 640 acres.

The Salmon River area recorded here reflects the full range of this changing pattern, from claims as small as 40 acres to others as large as 640 acres.

The following chart compares the rates of settlement in terms of percent of total area, by the periods diagrammed on the following township sheets. The much faster

Cumulative Record Of Patented Land Claims

Township & Range	1910 :	1915 :	1920 :	1925 :	1939
T 29 N, R 3 W -	:	:	:		
Number of settlers	5 :	14 :	40 :	58 :	66
Acres of patented claims	785 :	2,179 :	8,606 :	13,045 :	16,281
Percent of patented total	5 :	13 :	53 :	80 :	100
T 31 N, R 3 W -	:	:	:	:	
Number of settlers	:	26 :	87 :	94 :	98
Acres of patented claims	:	3,220 :	16,826 :	18,731 :	19,326
Percent of patented total	:	17 :	87 :	97 :	100
	:	:	:	:	

settlement of T31N, R3W probably resulted from its easier accessibility. The farthest reaches of this township were only 15-18 trail miles from the trading town of Forest, whereas ranches in T29N, R3W were 30-35 trail miles from Whitebird or Cottonwood, with the unbridged Salmon River to be crossed for either town. Family clusters were prominent in the settlement pattern. The Bottorf-Critchfield-Freeburn-Vallem clan patented a total of 17 claims in the Eagle Creek area of T31N, R3W. The McMahon-Platt cousins patented 16 claims in Townships 30 and 31n, R3W.

To visually illustrate the flow of settlement onto the area involved in this account, the lands homesteaded in two representative townships have been diagrammed by time intervals over the settlement period. Township 29 North, Range 3 West, where John Platt made his start in 1895, had only 5 homesteads patented up to 1910; T31N, R3W, where he ended his Salmon River sojourn in 1917, had none. Subsequent settlement moved swiftly, but especially fast in T31N, R3W. The following nine pages of diagrams graphically show the settlement progress in the two townships. The first page for each

TOWNSHIP 29 NORTH RANGE 3 WEST OF THE BOISE MERIDAN, IDAHO
PATTERN OF LAND SETTLEMENT 1910

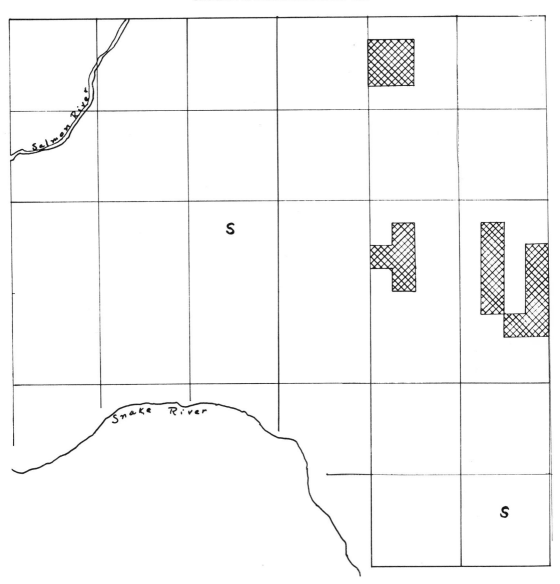

TOWNSHIP 29 NORTH RANGE 3 WEST OF THE BOISE MERIDIAN, IDAHO

PATTERN OF SETTLEMENT 1915

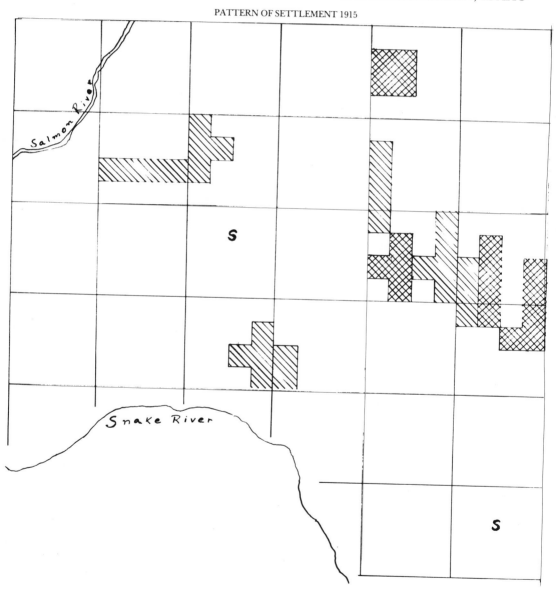

TOWNSHIP 29 NORTH RANGE 3 WEST OF THE BOISE MERIDIAN, IDAHO
PATTERN OF SETTLEMENT 1920

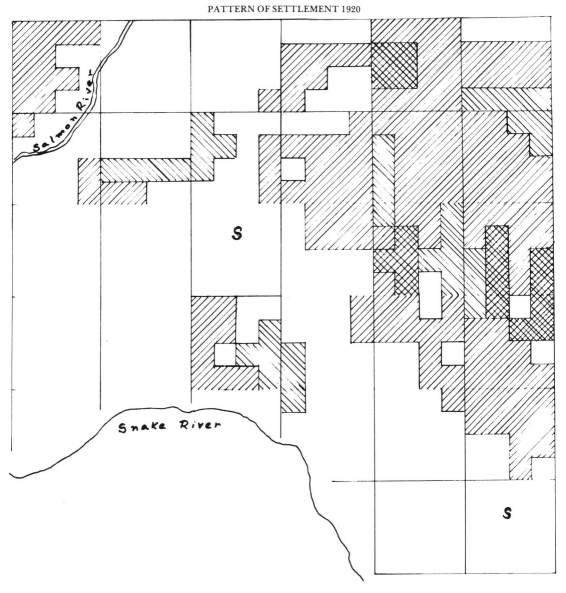

TOWNSHIP 29 NORTH RANGE 3 WEST OF THE BOISE MERIDIAN, IDAHO

PATTERN OF SETTLEMENT 1925

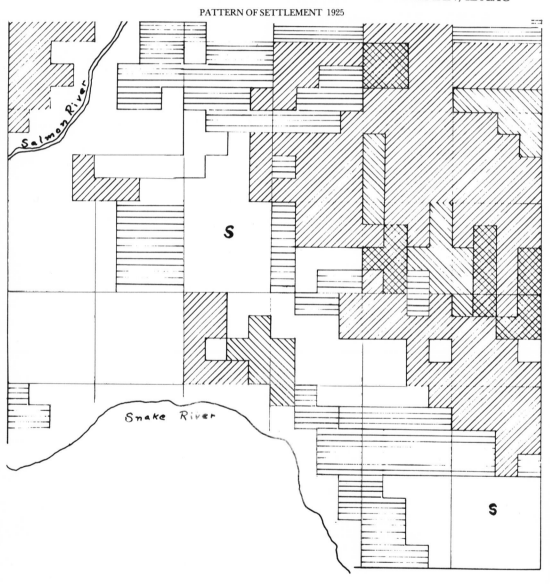

TOWNSHIP 29 NORTH RANGE 3 WEST OF THE BOISE MERIDIAN, IDAHO

PATTERN OF SETTLEMENT 1939

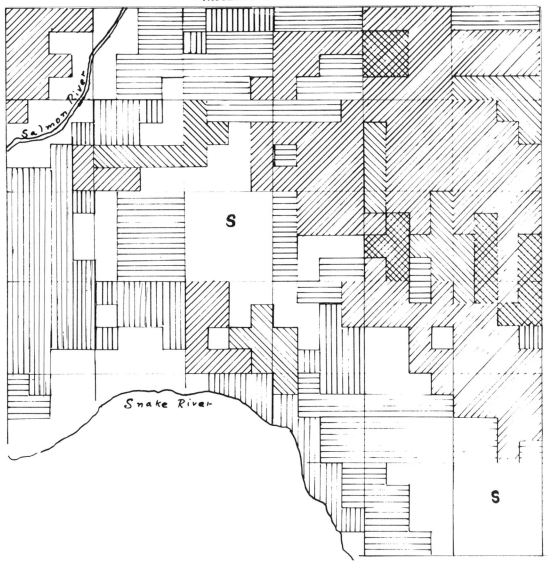

TOWNSHIP 31 NORTH RANGE 3 WEST OF THE BOISE MERIDIAN, IDAHO
PATTERN OF SETTLEMENT 1910

TOWNSHIP 31 NORTH RANGE 3 WEST OF THE BOISE MERIDIAN, IDAHO
PATTERN OF SETTLEMENT, 1915

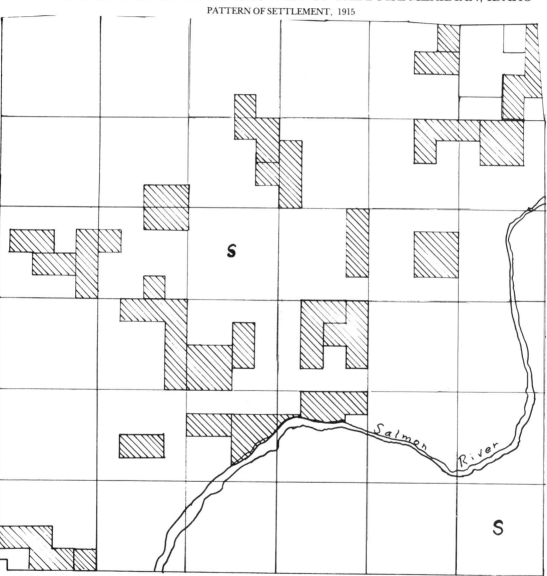

TOWNSHIP 31 NORTH RANGE 3 WEST OF THE BOISE MERIDIAN, IDAHO

PATTERN OF SETTLEMENT 1920

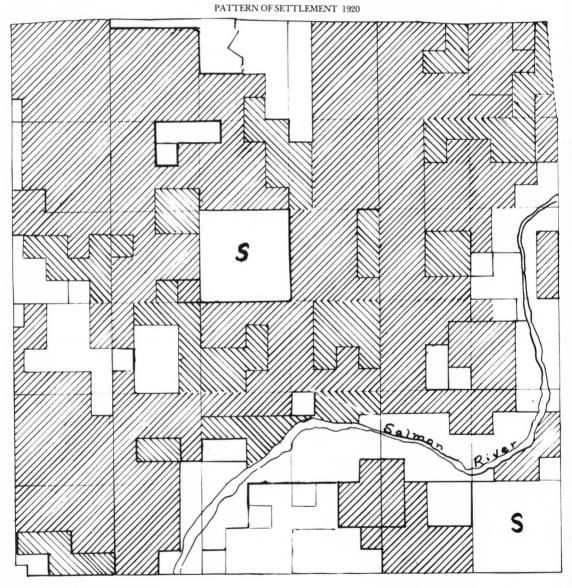

TOWNSHIP 31 NORTH RANGE 3 WEST OF THE BOISE MERIDIAN, IDAHO

PATTERN OF SETTLEMENT 1939

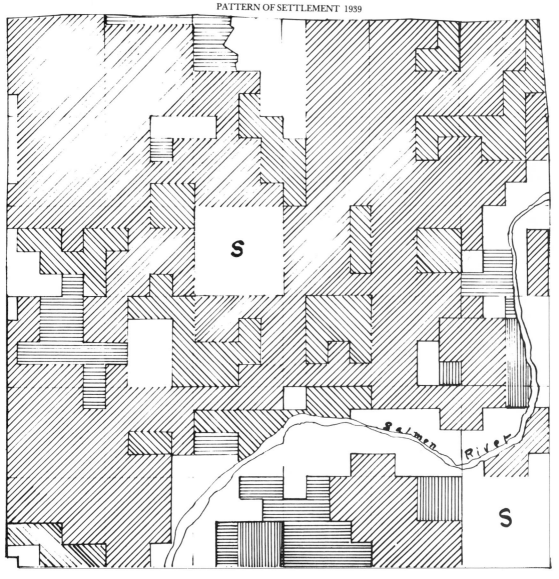

township shows the location of land claims patented through 1910. Following pages show cumulative settlement by 5-year periods through 1925 and for the period 1926-1939, after which no more homesteads were patented. A quick turning of these pages will give an effect of shadows advancing across them, until nearly all area is covered. The reader can then reverse this effect by visualizing the departure of nearly all land claimants from the area in the period from 1925 to 1940, leaving a white space on the map as already noted.

Earliest settlers were there before the lands were surveyed. The homes they built, no matter how crude, gave them squatters rights which were adequate to protect their hold on the sites occupied. Since the area was suited only for stock raising, and since the vacant government land all about them could be grazed without charge, they were in no hurry to own the land. Ownership meant paying taxes, an evil to be put off as long as possible. So it was more or less typical that the survey of Township 31 North, Range 3 West, done in 1905 and 1906, took note of 15 occupants already present. Only 10 of these eventually obtained homestead patents. Earliest patents among these 10 pre-survey settlers were not obtained until 1913, and the last one not until 1920.

The following table of land recipients lists all those recorded for the 12x18 mile rectangle that covers most of the story area of *Forgotten Songs And Untold Tales.* That area comprises six townships straddling the lower Salmon River from its junction with the Snake River up to the southern rim of Craig Mountain near the head of Deer Creek.

Many land seekers whose names are not listed came and went in this area during its settlement period. Some filed homestead claims but later sold, relinquished to others, or abandoned them. Others worked for wages while looking over the country, but never found land to their liking. Still others were miners, hunters or trappers, who moved on when the country began to fill up.

The 194 who left their names on the land records of this sector were those who established homes there, and stayed long enough to meet the Homestead Law requirements for gaining title to their claims. The following roster shows the land patent number, acreage, location, and year of patent for each name listed. It is included as an aid to any who might wish to pursue the history whose page is opened here.

Land Recipients In Six Townships Of The Lower Salmon River
(Townships 29, 30 and 31 North, Ranges 3 and 4 West, B.M.)

Name of Recipient	Land Patent No.	Township & Range	Acres	Year of Patent
Alles, Conrad	182334	29N/3W	160	1911
Alles, John	145595	"	160	1910
Alles, Henry	193144	"	160	1911
Anderson, Geo. F.	871794	30N/3W	320	1922
" " "	871795	"	160	1922
Ardinger, Roger S.	253332	31N/4W	160	1912
Axtell, Archie W.	945070	31N/3W	242	1924
Aztec Land & Cattle Co.	176734	30N/3W	40	1911
Baird, Charles H.	50174	"	160	1909
" " "	99463	"	160	1909
Baird, Charles H.	485128	30N/3W	160	1915
Baird, Lizzie L.	233458	"	80	1911
" " "	420308	"	160	1914
Bartlett, Harry G.	833206	30N/4W	160	1921
" " "	931633	"	481	1924
Bettison, Chas. E.	865409	29N/4W	164	1922
" " "	865410	"	244	1922
Bond, James L.	485126	29N/3W	120	1915
Bottorf, Martin A.	656544	31N/3W	315	1918
Bottorf, Wm. A.	416386	"	80	1914
Bradford, Leo R.	724277	31N/4W	320	1919
Branin, Alvertie	140817	"	160	1910
Brock, Daisy M.	829402	30N/3W	320	1921
" " "	942064	"	320	1924
Brock, Vernon C.	983680	"	320	1926
Brock, Vernon C.	1007583	30N/3W	320	1927
Broo, August F.	182477	31N/4W	160	1911
Brown, Frank E.	386552	30N/4W	142	1914
Brown, Fred S.	674596	"	320	1919
" " "	771458	"	160	1920
Brown, Harriet M.	650368	30N/4W	323	1918
" " "	781960	"	240	1920
Brown, Helen M.	725596	"	324	1920
" " "	830097	"	280	1921
Burns, Ernest R.	501840	31N/4W	160	1915

Name of Recipient	Land Patent No.	Township & Range	Acres	Year of Patent
Busick, Jefferson S.	966041	30N/3W	320	1925
Canaan, Floyd A.	674603	29N/3W	320	1919
Caldwell, Mose	568870	30N/4W	320	1917
Cantner, James E.	670846	30N/3W	329	1919
Cardwell, Wiley	236050	29N/3W	160	1911
Carrick, Bertha	801479	31N/4W	160	1921
" "	953696	"	320	1925
" "	958895	"	332	1925
Carrick, Thomas F.	412956	"	157	1920
Carrick, Thomas W.	758526	"	157	1920
Carssow, Mary A.	485106	31N/4W	73	1915
Cattron, Delvert M.	980522	29N/3W	334	1926
Cesar, Martin	758524	31N/3W	280	1920
Chaffee, Jerome B.	760556	29N/3W	320	1920
Clark, Roy	780215	30N/4W	320	1920
Clark, Roy	780216	30N/4W	320	1920
Coburn, Chester W.	1013488	"	614	1928
Cooper, Oliver A.	314799	30N/3W	160	1913
Cornwell, Henry	656542	31N/4W	321	1918
Cox, John W.	977989	29N/4W	320	1926
Critchfield, Daniel J.	416385	31N/3W	80	1914
" " "	441975	"	160	1914
" " "	633281	"	320	1918
Crum, Rufus C.	806347	30N/4W	280	1921
Dehning, Wm. H.	676299	31N/4W	320	1919
Deschamps, John B.	81079	31N/4W	160	1909
" Tillie	126006	"	160	1910
Duckworth, John L.	193972	"	160	1911
" " "	140823	"	120	1910
Eastman, Alseaba	743420	30N/4W	320	1920
Eastman, Alseaba	887085	30N/4W	320	1922
Eberhardt, Herman B.	938417	29N/3W	230	1924
Eberhardt, Hugo E.	938416	29N/4W	320	1924
Edwards, Phillip E.	675459	31N/4W	320	1919
" " "	778763	"	320	1920
Emerich, Samuel H.	556828	31N/3W	161	1916
Ferguson, Wm. A.	831685	30N/3W	327	1921
Fisher, Don C.	800210	"	320	1921
" " "	946485	"	320	1924
Flynn, Carl T.	455632	31N/3W	160	1915

Name of Recipient	Land Patent No.	Township & Range	Acres	Year of Patent
Flynn, Thos. H.	347841	31N/3W	160	1913
Forge, Hal E.	675450	"	320	1919
Forsland, Robt.	928733	30N/3W	320	1924
Fountain, Cora B.	999152	31N/4W	312	1927
" " "	999153	"	320	1927
Fountain, Wm. M.	819396	30N/4W	320	1921
" " "	819397	"	320	1921
Freeburn, Jacob E.	441974	31N/3W	160	1914
" " "	633282	"	320	1918
Freeburn, Wm. A.	633283	"	320	1918
Freeburn, Wm. A.	960690	31N/3W	280	1925
Frye, Tillie M.	781309	31N/4W	120	1920
Frye, Walter J.	762919	"	320	1920
" " "	892192	"	320	1923
Gibbins, James R.	886138	29N/3W	160	1922
Goodwin, Elva	725594	29N/3W	320	1920
" "	961079	"	320	1925
Goodwin, Vernetta	706396	"	320	1919
" "	946486	"	320	1924
Greenhagen, Geo.	732375	31N/4W	320	1920
Greenough, Wm. S.	711792	29N/3W	320	1919
Guthrie, Ernest	701881	31N/4W	320	1919
Guthrie, Geo.	833198	30N/3W	326	1921
Guthrie, Thos. J.	701880	31N/4W	320	1919
Guyon, Annie	612123	30N/4W	320	1917
Haddock, Zack	780985	31N/3W	160	1920
Haddock, Zack Sr.	631333	"	298	1918
Hall, Chas. G.	656533	"	320	1918
Hallett, Claude F.	47368	29N/3W	160	1909
Hardin, Jesse L.	633289	31N/4W	320	1918
Hardin, Walter H.	694489	29N/3W	320	1918
Harris, Elliott R.	871797	29N/4W	325	1922
" " "	871798	"	162	1922
Harris, Mark	604128	30N/4W	320	1917
Harrison, Clarence R.	833207	30N/3W	320	1921
Henley, James E.	314093	29N/3W	160	1913
Heselwood, Bertha	212043	31N/4W	160	1911
Heselwood, Robt. A.	356799	"	166	1913
Hoagland, Roy C.	531879	31N/3W	160	1916
Hollingsworth, Scottie	546330	"	160	1916
Hollingsworth, Scottie	590139	31N/3W	160	1917
" "	604131	"	160	1917
" "	985813	29N/3W	310	1926
Hubbard, Chas. N.	859848	29N/4W	320	1922
" " "	859849	"	120	1922

Name of Recipient	Land Patent No.	Township & Range	Acres	Year of Patent
Hubbard, Chas. N.	975882	29N/4W	200	1926
Hubbard, Thos. J.	829405	"	320	1921
" " "	829406	"	160	1921
Huber, Joseph	426560	31N/3W	49	1914
" "	501838	"	80	1915
Jackson, Herman	444254	30N/3W	103	1914
Jensen, Peter	486658	"	99	1915
" "	674991	30N/4W	80	1919
Johnson, Albert P.	640354	29N/3W	312	1918
Jones, Julian	833204	30N/3W	252	1921
Jones, Julian	977988	31N/3W	80	1926
Jones, Katherine B.	876823	30N/3W	320	1922
" " "	898756	"	320	1923
Jones, Roxey	650366	31N/4W	240	1918
Jones, Wm. C.	891058	"	320	1922
Jones, Wm. C.	891059	31N/4W	320	1922
Kane, Harold C.	473460	29N/3W	160	1915
Keane, Arthur C.	531351	31N/3W	160	1916
" " "	578893	"	120	1917
" " "	633285	"	160	1918
Keane, Arthur C.	847861	31N/4W	160	1922
Keane, Cora A.	859843	"	320	1922
" " "	859844	"	320	1922
Kemp, Leonard W.	501842	30N/3W	80	1915
" " "	620595	30N/3W	320	1918
Kemp, Leonard W.	951759	30N/4W	240	1925
Kemp, Percy	620484	29N/3W	144	1918
" "	656521	"	311	1918
Kennedy, John C.	827530	31N/3W	165	1921
Kittsmiller, Matilda	81081	31N/4W	160	1909
Kittsmiller, Thos E.	81080	31N/4W	160	1909
Knorr, Christopher B.	535650	29N/3W	160	1916
Knorr, Edward A.	1097179	"	473	1938
Landru, Merl E.	404196	30N/3&4W	214	1914
Lanser, Catherine	658121	31N/3W	320	1919
Lemons, Ernest D.	633295	30N/3W	320	1918
" " "	871796	"	320	1922
Lemons, Walter H.	535649	"	160	1916
" " "	535652	"	160	1916
" " "	667592	29N/3W	322	1919

Name of Recipient	Land Patent No.	Township & Range	Acres	Year of Patent
Lorang, Vincent F.	455631	31N/3W	120	1915
" " "	507000	"	40	1916
" " "	556372	"	320	1916
Madden, Clara E.	391851	31N/4W	158	1914
Madden, Geo.	60107	"	160	1909
Madden, James S.	189071	31N/4W	160	1911
" " "	279253	"	40	1912
" " "	693090	"	160	1919
" " "	819393	"	319	1921
Magginetti, Costanto	255058	"	160	1912
Magginetti, Elmer	674606	30N/3W	297	1919
" "	969920	"	336	1925
Malinek, Anna	1096044	30N/3W	330	1938
Manning, Frank A.	889884	30N/4W	480	1922
" " "	889883	"	160	1922
Mattingly, Geo. F.	744410	31N/3W	320	1920
Matteson, Thos. F.	622456	"	291	1918
" " "	778767	"	244	1920
McCoy, Guy D.	633744	"	160	1918
McCoy, Sylvia	656526	"	159	1918
McCracken, Loy A.	643556	29N/3W	320	1918
McCulley, Hattie M.	675605	"	321	1919
McCulley, Robt. W.	674602	"	320	1919
McGrubb, Alexander	454890	31N/3W	160	1915
" "	506997	"	40	1916
McGrubb, Alexander	656535	31N/3W	160	1918
McMahon, Elizabeth T.	489273	30N/3W	40	1915
" " "	501849	"	120	1915
McMahon, Wm. A.	431488	"	40	1914
" " "	485127	"	160	1915
McMahon, Wm. A.	674594	30N/3W	160	1919
" " "	882196	"	480	1922
Melkhart, Chas. H.	139718	31N/4W	161	1910
" " "	1003443	"	145	1927
Miller, Chas. A.	933562	30N/3W	320	1924
Miller, Chas. A.	1010704	30N/3W	320	1928
Miller, John	842330	29N/3W	321	1922
" "	842331	"	240	1922
Moffatt, James	525649	31N/3W	160	1916
"	622459	"	160	1918
Moffett, Amy C.	851759	31N/3W	480	1922
Moffett, S. Carson	403226	"	160	1914
Molloy, Joseph M.	206561	31N/4W	160	1911
Moulton, Mertie	972760	"	320	1926
" "	1013942	"	320	1928

Name of Recipient	Land Patent No.	Township & Range	Acres	Year of Patent
Moulton, Walter W.	850604	31N/4W	80	1922
Mounce, Arthur J.	819391	31N/4W	320	1921
" " "	839890	30N/4W	294	1921
Mounce, Carl R.	706399	31N/4W	320	1919
Munden, Noel A.	811523	30N/4W	320	1921
Murdick, Roy	682633	31N/3W	320	1919
Nash, Richard P.	664528	"	179	1919
Nelson, Arthur W.	569443	30N/4W	164	1917
" " "	807017	"	160	1921
" " "	807018	"	480	1921
Nelson, Eddie C.	631951	31N/4W	326	1918
" " "	755418	30N/3&4W	156	1920
Nelson, Merl E.	578674	30N/4W	160	1917
" " "	931637	"	400	1924
Nelson, Mildred	578675	31N/3W	167	1917
Northern Pacific R.R. Co.	470241	30N/3W	78	1915
" " " "	622266	"	40	1922
" " " "	882815	"	40	1918
Olson, Olaf	633274	31N/4W	160	1918
Paris, Joseph D.	675444	31N/3W	160	1919
Paris, Joseph D.	716865	31N/3W	160	1919
Peek, Ernest H.	931635	30N/3W	325	1924
Platt, Carrie	590136	31N/3W	320	1917
" "	675895	"	80	1919
Platt, Emma C.	675884	31N/4W	80	1919
Platt, John A.	416870	31N/3W	150	1914
" " "	433464	"	80	1914
" " "	535646	"	80	1916
Platt, Wm. T.	227426	30N/3W	160	1911
" " "	394185	"	40	1914
Platt, Wm. T.	884495	30N/3W	320	1922
" " "	884496	"	160	1922
Poole, Albert J.	481818	29N/3W	160	1915
" " "	748462	"	160	1920
Powers, Maria E.	495437	30&31N/4W	142	1915
Powers, Winfield S.	289325	30N/4W	160	1912
Prato, John	764939	31N/4W	322	1920
" "	764940	"	280	1920
Provost, Adena E.	675883	"	160	1919
Provost, Earle N.	1056834	"	634	1932

Name of Recipient	Land Patent No.	Township & Range	Acres	Year of Patent
Pruett, Levi R.	693081	30N/4W	320	1919
" " "	956197	"	320	1925
Radamsky, Richard F.	47383	31N/4W	162	1909
" " "	407550	"	160	1914
" " "	831683	"	160	1921
Radamsky, Richard F.	840928	31N/4W	160	1922
Radley, Dudley M.	730533	31N/3W	320	1920
Rawls, Roxie	933559	30N/4W	320	1924
" "	933560	30N/4W	320	1924
Read, Wm. H.	717723	29N/3W	40	1919
Reeves, Benjamin F.	339956	30N/4W	40	1913
" " "	426302	31N/3W	160	1914
" " "	472036	30N/4W	160	1915
" " "	501851	31N/3W	174	1915
" " "	564240	30N/3W	170	1917
Reeves, Benjamin F.	763993	30N/3W	158	1920
Reeves, Julia	420300	"	158	1914
" "	657632	31N/3W	160	1919
Rencehausen, Clyde	633286	"	338	1918
Rickman, Thos. H.	412207	30N/3W	160	1914
Rickman, Thos. H.	455628	30N/3W	160	1915
Ringer, Leonard E.	427252	30N/4W	160	1914
Roberts, Felix E.	356800	31N/4W	160	1913
Robinson, Francis E.	457389	31N/3W	160	1915
" " "	633280	"	160	1918
Rock, Cecil J. J.	674594	30N/3W	160	1920
" " " "	727347	"	320	1920
" " " "	951760	31N/4W	80	1925
" " " "	"	31N/4W	240	1925
Ross, Ralph T.	436911	31N/3W	160	1914
Rossiter, Otis	1073412	30N/4W	637	1934
Roth, Fred	578279	30N/3W	160	1917
" "	975878	"	480	1926
Ruddell, Clair I.	833205	30N/4W	320	1921
Rudolph, Michael	348894	31N/3W	156	1913
Rudolph, Michael	427276	31N/3W	80	1914
" "	931632	"	80	1924
Ryan, Simon E.	869743	29N/3W	160	1922
Scharbach, Fred H.	556370	31N/3W	319	1916
Schmidt, Adolph E.	861784	31N/4W	321	1922

Name of Recipient	Land Patent No.	Township & Range	Acres	Year of Patent
Soards, Wm.	457141	31N/3W	40	1914
Smead, Herbert	501139	29N/3W	160	1915
" "	643557	"	160	1918
" "	965465	29N/4W	320	1925
Smead, Warren	355277	29N/3W	154	1913
Smead, Warren	685172	29N/3W	149	1919
" "	965465	29N/4W	320	1925
Smith, Archie N.	669426	29N/3W	320	1919
Smith, Charles P.	675454	31N/4W	320	1919
Smith, Geo. J.	674604	29N/3W	315	1919
Smith, Geo. J.	675026	29N/3W	40	1919
Smith, Robt.	253327	31N/4W	160	1912
Smith, Thos. J.	862606	"	320	1922
Spivey, Lawrence	1074905	"	590	1935
Spivey, Wm. A.	841944	29N/3W	160	1922
Spivey, Wm. A.	977236	29N/3W	320	1926
Stearns, Harry A.	753988	31N/4W	320	1920
Stewart, Wm. R.	650371	"	320	1918
Stevenson, James R.	161457	29N/3W	160	1910
Stevenson, John S.	49292	"	145	1909
Stevenson, John S.	163432	29N/3W	160	1910
Stubblefield, Blaine	946488	"	320	1924
" "	981831	"	322	1926
Stubblefield, Fancho	537203	"	120	1916
" "	674612	"	200	1919
Stubblefield, Fancho	947904	29N/3W	323	1924
Stubblefield, Newell	882197	30N/3W	320	1922
Swearingen, Thos. O. M.	359642	"	160	1913
Taylor, Ben Franklin	726320	31N/3W	80	1920
Taylor, Ben Stillman	854800	30N/3W	320	1922
Taylor, Bud	834971	30N/4W	159	1921
" "	972759	"	478	1926
Taylor, Elmer	676303	31N/3W	320	1919
Taylor, Esther F.	653896	"	80	1918
" "	657013	30N/3W	325	1918
Taylor, Margaret	485107	30N/3W	120	1915
" "	591862	"	85	1915
Thiessen, Sydney S.	403215	31N/4W	160	1914
Thomas, Joseph	674608	29N/3W	160	1919
" "	962319	"	160	1925

Name of Recipient	Land Patent No.	Township & Range	Acres	Year of Patent
Thomas, Joseph	962320	29N/3W	320	1925
Toman, Henry	1059608	30N/3W	490	1932
Toman, Michael	1081947	"	591	1936
Twogood, Harry P	874355	29N/3W	110	1922
Tysonm, Geo. W.	769320	31N/3W	326	1920
Vallem, Agnes M.	431503	31N/3W	80	1914
" " "	568873	"	320	1917
Vallem, Geo.	416869	"	160	1914
" "	426295	"	80	1914
" "	532065	"	40	1914
Vallem, Geo.	725595	31N/3W	40	1920
Vallem, Robt. W.	693080	30N/4W	320	1919
" " "	764493	"	320	1920
Vanetter, Anna	675446	31N/3W	333	1919
Vanetter, Ben	669424	"	320	1919
Vanetter, Geo. R.	506996	31N/3W	120	1916
" " "	556370	"	320	1916
" " "	556371	"	280	1916
Van Pool, Earl	716871	29N/3W	320	1919
" "	923181	"	320	1923
Verzani, Ernest G.	534101	31N/3W	160	1916
Vidrick, John	675457	"	320	1919
Vincent, Tammany	633296	"	320	1918
Walker, Chas. C.	813507	29N/3W	320	1921
" " "	931674	"	240	1921
Walker, Fred E.	834968	29N/3W	320	1921
" " "	1003865	"	320	1927
Walker, Omer C.	905089	30N/4W	640	1923
Washburn, Chas. W.	260943	31N/4W	160	1912
Washburn, Rachel	676293	30N/4W	320	1919
Wayne, Gilbert	69103	31N/3W	300	1919
" "	1101161	"	154	1939
Wayne, Olive B.	355826	"	171	1913
Wayne, Wm. W.	778768	"	120	1920
" "	501837	"	160	1915
" "	622457	"	320	1918
Wedge, Isaac	675458	31N/4W	320	1919
" "	725559	"	160	1920
Weller, Dosia	674228	"	160	1919
Weller, Harry E.	535651	31N/3W	160	1916
" "	633287	"	334	1918

127

Name of Recipient	Land Patent No.	Township & Range	Acres	Year of Patent
Wiley, Edward	781956	30N/3W	322	1920
" "	902022	"	324	1922
Wiley, James	743239	"	322	1920
Wilson, Clarence E.	1072961	"	639	1934
Wilson, Franklin B.	973350	29N/3W	302	1926
Wilks, Geo. F.	675452	31N/4W	320	1919
Wise, Harley	693066	30N/4W	324	1919
White, Chas.	831691	"	161	1921
" "	831692	"	480	1921
Wood, Fen	649430	30N/3W	320	1918
Wright, Burton E.	693075	31N/4W	320	1919
Wright, Chester H.	1077191	29N/3W	600	1935
Wright, Elizabeth A.	145592	30N/3W	160	1910
Wright, Howard	709977	29N/3W	314	1919
Wright, Nicatie B.	1104035	30N/3W	562	1939
Wright, Sample H.	830774	29N/3W	165	1921
Zumwalt, Martin C.	798923	30N/3W	324	1921

"Looking toward the Salmon"

shears

Wm. T. Platt when first on Salmon River,
about 1904

Martin Bottorf at his homestead
on Eagle Creek, about 1915

129

Esther Taylor near head of Skeleton Gulch, first Platt location
SE of Salmon River, 1895-1900. Photo about 1915, courtesy
of Esther Taylor Emerich.

Looking west across Cottonwood Creek at the B. F. Taylor ranch, 1906 L-R, B. F. Taylor, unidentified, Mrs. B. F. Taylor, Stillman Taylor. Photo courtesy of Esther Taylor Emerich.

View up Salmon River from Deer Creek Ranch in late summer. White band along left bank shows height of flood season flow, about a 20-foot rise here. In narrower gorges the flood rise sometimes exceeds 30 feet.

John Platt driving cattle to summer range on Craig Mountain, 1913. Note back end of dog in edge of brush below cattle. Dogs were essential for bringing up stragglers.

Ready to brand a cow at Moffett ranch, near Deer Creek mine, 1910. L to R Frank Stackpole, Tom Platt, Carson Moffett holding branding iron, "Yank" Robinson kneeling, "Cody" Raeder at right.

Tom Platt (L) watching his father prepare to "flank down" a calf for branding. The unusually docile heifer poses, too. Steer in background plainly shows the Platt brand, read W-cross.

Branding larger calves required a 5-man team for fast work. Here two riders have roped the feet and stretched the animal on the ground, the hatted man squats on its shoulders and doubles back the unroped front leg to hold it securely in position, the front man notches ear and wattle marks with a sharp knife, and the back man burns on the brand with a hot iron. Power chutes and presses now enable one man to do the whole job in about the same time.

Bull fights frequently livened the branding corral scene.

Wedding Picture
John Albion Platt - Emma Caroline Batdorf
Genesee, Idaho July 11, 1900

Emma C. Platt with children Tom (3½), Mary (2) and Frances (6 mo) at Wickiup summer camp, Joseph Plains, Idaho County, August 1906.

Skeleton Gulch home base of John and Emma Platt, 1900-1906. Mary Platt between first two horses, Frances at head of white horse, Tom at front leg of white horse. Packstring being loaded for family move to Deer Creek Ranch, February, 1907. Grandma Batdorf (mounted) returning to Berkeley after a working visit of several months.

John Platt and Emma Platt at Wickiup camp in 1956. Remains of
saddle shed built by Platt in 1902, collapsed by snow.

John and Emma Platt at Golden Wedding anniversary, Spalding Park,
July 11, 1950

137

Elegy Without Words

III
LEGENDS THAT LINGER

VERY MAJOR AREA in our country has its legends, usually fitted to the regional folk history. In the East are the buccaneer tales, the derelict ships, the lost colonies and the deep woods frontiersmen. The lake states forests produced their Paul Bunyan. In the West are the famous bad men, the lost mines, the mountain men, and "the gun that won the West." In smaller areas the legends attach to local heros and mystery figures. Apart from all these each generation has its legendary "good old days" when things were so much better than now.

Part III examines some of these legend concepts as found in the frontier life recounted here through the eyes of some who were there.

The "gun that won the West" is held up for review in the experience of one Idaho settler as told to his sons.

The romantic homestead life is rubbed down to reality in the recollections of a pioneering school teacher.

These samplings are not intended to debunk. There *was* an authentic lure of the West or it would not have been peopled as enthsiastically as it was. There *were* real characters behind the legends. But the real can be better appreciated when seen as it really was. Each reader then can color it any shade he likes.

"THE GOOD OLD DAYS"

The golden age of any culture always lies somewhere in the past. The aura thickens with distance. Ordinary people grow to hero figures, their exploits more than life size. In time, their deeds overshadow the difficulties that made them memorable and their times take on a golden glow in popular thought.

The American West has been and still is particularly romanticized in song and story. The "Western" as a realm of literature and entertainment has assumed classic lines, where right always prevails, an alternately reluctant-beneficent nature yields prosperity, and the good guys make the whole outcome look inevitable—even easy. Those were "The Good Old Days," a built-in assumption in the latter day popular recall of our pioneer era.

How to get behind this myth and convey the realities of the past to people whose only direct experience is the present, and whose dominant interest necessarily is the future, is a special challenge. The present too easily is taken without much thought about how it came into being. The past too easily is romanticized into hazy unreality.

In this day of crowded, hurried living, neon scenery, trashed environment, impersonal technology, and transient social relationships, who has not yearned for a way to step back into the calmer, cleaner, more stable past? Those days of country living! Then neighbor could depend upon neighbor. Daily life was not hectic, simple honesty prevailed, and---.

But wait! Before we go all the way back to the unturned sod, let us take a look at pioneer life as seen by people actually involved in it. The following three letters by pioneer women convey the story as no amount of literary erudition could do. Written from widely different settings, each limns a real page out of pioneer experience.

The first, dated November 17, 1890, was written from Southwick, Idaho, by Mrs. Benjamin F. Jacks to her son James. Here is her unpretentious report:

Home, Sweet Home

Dear son -

I will try to answer your letter. I entended to answer yesterday but had company and could not we received your letter several days ago, but Pearlie is oh dear so cross and requiers so mutch care, tho she is better, in fact she seems like one from the grave, she has bin so near there. She has had too spells that I thought she would never breath any more one time I enserted my finger in her mouth to try to get the phlegm out of her throat, and her jaws set and she set her teeth on my finger, I was sure she was gon. I screamed oh Pearlie are you dead and my finger fast in your mouth, and just then I gave my finger a twist, and that loosened her jaws anuff that I thrused my finger as far down her throat as my finger would reach and oh dear the phlegm blood and corruption, did come.

That was just a week after the time that I wrout you about. I tell you my finger hert she had it fast right threw the first joint and it swelled as tight and hard she mad impration anuff that she reached blood. Orrin has bin very bad he coughs so heard and his lungs bleeds every on that have seen them say that they never saw any worse. Essie keeps up she confes heard but not like the other too.

I hav bin confined in the house so long and so clost, and yesterday Jess went for medicin and of coors your Pa had to go to meeting, and I had to run out too or three times to set the dogs on the stock to keep them where we wanted them to stay, and I took a dreadfull cold, my head and ches, and I feel real badley but will get all right as soon as my cold gets ripe anuff to pick. I tell you, we have a fine doggie he could not be bough today with ten dollars. Yesterday the cow was a quarter of a mild north of the house, and I called the dogs they came to me I said Bess, Prince, look see that cow they looked at me I said take her. Away they went. I stood in the dore-yard, and wished Jim could see the way that dog run. Bess let Prince lead out, but the cow come a bobbing you bet. He would bigh her heels and purk her tail once in a while he would run to her head to turn her. Oh we love our dogies. Mrs. Rice was hear, and they have a brother to Prince. She says he is one of the smartest dogs, and that they would-not take ten dollars for him.

When Perlie was so bad choked and the children was crying bess seemed to know that sompthing was wrong with her, for she sat back on her honches, and oh dear how she howled. That made us all have a more tender feeling for her she watches her chance and comes in and licks Pearlies hands and will give her a lick in the face to. Well we will tell you lots of Bessies pranks when you come home.

I was seting one day, seting back from the door. I looked at her just kept looking at her didnot say a word nor make a motion. She looked as solm. A casionally she would twitch her lip just a little I looked at her and frowned. She showed signs of fear or sompthing for her eyes would look sad. I sat there just experimenting, finley I camenced to look pleased her ears commenced to twitch and trin and I still eyed her and she eyed me, and as I alowed myself to look more pleased she took on as it seamed the same feeling finly I just chuckeled to myself. It realy seamed so funy that I had to laugh hear she came whinig and frisking, and she wasnot content untill she sat her fore paws on my lap and wanted to kiss me but I said that will do bessie get down, you are a smart dog.

Well Jimie we have writen and found out that there will be nothing dun about the school land untill after the Legeslature next January that will give us all a better chance. Why not come and work in the Lueston Teller office it is a good Republican paper, double sheet and a fine paper. I wish you would get nearer home Moscow runs a good paper, and so does Kendricks. The R.R. is at work and say that the wistle will blow in Kendricks this fall or forepart of winter.

Cannot tell sure just when we will thrash this week. Your Pa has gon for a tank of water he holls water about three milds. Old Mrs. Hartenges has a new well 39 feet of water, dont you think she is glad. Charlie Black has a boy kid John Huett has bough Albert Huetts farm and has moved up. Henrie Jacks has lost old dexter didnot know that there was any thing wrong, went to take off his bridle and found his jaws locked. he lived about aleven hours and died he has lost a nice colt and a good cow all clost together Mary and all the children have the whooping cough

Mary branderberg is very sick she is in a sad fix she had worked heard and got a big flock of fullblooded brown laghorn chickens and some one stold all of them one night and she cryed so mutch about that, and she works awfull hard, and she works of so hard, and she has bin very porley all the summer, and she has a young baby about 3 months old and she is so anxious for money and over worked her self, when she ough to rested all things together has about unnerved her mind and boddley to. Her recovery is doubtfull she has not her right mind a part of the time but she new your pa when he was there last week

Well we are going to kill a hog this evening, and I will have to help get the water hot Come over for breakfast and eat rosted ribb! Well Jimie it just seems as I am never to get this letter finished Monday night after we got threw butchering, Frank Ferington, a 'wood rat,' came and put up for the night and C. Landing and Jack Sotherland came to see us I think that they were real kind to take the trouble to come so fare Charley tole Pearl that he came to see her

Your pa has gone to Fairview with wood. Jess has gon to the post office, and Pearl and Essie and Orrin is trying to see which can bother me most Pearl is oh so cross, if you could hear her just now, oh dear, she is so spoilt. We got a letter from Allie Monday They was all well well I have comenced to cook grub for the thrashers. I have a pot of pumpkin cooking. I am going to give them pumpkin pies Oh well I will have to quit for Pearl is yelling and Orrin is coughfing and vomiting dear dear it is awfull, but I feel like that they are so much better that i feel like singing a long meter doxolegey prais god from whome all blessing flow god bye must get supper, your mother in hope of seeing her absent boy soon,

Mary M. Jacks

(The above letter was obtained from the Rural Women's History Project, University of Idaho, and is printed here by permission of Mr. Frank O. Jacks, Clarkston, Wash., who supplied it to the RWHP. No changes have been made in capitalization or spelling, but spacings have been adjusted to facilitate reading. The author hereby extends his appreciation for the courtesies that allowed this usage.)

141

KENNETH B. PLATT
Hands Across The Canyons

To the pioneer generation that settled northern Idaho the precipitous river canyons of the region were just part of a package of hazards that somehow cemented frontier relationships into a code under which open handed living and mutual aid in emergencies were implicit. Each frontier area in its own way produced the same code. Here we have a brief sample of pioneer ranching experience in Nez Perce County as recorded in a letter written by Mrs. Lucille F. Clark, who lived as a teen-ager and ranch wife in the canyon and ridge country of upper Tammany southeast of Lewiston from 1898 to 1910. The letter was written in response to her reading of John Platt's *Whispers From Old Genesee And Echoes Of The Salmon River* when it was first issued. It reveals many facets of Idaho ranch living around the turn of the Century.

Santa Monica, Calif.
10 21/62

Dear Mr. Platt -

I have just finished reading the book and it was like getting a letter out of the past. The Clarks went to Idaho from California in 1878 . . . My family came from western Oregon to Tammany in 1898. Mother's parents crossed the plains from Ohio in 1852. My grandfather used to tell me it took them six months, and that I would live to see the time that we could make it in two hours . . . We went to Alberta and bought railroad in 1910 . . .

I never knew any of the Caldwells, but did know John Cambell and his beautiful white horse. When they were shipping cattle from Lewiston once, Hawley Wickham of Grangeville, George's brother-in-law, roped one of Caldwell's steers and sheared the brand. Cambell called him a name no man takes, so they had a fight. Both had been drinking. Hawley had old John down and had his thumbs in his eyes. Bill Caldwell was outside the fence, but reached through and knocked Hawley off, then the crowd stopt the fight. As they were leaving the corral Cambell jerked Lafe Mounce's gun out of the holster; George was right behind him and grabbed the gun. That must have been in the late nineties . . .

During the Indian War the government sent out a lot of old Civil War guns to the settlers and the people of Lewiston. The guns had been converted from muzzle loaders but still were a one shot gun. When George was running cattle in the mountains he bought three of those old guns to set for bear. He sawed the stocks from two. The other one we still have. One year the bear had been bad, and Jim Lambert, George and two other men were in the woods looking for a place to build a pen where they could set the trap. In setting a gun they always built a pen, so as not to endanger a man or livestock.

They came onto a grizzley eating on a steer that he had killed. The only gun they had was that old Civil War gun. George shot him and killed him with the one shot. I thought they took quite a chance. If he had wounded the bear he could have been onto them before George could have got another cartridge in the gun. Lambert hit the bear over the head with the back of an ax, which was another bad chance. George said he yelled at him not to go near till they made sure he was dead, but should look for a tree that was easy to climb. It was summer, but Lambert wanted the hide so they skinned him out, and there wasn't a bullet hole in the hide. I told George that was bad shooting, if he shot at the chest and hit the bear in the mouth.

SALMON RIVER SAGA

We still have the Winchester shotgun that George bought in 1885. I used it quite a bit in 1914, in Alberta. We had built a house that summer and moved out of the shack we had been living in since 1910. We had planted shrubs and trees but they were not large enough to give protection to the chickens. I had raised 300 chickens and wanted them for harvest. The hawks started carrying them off. I kept the gun in the kitchen, not loaded, but it was a pump gun and could be loaded fast as I dashed for the yard. The hawks were like General Chennault's Flying Tigers, if they missed they did not make another try for an hour or so. There are two breeds of hawks that we try to protect, a big gray and the red tail. They never bother chickens, but would follow the men at haying time and grab mice from under the pitch forks. I had to kill the chicken or Cooper hawks, I believe they are called, or I would not have had a chicken left.

One day I heard the chickens squall and dashed out the kitchen door, to meet a Blackfoot Indian. They were haying for a rancher north of us. He could not speak English and I could not talk Blackfoot. All he could say was, 'Bassano me.' There were only trails across the prairie. I pointed to the gate that would take him out of our pasture onto the Bassano trail. Three days later I heard the chickens at the front and run for the door only to meet the same old Indian. All he said was 'Pony me.' I thought he wanted to feed them and pointed the way to the barn. When he got there he could see the watering trough. All he wanted was to give them a drink. I wondered what he thought to be met twice with a shotgun.

I have never been past the old Clark ranch since a new house was built. I always wanted to build above the small orchard where the ground sloped, and get out of the mud. I believe that Lafe Mounce Jr.'s son-in-law owns that part of the ranch now. The Lloyd Bros. have the Tenmile part, and the 120-acre field that joins the Jap Mounce place. My father-in-law scripted that field. They may have the west field that George bought from Frank Kettenbach, before George was of age. His sister held the deed till George was old enough. There was 90 acres of farm land on it, the rest a rocky pasture that run down into Tenmile. That part of the pasture could be used in the winter, while the other side, where there were no rocks, the cattle had to be taken out of there before the frost.

George rolled three horses on the brakes of the Snake River. One was stepping up over a rock and got his foot in the ring stirrup. The last one was after we were married and was one of my favorite horses. George called that a case of horse suicide. His hind foot slipped off the trail and he made no effort to get back, but just sat down. George hung onto the bridle reins as long as he could. The horse went over backwards end over end. George borrowed a pony that was just big enough to carry the saddle, which could be repaired. He walked the rest of the way home. However the cattle thought he had a horse, went along without giving any trouble . . . .

When my folks lived on the old ranch from 1902 till 1905, Warren was still running a stage to Cottonwood. He used a spring wagon and not a stage, with only two horses. The horses would be played out by the time they got within a quarter of a mile from the house and the driver would be up to get someone to pull them out. My job was to go bring a team in from the pasture and Dad would pull the stage out. It got to be such a regular thing that we would keep a team up till after stage time. We would take them to the top of the gulch, then they were on the level and could go on to Jap Mounce's place where they changed horses.

In the spring when the snow went off with a rush, so much water went down the road that holes were washed out deep enough to bury a horse. I may have had something to do with having the road changed. When that highway district was formed two of the commissioners were Jack McCormack and Horace Nelson. I told Horace that the road should be changed, that in the long run it would be cheaper to make that grade than to build up a grade in the gulch and have to repair it every spring . . . . I never

143

"whoa -- you crazy horse!"

could see any reason for opposing it. It did not take any farm land. In fact it would have benefit to the ranch back in the days of the freighters. There was a wide place in the road where they could camp over night.

Most of them were all right, others helped themselves to a horse collar and a few halters from the barn. One man and his wife that both drove a six-horse team often camped there. One evening she came to the house for a little flour to make gravy. The next morning we saw where they had picked one of our chickens and never bothered to burn or bury the feathers. It used to make me sick to see those people go past the house, and hear the horses groan when they went up against sore shoulders, and see the blood on their sides where the blacksnake had been used. No. S.P.C.A. there in those days, and the poor beasts had no redress . . . .

We were never bothered with cattle thieves in Canada. I guess in the real early days there were, but when they started sending them up for 21 years it stopped it. The wolves were bad when we first went there, and the stockmen put such a large bounty on them that it brought in expert hunters. They are not like a coyote, they never come back to a kill. I don't know if the hunters got them or they couldn't stand civilization. A few years ago the government sent in men to poison the coyotes. It is a method that I never heard of. The bait sticks up on something and when the coyote takes it a needle hits him in the mouth and he gets a dose of cyanide. They were good mouse catchers, but were getting too many calves, and some of the farmers wanted to keep a few head of sheep . . . .

I always liked the old ranch in Idaho and hated to see them sell it, but we could not run the two places so far apart. George never wanted to go back to it. As cold as it got in Alberta, he liked it better. The barnyard was never muddy. We had storms at harvest time but it was never hot. He said, too, that it was nice to be able to pick up a board and know that there was not a rattle snake under it. Snakes must have been a worry to you and Mrs. Platt with those young children on the River.

A cousin of my mother's lived on the Oregon side of Snake River. They had a two-year-old child bitten by a rattler, and the Nez Perce saved her. Their cabin was on a hill a quarter of a mile from the corrals on the river. The mother heard the child scream. She had been hitting at the snake with a short stick and was bit on the thumb. She panicked, put the child in the house and told her to stay there, and ran to where she could see the men at the corral, where they were branding, waved her apron and screamed. The three men rode their horses up over the rocky trail as fast as they could. It was hot and they met the baby coming after her mother. Sam picked her up and sucked the wound, told one man to go across the river and ask a camp of Indians for help, and the other to ride 20 miles to a phone and call a doctor from Lewiston.

An elderly squaw and her husband took charge, the others took sacks and started gathering cactus. The Indian would burn the thorns off and split the cactus, and the squaw would slap it on the baby's thumb. She also kept the baby's body wrapped in hot towels. They kept that up for three days and nights without a rest. The third day the squaw said, 'She live now.' It was 75 miles from Lewiston and the doctor told the rider that unless the Indians could save the child she would be dead before he could get there, but he would send out a rider with medicine that might help if she was alive . . . .

I have been writing at odd minutes and will not read this over or I probably would not send it. November 7th. Election over and it did not go to suit me here in California. Only four that I voted for were elected.

Sincerely,
Lucille F. Clark

A Letter from Jennie

Jennie Batdorf was my mother's older sister. The Batdorf family passed through Genesee, Idaho, in the mid-1890s, there making acquaintance with the Platt family that led to the marriage in 1900 of my parents, John Platt and Emma Batdorf.

The Batdorfs had wheeled their wagons from Lawrence, Kansas, to Lewistown, Montana, in 1889. Over the next several years they lived there or in the neighboring communities of Cottonwood and Beaver Creek. In 1894 they drove from there through Yellowstone Park to the Boise Valley in southern Idaho, then on to Genesee. Working at fruit picking, haying and grain harvesting, they earned their keep as they traveled. Jennie by then was Mrs. Will Lewis and mother of her first child, Jesse.

145

In 1897 the Batdorf family—father Jesse S., mother Mary C., Emma, Sam, Charles, and Bertha, and the Lewises, drove south across the Blue Mountains and High Desert of eastern Oregon, and on through northern California to Hollister, south of San Francisco.

The letter from Jennie here reproduced was written from Hollister the year after Emma had gone back from there to Genessee to marry John Platt and settle with him on a cattle ranch in the isolated canyon country of the Salmon River near its juncture with the Snake. As the letter shows, ranch life in the Hollister area was not the "sunny California" picnic so often pictured. Busy with three small children, and with endless house and outdoor chores, Jennie had no time for letter writing. This letter could be written only be neglecting the demands of her own household.

So, at intervals over several days, and in sessions deep into the night, the letter was written. An intimate communication between sisters, it reviews shared acquaintances of both their Montana and their California years. Candor finds few saints as Jennie turns the leaves of both family and friends with an impartial rake. Always in the background are the hard conditions of pioneer life, a too-often losing tale of brinksmanship on almost every front.

But there is another and less somber side of Jennie's background that we need to know before we read her letter. The glimpses of warm love and sympathy, of nostalgia for distant friends, that lighten her story bespeak a once carefree girlhood. In her memory the years in Montana were golden years. There she arrived as a young teenager, joined in the bustling social life of her age group, found her future husband, matured to womanhood and married.

In those years her autograph album—then the young girl's personal social register—accumulated the names and sentiments of many who were to be lifelong friends, as well as those of her own family. Treasured through four generations, the album now yields its once inconsequential entries as lamps to the page of history from which Jennie steps. Most were copied pieties or familiar jingles used by many; a few were original. Together they go with Jennie from her 1891 first acquaintance with her husband-to-be to their marriage in 1893. Fittingly, the first entry is her own dedication of the book to its purpose. Following in chronological order are the entries that introduce us to the friends and relatives mentioned in her letter.

Miss Jennie Batdorf
Beaver Creek, Mont.

Go forth thou little volume,
I leave thee to thy fate,
To love and friendship truly
Thy leaves I dedicate.

To Jennie—

Since scribbling in albums remembrance assures,
With the greatest of pleasure I'm scribbling in yours.
W. H. Lewis, Cottonwood, Mont.
May 14th, 1891

KENNETH B. PLATT

Dear Sister —

> Remember me when far away
> And only half awake.
> Remember me on your wedding day
> And send me a piece of cake.
>
> > Your sister Emma
> > Beaver Creek
> > May 22, 1892

Dear Sister —

> Within this book so pure and white
> Let none but friends presume to write,
> And may each line with friendship given
> Direct the reader's thoughts to heaven.
>
> > Charles Batdorf
> > Beaver Creek
> > May 23, 1892

Dear Sister.

> Remember me dear sister
> When on these lines you look;
> Remember it was your dear brother
> Who wrote this in your book.
>
> > Samuel L. Batdorf
> > Beaver Creek

Miss Jennie Batdorf —

> Ever keep before you the vow you have taken;
> live to make the most of your life by keeping
> close to your Savior's side, is the advice of
> your friend,
>
> > N. S. Hawk
> > May 23, 1893

Dear Jennie —

> Remember me when this you see
> Though many miles away
> Remember me and so will I
> Remember you until I die.
>
> > Your friend,
> > Vilenna LaFollett
> > Beaver Creek
> > May 29th

148

SALMON RIVER SAGA

Friend Jennie—

           Sailing down the stream of life
              In your little bark canoe,
        May you have a pleasant trip
          With just room enough for two.

                       Your friend,
                       Francis E. Lafollett
                       Beaver Creek
                       May 30, 1892

Dear Jennie—

        When the name that I write here is dim on the page
           And the leaves of your album are yellow with age
      Still think of me kindly and do not forget
          That wherever I am I remember you yet.

                       Your sincere friend
                       Eliza A. Deffenbaugh
                       June 5, 1892

Friend Jennie—

        When I am in some distant land
           And my face you cannot see
      View the writing of my hand
          And give one kindly thought for me.

                       W. H. Lewis
                       Cottonwood, Mont.
                       June 11, 1892

Dear Jennie—

        Fourth in your album may I be
          Fifth in your thoughts
             Sixth in remembrance
               But last to be forgot.
                       Maud E. Whipple
                       Cottonwood
                       June 25, 1892

Friend Jennie—

        Think of me ever in kindness I pray
      Forget me oh never though far far away.
                       E. E. Lewis
                       Beaver Creek
                       July 8, 1892

Jennie—

> Whether in midocean or on land
>> Our friendship true shall ever stand.
>>> W. H. Lewis
>>> November 28, '92

Dear Jennie—

> May your life be pure and noble
>> A life without a pain
> A life that's free from sorrow
>> And may heaven be your gain.
>>> Alice Kelly
>>> Cottonwood
>>> March 7, 1893

Friend Jennie—

> Be always good. Lead a good life.
>> Get a good husband and be a good wife.
>>> Your friend,
>>> Mabel E. Bean
>>> Cottonwood
>>> March 22

Miss Jennie Batdorf—

> I am not sure that life to anyone
>> A fuller measure of contentment brings
>>> With all its gifts, than in the draft which springs
>>> From honest work well planned and bravely done.
>>>> Your friend,
>>>> Isabella M. Bean
>>>> Cottonwood
>>>> March 27, 1893

Dear Jennie—

> Lover's eyes more sharply sighted be
>> Than other men's, and in dear love's delight
>> See more than other's eyes can see.
>>> Yours truly,
>>> Grace Scovel
>>> Lewistown
>>> June 1, 1893

SALMON RIVER SAGA

Dear Sister —

May happiness ever be thy lot
Wherever thou shalt be
And joy and pleasure light the spot
That may be home to thee.

Your sister Emma
June 2nd, 1893

Dear Jennie —

The eternal stars shine out
As soon as it is dark enough.

Your Father-in-law
J. Lewis
Sawmill Gulch
June 16, 1895

Dear Jennie —

Remember me in friendship
Remember me in love
Remember me dear Jennie
When we shall meet above.

Your mother
Charlotte Lewis
June 16, 1895

And now, the letter.

Hollister, Calif.
Oct. 27, 1901

My dear Sister Emma & Brother John

I believe I promised to write to you when I got home from San Jose, but at least a period of time four weeks in duration has elapsed and I can't bring myself to think that I have time to write to you, as much as I want you to hear from me. When I get a letter I don't answer [illegible] hear and I am sure you all will be thinking ill of me long before I get done writing and I am afraid you will get disgusted and quit long before you get done reading it. I have been going to write to you for months and now I thought I would take the whole day for it but it is three o'clock now.

Let me tell you just how we look in this room. This is Sunday and the floor has not been swept since Friday noon, my hair is uncombed. Will sits there half-soling his boots. The baby is in the rocking chair. The girls are running around their hair not combed. The stove is in need of a fresh coat of blacking and the blue kettle sets on the same with nine peaches in it of our own drying and they smell nearly like the ones we dried in the Sacramento valley. I don't believe we will like them.

This house has not been cleaned since we came here. There are only two rooms that there is any wood work to wash. One bedroom has a hole cut in the side and a piece of screen nailed over it for a

151

window and the other, the one we use for a milk room and store room, has a little window in it but the walls are just rough boards. The other three rooms are papered. I have washed the windows several times and scrubbed the floor several times but I am going to get at it and clean house in earnest before long.

Sat. the nineteenth Will went to town and Bert [teen-age sister Bertha] came up with him and stayed a week. She went home yesterday morning on the stage. She got a saddle horse and rode every day. She got poison oak on her hands too on Wednesday and she couldn't help with anything. We had a box of poison oak cure which made her life easier or she couldn't have stayed here. Pa had told her to come home Thursday and help Ma, but she said she wasn't going to. We raised a few pie pumpkins this summer and I cooked them while she was here and was going to send some to Ma and then she didn't go Thursday so I sealed it up boiling hot but it spoiled and I couldn't cook the germs out of it so I threw it away.

Will had lots of nice lettuce while I was in town last spring and soon after I came back, but the birds eat it up before I could have any. We had some nice beans this summer, lots of sweet corn, a few little musk melons and a watermelon or two that didn't amount to anything. We had one row of cucumber vines and they are still bearing, though we haven't had a gallon of pickles off the whole row. There was some spinach last spring too but I wasn't here to use it so it went to seed. We planted a patch of onion sets too and some of them made big onions. The birds eat the onions that came from the seed and the beet seed didn't come up at all. There was quite a few peas too, and we raised about 8 sackfuls of potatoes. There was a few carrots came up, and a few turnips. I cooked the turnips but they were bitter. The carrots are in the garden yet, maybe I'll cook them some of these days. The birds, squirrels, gophers, rabbits, rats and mice bothered the garden, and the cow got in once and eat corn too.

We raised about 80 chickens this summer. The hawks have bothered them a good deal. Two different times a hawk took a chicken and carried it a ways but had to let it go. The chickens didn't get hurt. A small hawk got after an old hen out in the brush but we scared it away, and Will found a half grown chicken partly eaten out in the brush. We thought a hawk did it. We have not had an egg from our chickens for two months. When we came to investigate we found they were alive with lice and mites. Mr. Day (a neighbor and chicken man) told Will to get crude carbolic acid and take an equal amount of coal oil and paint the roosts. He did that and fixed the roosts to swing but the hens have not sufficiently recovered to bear fruit yet. They are moulting now and there is no green feed except when they fly into the prune trees and eat the leaves. There are 27 little chickens with two hens. They are about 3 weeks old.

It begins to look bare up here; the hills are brown and the leaves are falling off the trees. It rained Friday night and at intervals today. The young ones have been teasing to go out all day. Just now they are regaling themselves with bread and jelly. I made some jelly from silver prunes and some from quince and apples. We got some of those sour apples from the Gross place and the first jelly I made I used a third quince juice and the jelly was awful nice. The next two batches were half quince and they both got burned a little, not near as bad as that out at Bibbe's. I didn't get any as nice or good as that Ma made.

Well I suppose you want to know about my trip to San Jose. It was just splendid for me, as you will know. I took the boys. Jesse said it made him a little bit sick to ride on the cars just at the last and he didn't like it very well. He liked to ride on the electric car though. It didn't make him sick. In fact I liked it so well I wished I could go on forever. We started Monday morning on the early train, (Charles took us to the depot in the buggy) and came back Wednesday evening on the last train. I wanted to ride after dark when the lamps were lighted. When we got to Hollister nobody was there to meet us so I was about to climb into Mr. Wynn's wagon and ride down when Charles loomed up in the darkness on his wheel. Then we had the satchel, the baby and the wheel to take and I couldn't make the wheel go so part of the time Charles carried the baby and the satchel and rolled the wheel too. (What an expression "rolled the wheel") but you know what I mean.

SALMON RIVER SAGA

I found Aunt Mattie [widow of Uncle Sam Batdorf] in bed. I expect Ma has told you about it so I won't say anything about it. I will whisper to you that I didn't hardly have enough to eat while I was there and Jess was hungry most of the time. He is so particular what he eats. We couldn't leave Aunt Mattie to go to the parks or any place. John [son of Mattie] wasn't there, a circumstance of which I was very glad. They only had a gasolene stove too and the weather was cloudy and cool so it was too cold for the baby. He took cold and his eye was awful sore. It had never been well anyway, it was just like Helen's [Jennie's second daughter]. The change in the milk too didn't agree with him, and there was no place to put him down only on the bed with Aunt M. so altogether he was cross. I gave him a dose of castorie before we started home and about the time we got to Gilroy it commenced to gripe him and he cried without a stop till we got off the train at Hollister. As soon as we got home he was as good as could be.

That is a dismal house they live in. The walls are calsomined but it is dirty and marked up with all colors of lead pencils. It was so cold too that I just shivered and yet Aunt M. had to lie there without fire and she wouldn't wear a night gown. She had her flannel underclothes on. I guess the reason she wouldn't wear one was that it would make more work for Mary [Mattie's daughter], and Mary was all the time talking about what she had to do and didn't have time to crochet and learn drawn work and ever so many other things.

Em I wrote to you before that Aunt M. has consumption. Ma told me she had. But she has not, and I am glad of it. They have a parlor and I didn't notice much what was in it but Mary has Charles' and Sam's pictures in celluloid frames setting on the organ and your picture taken in Boise in a metal frame on a little stand. I wanted to hear Mary play but I had taken a tennis [a heavy cotton flannel] nightgown along to make for Aunt M. and I wanted to finish it so I didn't take time to listen. I felt obliged to stay by Aunt M. all I could too.

But enough of this: I must launch out on something else. I had to quit to get supper, and now they are all in bed but I. Will sat here and read what I had written without comment except to tell me I had Mr. Winn's name spelled wrong. I have been reading your letter but I guess I will have to read it again. Yes I have seen a dutch oven but am glad I don't have to use one. I ought not to have asked you the name of your stove. I guess Noah had something else to do besides give it a name.

You must sterilize John since he had the measles so we won't take them when we visit you. About the time he had boils, Will had one on his jaw which was very painful. 'I wish it were now so I could eat some berries.' That sounds just like child talk. We were all surprised to hear that you eat fish. Whenever you get enough yourself eat some for us. If you shoot grouse like we did up above Whipples I guess you won't get fat on them. Jess and Verna [Jennie's first daughter] look at the pictures through the stereoscope whenever they want to. I thought I would write a whole lot but I am so sleepy. Cora's boy is a girl this time and Mary sent the name Gladys Eva and Cora [Mattie's daughter] changed it to Dafny Eva and Addie calls her girl Nancy Estelle Caledonia. Dafny Caladonia would be a nice name for Miss Platt [Emma's first child, born 10/16/01] since you are so kind as to suggest the name 'Tink.'

Mary said they think Addie is about to have another baby. Mary has three boys. I will tell you what I meant about Charlie Scovel and the family. He died of consumption and Maggie traded the ranch for town property and moved to town and took in sewing. Then she was sick a good deal and she married a man that had a ranch over near the Moccasin Mts. [Montana]. I forget how many children Mary said she had and I do not know if she took them or not. She must have I guess. They would not have any place else to go. I know I told you about Elf Whipple the other time but I am sure there are questions on your mind which only a fuller explanation can set at rest. Mary told me more completely.

It happened on the bench back of John Whipple's place. She was riding a bronco and had a side saddle on and Ruby (the one after Addie Cora) was with her on another horse. Ezra Hawk had just drove out there to plow, leading a harnessed team. Elf and Ruby had been out there talking to him and started home when the saddle turned and the bronco bucked and kicked and her foot hung in the stirrup. She was kicked on the head the first thing and lost consciousness. Then the horse got its front hoof in the placket of her dress behind and that is how it come she lost her clothes. Ezra saw all this and left his team standing and drove as fast as the horses could go, to her. She was lying on her face with blood all over it. He turned her over and wiped the blood off with his handkerchief. He sent Ruby to Pintler's after Della who happened to be there, and a quilt to wrap the girl in and they loaded her up and she was at home in bed before she knew anything. Pintler's were living on the place Shortley's lived on back on the bench a mile or two from Whipples. Whipples live there now and I don't know where Pintler's went. You know that Whipples rented a hotel in Lewistown and somebody brought them the smallpox and they all had it. Ann was marked up a good deal. Then they were willing to quit and moved out there such a short distance from their old place.

Ruby died the 24 of August and was buried the 25th. She had appendicitis and peronitis, was sick five days. At first they didn't know what was the matter with her and didn't think it necessary to call a Dr. but they got a doctor then and he told them what ailed her and thought an operation would save her. They made an opening in the abdomen and the pus and corruption gushed out and she just screamed. They had to close it up and she became unconscious and would have died with a sweet smile on her face but the Doctor roused her up again and she screamed from then till she died and had a look of misery on her face. I read this in Cora's letter when I was to San Jose.

I read lots of Cora's letters and some of Addie's and Lena's and Lizzie Deffenbaugh's. She said too that when Ruby died Elf went into a kind of trance and didn't know anything for a while. I can think of so many things now that I was going to ask Mary so I could tell you and I forgot it while I was there. Elf shot Ed Shortly in the leg too. That was before Aunt M. left there. They two, with others were out toward the barn shooting at a mark with a pistol, one that the cartridges turn around and a little pressure on the trigger causes an explosion. She said to him "I'll shoot you," and all at once he grabbed his leg and doubled up and she said "What's the matter." He answered, "Oh you've shot me." They sent for John and Ed walked into the house and Mrs. Whipple and Ezra D. held him while John cut the bullet out with his razor. It was about halfway between the hip and knee and it came through far enough so they could see it.

Then Mrs. W. gave up her bedroom to him which was next the girls' room and they hung a cloth up to a window hole between the rooms, and one night after he had been there a few days they were wakened and Ann said "Elf there's somebody looking in there" and just then the curtain fell and Ed went back. They told Mrs. W. next day and she run him off. He was well enough to ride his horse away. I asked Mary what Mrs. Shortley thought about it and she said Mrs. S. did not care. That Ed had run away from home to escape putting in the crop and he could take what he got. Mrs. S. and Susie had to help Mr. S. put in the crop. A laughable circumstance about it was that one day she had been raking and it started to rain and she unhitched and got on the horse and it wouldn't go good so she give it a cut with the whip which sent it across the field at a good pace and her bouncing up and down. She was not riding sideways either. Ben saw her coming and he stood and looked with his mouth open.

Mary and Ed live up in the neighborhood of Key's and Lisbe's. Bud L. and wife lived up there but have moved to town now. Bean's moved to Lewistown soon after Aunt M. left there. Bernie Whipple came home from the Klondike as poor as he left. He and Blanche still have an idea they will get married but the folks on both sides fight it. Blanche is awful lazy. Her own mother told that she wouldn't wash a dish or sweep or hardly comb her own hair. Earnest is wild and stubborn. Merril W. is going with Letha Batdorf. That family of Batdorf's are Pa's third cousins and they live in that house by Morris Sloans. It is the one Shortley's used to occupy but Morris tore down the old one and built a new house. Letha is 16 and I don't know how many more children there are. That is one of the things I forgot to ask.

John and Maggie are the old folks names. They helped to swell the number of guests at Dettie's wedding and also the presents. She got lots of nice presents. I can't think of them all but Frank's present to her was a set of dishes, a dinner set. John, Cora, Mary & Aunt Mattie gave her a set of teaspoons that cost six dollars. Lou Eldridge gave Frank a set of silver knives and forks and Frank bought the spoons. Lizzie and Bertha gave her a beautiful light blue water set china and decorated with gold trimmings. After the wedding they visited John and Cora Alibele a few hours before starting for their home on Cottonwood. Dettie said she never was so surprised as when she beheld her new home. The stove was polished, the floor had linoleum put on (what an expression), the bed was made, the bedspread and pillow-shams on, the windows washed, shades and lace curtains up, the table set for twelve (he expected the shivari crowd), napkins laid to their places, and everything as nice as if a woman had done it, and Frank was nearly late for the wedding because he wouldn't leave till he had everything fixed.

Mary said he had an awful nice bedroom set. Mary said Maud and Dave moved up in the Mts. as far as they could get. They have a sawmill up there. I do not know what mountains. Aunt M. said that one summer before they left Mrs. W. said Dave and some of the Whipple children went berrying up in the Mts. and being short of beds Mrs. W. and Dave occupied the same one. The children told it the next day. John and Mrs. W. had high words about it. To quote Aunt M., "Oh John was awful mad." It came near making trouble between Maud and Dave too. Mary says Maud is queer about her children. She never kisses them and plays with them, she takes care of them what is necessary and puts them down again. She thinks lots of them too.

Grace and Jennie S. bid fair to be old maids, and Lotice got sick and her father came and took her home. Steven and she tried twice to get married but as they were cousins the law allowed them no license. Lotie was awful mean to Grandma and I asked why she didn't make her go away and Mary said Steve had her hired there to help his mother. One time in the winter the old lady had been sick and Lotie went away in the morning and left her without any breakfast. After while she got hungry and after many times resting she succeeded in dressing herself and then had to go down into the cellar and get butter and other things, and she fell when she was nearly to the bottom, and couldn't get up. She was soon chilled through and thought she would have froze to death if Steve hadn't happened to come and find her. He scolded Lotie that time.

Ida Scovel died of blood poison. She left a baby two weeks old. She hadn't been up yet and had not got along as well as she ought to and one evening she said to Frank she would soak her feet in mustard water, which she did. Then she said she felt as if she could sleep if he would help her to bed, and as he was helping her she asked him what that plate was on the wall for. He said what plate. Ida that's a board you had painted. That was the first he noticed that she hadn't her right mind. In the night she was delirious and waked them up. Mrs. Scovel was there (Frank's mother). She said she was hungry so they got her a lunch which she ate ravenously. They sent for the doctor, (I don't know who they sent) and when he got there he said it was too late, she was dying. There were some that said his show of grief was all put on, he didn't care a cent. Maggie S. was there with Blanche the day of the funeral and Frank came to where they were and told Blanche he wanted her to dry that up now, that was just enough. Maggie told him to go on about his business, she was taking care of Blanche.

Herbert and his wife wanted to adopt the baby but Frank wouldn't let them. He said they could keep it till it got old enough to come to him then he wanted it. They kept it two nights and concluded it was too much trouble to raise a baby if they couldn't have it, so took it back to him and his mother took it. She already had the next youngest child and she got sick so Frank took the little one to the asylum and brought Blanche to help take care of the baby. He took four of them to an asylum some place.

You remember that Will Roberts married Sadie Lutz and they had a little girl in less time that they ought. He went to the war and was sick when he came back, and died. He had his life insured and his wife only lived three weeks after he died. I don't know where the child is.

It is ten minutes past twelve and cold in here so I think I will close this chapter and begin on something else. I guess I have put an "e" to "her" everytime I have written it this evening. You can see where I rubbed it out. Miss Hatch, an old maid, lives with Mable and her husband. Mary said that Mable had several dishes scattered around, each with catnip tea in and every time the baby cried a little she gave it a dose of tea. Her last baby died. It was born since Aunt M. came out here.

Friday evening: It seems that I have not had time to write any since last Sunday night. I said I would begin on another chapter but I have thought of more Beaver Creek news. Annie Guess has left her husband. Mary told me when they first came out, what an awful man he was, so wild looking and profane. She says she don't blame Annie but I guess Annie is not much better. They told about how she acted at a dance and talked about getting rid of Guess. She kept the child and I don't know where she is living or where they were living before she left him.

Walter S. has traded his share in the big house for Lisle's place across the road from it down in the field a ways, so Mary says. They didn't write it to us and from their letters we could not tell where they were living. We got a letter from Mr. Lewis [Will's father] and he said they were down on Flat Willow looking for a location for their cattle. Will has invited them out here for a visit and we haven't heard from them yet. Lisle & wife are awful stylish, Mary says. John Whipple was down there for dinner one day and when he got home he told them Mrs. L. was asking him how old a baby ought to be before she should put short clothes on it and several suggestions similar to that. He did not know and was asking Cora about it. Simple should have been her name, instead of Sipple. Lib has not sent that picture of Lisle's baby yet. I intend to send it to you if we ever get it, to be returned of course.

You know May Rohabacker died. Harpers have the children. Dorra is sixteen now. I do not know how many children there are. I would just love to see my old schoolmates and friends' babies. Wouldn't you? If we could afford it I would have lots of pictures of my children taken and exchange with them. Mary said that Annie would have become a mother as a result of her first marriage and Mrs. Shortley and she both said so when her husband died but nothing came of it and after a while they denied it, so Mrs. S. must have been instrumental in that abortion for they had no money and I know for a fact that Mrs. S. is possessed of the knowledge.

You haven't paid Mrs. Clark a visit yet have you? Did you know she calls her boy Tommy? I know not what other name. I did know what Lena calls her girl but forgot. Perhaps you know.

I believe I have hauled every one of the Beaverites over the coals and back again so I will let them rest awhile. Sam's short visit was over before we got your letter (Say can you sympathise with me, the fleas are crawling on me). They (Charles & Sam) came up for breakfast Monday morning. I had left the supper dishes expecting to get up early and wash them and sweep the floor and comb my hair, and imagine my discomfiture when they caught me in the mess. I was up and had made the room presentable, though it was a chilly morning and Will's fire had gone out and he had went to milk. Sam whittled shavings the first thing and started the fire and then as the dish water had gotten hot before disaster fell over the fire I washed dishes and Sam seized the cloth and wiped them. In a few minutes he took a sidelong glance at me and said, 'If you keep on you will be the biggest member of our illustrious family.' Then we laughed. (Just now I separated the head of a flea from his body. He was audacious enough to bite my wrist.) He said none of us had changed much except me. I was as fat as a pig and I am awful wide out. It seems to me though that I am as poor as ever now.

But to return, I think Sam has changed considerably. He is not so slim as when he first went away. He is more like Uncle Sam, though not bent over with hard work. And he sings splendid. He had such nice songs. Among them was *Just As the Daylight Is Breaking*, companion to *Just As the Sun Went Down*. We wanted to be down home and hear them all sing together but we couldn't get there, his stay was so short and we had no rig to go in. We can't all go in the buggy any more.

We had some fun anyway. At first I was inclined to laugh at the self important way in which Sam spoke of his singing. If it hadn't been my own brother I would. Charles said something to Will about playing the accordian and Will did not comply immediately, and Sam said, 'If you don't play for me I won't sing for you, and you bet I can sing, too.' He was so anxious to sing he couldn't wait till evening. He got a song and sang it to me in the afternoon. (Oh, Em, the fleas, come with your fly brush and shoo them off while I write.) Directly after breakfast the first morning the boys and Will went to look at the place, and Sam said to me 'when you get ready to wash dishes call me.' But I didn't get ready and after while they came again and the dishes set there and I was busy at something else so they went down to the creek and were gone till after eleven o'clock and when they came back the dishes set there yet. I had to wait on the girls and wash the baby and clean rabbits for dinner, and other things too numerous to mention.

Sam had torn his pants leg like 60 below the knee, and after pinning that up he started in on the dishes and got them all washed and wiped before I got ready to help. Perhaps you think I did that intentionally. Charles had sent up word before not to kill myself cooking but that didn't make any difference to me. I cooked all the same. I think perhaps I would have fainted if it had been anybody but my brothers at the speech Verna made when she came out in her night dress and cap the first morning. She looked up at them with her eyes wide open and said, 'There's pie, there's cake.' (Oh, it was mortifying.) I can write the words but not the expression that she had.

After dinner Sam wiped the dishes, Charles went hunting and Will went to work. Then I started to make cream cake and asked Sam if he liked whipped cream. He replied, 'No I don't like it at all.' I said, 'Is that so, why didn't you say so before. That's just what we were going to have for supper' (just as if he could have known what I expected him to eat.) Then he commenced to back out and said maybe it wasn't whipped cream that he meant — said he would eat some anyway. He did eat some and said it was fine. I don't know that he wasn't trying to make amends though, for his quick speech.

Charles had brought in three rabbits and I told him that anybody that killed rabbits up here cleaned them, so he skinned them before supper and after supper he got them in a milk pan and poured boiling water over them first before the cold water. Sam yelled to him that he would cook them before he cleaned them, but it was too late. He stuck to his task nobly and cleaned them as good as anybody could after night. Right away after supper Sam proceeded to give us a vocal treat and Will was undressing the children so Charles wiped the dishes then cleaned the rabbits.

They brought up candy, oranges and peanuts with which we regaled ourselves during the evening. It was after twelve o'clock before we went to bed. But I have left out what he [Sam] said about his girl. He was showing Will some papers of the Moon Mining Co. and I said 'I thought you would have a picture to show us.' He grinned and replied, 'Well maybe I have when your fingers are clean.' (I was making corn muffins at the time.) He immediately produced it and we looked at it. I said 'She must have an awful long neck to wear such a high collar.' I thought afterwards what an ungracious comment. I ought to have been slapped. I asked him if she was high toned and he said, 'a little, not much.' I said too 'Is she going to be your wife?' He blushed and said 'I guess so.' Shortly afterwards he said 'I don't know, I may get badly left.'

While he was wiping dishes after dinner he said he was big-headed enough to think that he knew a lady when he saw one and he told me that 'she was just a little bit different from any girl he ever saw before.' Of course. (It is past eleven and the fleas are just getting a good grip on me). We talked quite a little about her in the afternoon and I asked him lots of questions. Once he said 'You think I'm engaged don't you.' I replied 'Yes I do.' He laughed and did not reply. Once he said to us all, 'Well when I'm a married man you'll know it.' I sincerely believe that he has not asked her yet because he is rather young and has not his debts paid and has to help his folks too.

It must be you don't think much of married life since you are so hostile to the idea of Sam getting married. Not that I think its an 'idea' with him. We talked over our folk's affairs some. I told him how Ma has to fight to get to use the money he sends her and he feels blue about it because he has to send so much every month and it is just like throwing it away. Pa don't get ahead a particle, just pays it out for rent. He said if it was doing a bit of good he wouldn't care. I told him too about the five dollars he sent to Ma Christmas to get a dress. She wanted to go to the store and buy it herself but she was sick when the money came and Pa had no rest in his soul or any place else till he got that money and bought the dress for her. He went to Lauritzen's and brought down two samples just as though her choice had to be limited to two. She chose the gray and then she wanted gray silk but Pa spent the five dollars and didn't get the silk either so she had to give him some more money. Then the lady clerk said she would rather have black silk so Pa took that and Ma had to put up with it.

I said to Sam, 'You and your wife will never be that way will you?' and he replied, 'No, you bet we won't. We'll understand each other before we ever are me and my wife.' After he left he wrote to me that he didn't realize how much he had missed you till he got back to work again. I must tell you about the goodby. He put his arm around me and took hold of my hand and kissed me as tenderly as you please. It was quite different from the violent hugs and kisses which Will bestows upon me. There were no tears shed.

I must tell you about Will's bee trees. It was the fourth of July. He went down to the lower place to finish haying and they got done early and cut a bee tree. There was Mr. Maice, Mrs. Maice's brother, and another man. Mr. M. wouldn't go near the tree and the brother (George) was afraid too but he was there awhile and Will had been chopping till he was tired and turned to give George the ax and he wasn't there. He was over on the hillside with the rest, watching Will. He finished felling the tree and then went to where the others were and commenced to slander that coward right to his face. He took it good naturedly. Will came home and milked then took our milk bucket which holds more than that U.S. bucket that spoiled the cider at the Sally place, and went again to the scene of buzzing. He was the only one with a mosquito net so he took the honey out and filled our bucket first which proved to be the best. Some of the comb was nearly as nice and white as boughten honey. The bucket was full. The way we strained it this time, we put it out in the sun in tin vessels till it got warm, then put it into a cheese cloth sack. It was very easily done.

Then in August some time they wanted to cut another and because it was so much larger and had been there 7 years they thought there would be lots of honey. There was a better man helping cut it this time. Will took Hawkins' wash boiler, a big butcher knife, a table spoon, the lantern, and had it all strapped around his shoulders so it would be easier to carry. He had to walk and it was a mile away. He came back at eleven o'clock and didn't have a smoogen of honey. They had scarcely got what they wanted to eat. We had went to all the trouble to make a bee rig too.

Never saw one? Well this one consisted of a gunny sack with a hole cut in one side and a piece of screen sewed in for ventilation and a skylight. He made that and I made two pairs of ticking mittens one to be worn over the other. We were surely disappointed at the result of that honey hunt.

It is after twelve o'clock and Will is going to town tomorrow to buy grub, so we have to rise early. I ought to go to bed but I will write some more. Last week I made some bread, mixed it up at two o'clock in the afternoon and it wouldn't rise only very slow so I left it all night. The next morning it was raised nicely but as cold as ice, if I be permitted to use that expression in California. I made it into loaves and set it over the stove on the bracket and a kettle and it rose again. I baked it and it is as good bread as I have made since I came up here. I can't make good bread any more. I do not know the cause; perhaps the yeast is too old. When we came up here after the baby was born I wrote a bill of stuff for Will to get and I wrote yeast cakes and opposite I wrote three boxes. I wanted three store boxes [for storage] but Will didn't understand and bought three boxes of yeast cakes. I have one yet and a little besides.

There are only a few words that Verna [baby daughter] can say. She says aurels of laurels, and she can't say Elizabeth. Helen talks plain too, although she gets 'll' as 'z' every time thus: Dozzy, azz, shazz — for dolly, all, shall, etc. Some people say she looks just like Em. Verna can't hurry and grow, she don't eat enough. Helen has a better appetite than she has. They are the greatest girls to get uncovered in the night I ever saw. Nearly every morning Helen is on top of the cover as cold as ice. Helen didn't take very kindly to the mercy seat so I have had lots of washing for her all summer. She is doing better now.

Jess picked up prunes enough so that he earned a dollar. He has not got his money yet. He wants to buy a 25 cent knife. Perhaps he will go to town with Will. Ma and I were out to Messar's and Evan's last July. They had just heard that Ollie Divana was married. He married a Kingsley girl at Santa Cruz. Mrs. M. said the family were old friends of Messar's but that they did not fancy the marriage much. Ollie was 21. Will saw him in Hollister one day in August. He had a hay baler and was operating it up in that part of the country. To be more definite, up the San Benito. His wife and her unmarried sister were doing the cooking in the cook house. Will invited them up to see us and he said they would come this winter.

Will went to town about a fortnight ago and brought up a four horse load of stuff, and it was a heavy load for the four too. Chicken and pig feed formed a part of it, and our fruit that Ma canned and our winter's grub, some of it at least. He also brought a nice oak extension table, cost 6 dollars. There are four leaves though we only use two, and of course a new oil cloth, white with blue lines running through it. Running I say, and yet they always stay at the same place. We got a new table cloth and dozen napkins some time ago, and now use tablecloths all the time. Have not used the napkins yet for the reason that I think they must be overwhipped all around the edge and I don't have time to do that.

I have lots of sewing to do but the mice got into the house so bad I have to let it go and clean house awhile. I started in this afternoon, on the milk room. Ma and I finally got Verna's pink percale dress done and she wore it once and got it dirty so I washed it and have not ironed it. I took out that yoke I had started and put a solid tucked one in. I guess I will let Verna go with Jess to school some of these days.

Now Emma it is one o'clock and you can't say that I don't make an effort to write you a letter. Don't let little Dafny Caladonia cry while you read this, the letter is not worth it. The word 'Dafny' should be spelling Daphne. I don't know where Cora got that from — certain it is she knows not how to spell it. Don't you be naming baby after me. My name is not nice enough. I thought I would tell you about Harold William this time but I must put that off till Sunday. I will try to send the third and last consignment Tuesday. I must divest myself of these flea laden clothes.

Jennie

159

Jennie Batdorf Lewis and family, 1918

Left to right
Back: Jesse (seated), Arthur, Verna, Harold, Alice, Carl, Helen
Front: Lloyd, Will, Thelma (glasses), Ethel, Jennie, Darrell

At the Lewis farmstead, Kermin, Ca., 7/8/31
L-R Carl Lewis, Darrell Lewis, Kenneth Platt, Jennie Lewis, Will Lewis

A Salmon River Homestead Teacher

Many accounts of frontier teaching have stressed the difficulties of discipline among the frequently over-age pupils that accumulated because schooling was given so little time. To cope with this problem, men commonly were employed as teachers. A typical example has been described by Garret D. Kincaid, a pioneer of Palouse, Washington.[1] Listing a succession of 12 men before the first woman teacher in Palouse in the 1870s and '80s, Kincaid remarks:

When the public schools were first established in the new community where every man was a law unto himself discipline had to be enforced by the severest methods. The teacher was forced to be 'boss' — boss in every sense of the word, because there were a great many young people who did not attend school, and in their contempt for higher learning did everything in their power to disrupt the class room. Beside the outside forces, the students themselves made life miserable for the instructors — if they found they could get away with it.

[1]Garret D. Kincaid, "Palouse in the Making," *Palouse Republic* (July 6, 1934), *44* (18[19]), pp. 13-14.

161

KENNETH B. PLATT

With children's utter disregard and indifference for discipline most parents and school directors gave the teachers full control of the school's law enforcement, no matter what means he might use . . . . One case is told of a school in a neighboring county whose so-called students had beaten up every teacher who dared to take over the job. Finally a barkeeper was obtained who had an outstanding record as a former pugilist, which was perhaps his strongest recommendation for the position. The directors even approached this man with trepidation, because of the unrivaled teacher-threshing record of the school boys. But the barkeeper merely took a week's vacation from his bar, saying that within that time he could quell the toughest school. He started by threshing each and every boy in the school and asking them if they wanted to come back for more. They didn't. When the youngsters found that their instructor was a former prize fighter and could floor the best of them they became meek as lambs.

One day the new teacher saw a wagon drawn by a pair of white horses coming down the road. He inquired from the students who it was, and one of the boys who had been among the hardest to subdue, answered that it was his father, one of the school directors. This man, although a director of the school, had upheld the children in their lawlessness, encouraging them to beat up on their teachers. With this in mind the pugilist teacher met the visitor at the gate and soon had him rolling in the dust. After this, little or no trouble was had in the school, and the children, if not enthusiastic about soaring into the higher realms of knowledge, at least offered no violent form of objection.

. . . In spite of the tumultuous picture painted of early school days, and although these episodes stand out most vividly in the minds of those who attended the pioneer schools, all the teachers who ruled in the first Palouse classrooms had nothing but the good of the children at heart. Every one was a remarkable man and wonderful teacher striving to lift the minds and ideals of their students to a high point in spite of the harsh means many were forced to employ.

When the Salmon River area of this account was ready for its first teacher some 35 years after the above Palouse experience, classroom conditions were much different. Most of the students there were beginners, and discipline problems were minimal. Outside the classroom, however, the teacher's life was the same as that of other members of the community, with extra-curricular duties often demanding equal time. Such duties were taken in stride, and not viewed as an imposition. Rather, as a member of the community the teacher was expected to do about the same round of "living" chores as everyone else.

Having grown up in similar circumstances, Winnie Spurbeck came from Genesee to The River in 1912 fully accepting these conditions. Her story of her teaching years is a happy one. The many sidelights on social life and living conditions of that time, and the frequent glimpses of her own inner thoughts, convey a frankness that invites the reader to relax and enjoy the whole experience along with the central character. Her account follows.

SALMON RIVER SAGA

Memories of Salmon River Ranch Life

by Winifred Spurbeck Freeburn

The fall of 1912, shortly after September 1, I was informed by the school board of the Yellow Rose District that school would not be held that fall, because only two pupils had enrolled and these children would be transferred to a nearby school called Union. Since I had been promised this job, the late notice left me without much of a chance to apply for another position. Shortly after this date I was given the choice of being the mistress of the Genesee, Idaho, Post Office, or of going to Salmon River to take employment as a teacher to the John Platt children, as otherwise they would have to move out to Genesee to send them to school.

Winifred Spurbeck, first Salmon River school Teacher, as she appeared in 1912.

Security, No; Adventure, Yes!

Being a lover of children, outdoor life, and horses, it seemed much more acceptable to me to choose to go to Salmon River. Who could tell, being single I might meet my future mate and decide to settle there! Cowboys were numerous and, being young—just out of normal school—romance might blossom.

163

My mother was a little doubtful of my selection. She had heard that there were places going around cliffs that a horse might slip and rider and horse fall in the river. Father was more in favor of my going. He made me two coal oil can boxes, each of which had originally held two 5-gallon cans of oil, with handles obtained from two unused tubs. He fastened a lid on each box, secured with hinges and fastened with a hook. These boxes were constructed to carry my belongings and to fit easily on a pack horse, as there was no other way of traveling to my destination save horseback.

As it was the day when hobble skirts were the fashion, my sister and I made a divided skirt for me to wear. Side saddles were out of the question for riding the rough trails one would encounter on the way down. I collected some books and materials that I would be using and placed my clothing in a suitcase which would fit nicely on the top of the two boxes. I had also packed an unloaded revolver which I thought I might use to scare an intruder even if I didn't have any bullets. On opening my suitcase when I arrived I discovered the revolver missing. I guess my mother must have thought it unnecessary and removed it. She knew the people I was to live with were very respectable, because their folks and ours had been two of the pioneer families that settled in Idaho when it was a territory, and we as children had spent happy hours at their home.

When the day arrived for the start of my journey my father drove me to Juliaetta to the train. We still drove buggies as cars were not plentiful at that time and still considered rather a novelty. I rode on the Grangeville train as far as a branch siding that took me into Winchester, a logging town, where I would catch the horse drawn stage the next day for the town of Forest to meet Mr. Platt. I was a little concerned whether my baggage was transferred so I inquired of the conductor. He laughed and said, "Oh yes, those ninety-nine dollar trunks are aboard." When he learned my destination he agreed that I had the right equipment for such a pack journey.

The Winchester Inn proved to be a very nice place to stop and the meals were delicious. My room was clean and warm, which felt refreshing after the day's ride on the train.

The next morning I rode the stage which stopped several places along the way to deliver the mail, packages ordered by farmers who lived near the road. When we arrived at Forest I found it to be a small town with a hotel, store, post office, livery barn, a few scattered dwellings, and a two-storied school. I was told I could not stay at the hotel because some man had just committed suicide there. I was invited to stay with a Mrs. Fisher, the post mistress, who lived in the rear of the postoffice building. As I entered the building I noticed the room contained the postoffice, candy counter, a few useful trinkets for sale, a stove, and several chairs for those wishing to rest or visit. Mrs. Fisher and her two children, Archie and Marjory, were in the room. As the mail had arrived on the stage, the mother sorted it until supper time. After the evening meal was over and the dishes cleared away we returned to this room as the townspeople came to collect their mail and, also, those who were late in reaching town from the outlying ranches or homesteads. Thus I was introduced to several people who had come for their mail. There was one in particular, that I noticed was very handsome, which she introduced as Harry Weller, but to the embarrassment of both of us she said, "Don't make eyes at him as he is a married man."

There was a man doing chores around the place and I asked the children if that was their father. It was puzzling the way they acted, no answer but a lot of giggling, until I found out later that his name was Mr. Farr and he was to be their future stepdad.

It was that same evening that Mr. Platt had come out from the river to attend his lodge meeting and to show me the way to his home. When he saw me he asked if I had something different to ride horseback in. I guess it did look as if I would have trouble getting into a saddle with a hobble skirted dress. He said he would be by in the morning, as it was a good many miles by horseback on the trail.

I was up bright and early and ready to start on my way. It came ten o'clock and no Mr. Platt, but I asked for a lunch as I was a paying guest. She said he wouldn't be along before afternoon, but I wanted to be ready so I ate the early lunch. Noon came and with it a chicken dinner which I wasn't hungry enough to enjoy after my generous sandwiches. He finally came about two o'clock and we were on our way with a sack of mail. It was the custom for whoever was out to Forest to bring down everyone's mail to be passed along among the homesteaders. This was the way I received a lot of my mail while I was there.

As we left Forest I noticed a rail fence which made me think of pioneer days. It was a very picturesque scene with moss clinging to the trunks of the huge virgin forest trees under whose limbs we rode.

When we had passed through these trees we came to a building called the Weller House, whose occupants had moved away. It made a very good place to store supplies as they could be hauled out by team and loaded on pack horses later. We were met there by Tom, the eldest Platt boy, with a pack train. Each horse had two coal oil boxes roped to his pack saddle, which were filled with bricks to use in making a chimney in the new house then under construction.

When those were loaded we headed for the zig zag trail that meant home to them. After some time on the trail we came to the Deer Creek Mines, which were active in tunneling out silver and gold ore. Going on a little farther we came to a Mr. Moffet's ranch where he and Mr. Platt put a large amount of beef on one of the pack horses.

By this time it had begun to get dark. I was soon unable to see much of the scenery along the way. We hadn't gone too far in the dark when Tom called to me. Mr. Platt was in the lead, then a few pack horses, then Tom and a few more pack horses between him and myself, who rode at the end of the train. "Miss Spurbeck, better look out, a rock fell off the pinnacle and rolled across the trail when I came up today." Keeping my ears alert we soon passed that false alarm. Then further on my horse suddenly just sat down and slid down between two rock formations until it hit the trail below. Since I had not been warned of this, when the horse began to slide and I could hear water rushing by, for a minute I thought of my mother's suggested idea of falling into the river, but when I took my feet out of the stirrups and felt the rock formation on each side of me and realized it was only a rock formation that couldn't be bypassed on the trail, I was again convinced of my survival.

Everything was peaceful after that until we had just about reached our destination, when Tom hollered to me again. "Watch out, that horse you are riding jumps the irrigation ditch." He had hardly said it when we rounded a bush and my horse reared up and jumped. This didn't bother me very much as I had ridden horses my brothers broke that did a lot of jumping, but it was a welcome sight to see a light in the distance. Our meal that night was served in the old house, but we slept in the new one until it was finished and ready for occupancy.

The next day I rode up to see that rock formation by daylight. Our school started Monday with Tom, Mary, Frances, Kenneth and Lorene Platt. They were very attentive children and I enjoyed teaching and being with them. We gave little entertainments to whoever wanted to listen. Some of the cowboys seemed to enjoy listening to them. The program was singing, reciting a piece, or a display of their school work.

Enter, Dashing Cowboys!

One evening as I was watching a cowboy, Mr. Kennedy put some matches on the stove, which when they lit, he claimed, would fall toward the person's home you might meet, a knock came on the door. There stood the most handsome young man I had ever seen. He had strikingly beautiful blue eyes and light brown wavy hair. He wore white curly goat hair chaps and held the reins of a beautiful sorrel horse in his hands. I had promised the children I would put them to bed that evening, so excused myself and went with them. When I returned, Mr. Billy Freeburn, as his name turned out to be, had gone to the bunk house. I said, "Who's that handsome man? I'm going to try to go with him while I am here." Mrs. Platt told me he was single and the son of one of their best friends.

A few weeks after this Mrs. Platt became ill and Della Freeburn was asked to come help with the work. Naturally the brother came to see his sister. Almost every Sunday after that, we three went riding. Billy brought along an extra saddle horse for her, while

I rode one of the Platt pack horses called "Hatrack." His hips did protrude but he was full of life and made a good saddle horse.

We three had been invited to dinner with different bachelors. In this way I was able to observe the method of their house cleaning, cooking, and hospitality. The main company meal usually consisted of beans, biscuits, bacon, sometimes fried eggs, syrup and honey. One homesteader named Jimmy Moffit decided to make a custard pie. He put baking powder in the crust, which raised up so much that most of the filling was over the edges and into the oven.

The custom those days was that the door was always unlocked, so that anyone happening to be far from home was welcome to enter and cook himself a meal. Della and I found this out when Mr. Platt heard of someone who was going to jump a claim he had in mind. He sent us up there with a loaf of bread and a jar of milk. Finding the cabin was difficult, as the snow had covered up the landmarks. Eventually we arrived and found some beans and bacon in the cupboard, and plenty of firewood. We put the beans to soak, then started to cook them. While they were simmering we made a bacon sandwich which tasted real good, but the next morning we wondered how we ever could have eaten it the night before, as it had a very strong taste. The next night just Frances and I went. We had just about reached the cabin when, on going up a small slope, she slid off into the deep snow and I had to dig her out.

The only recreation was an occasional dance which everyone seemed to enjoy. The music consisted of two violins and two hollow handled knives that, when beaten on an empty coal oil can, gave the sound of a drum. The dance started early and lasted until daylight. There was always enough food for an evening meal, a midnight snack, and breakfast. The men always outnumbered the women, so no lady was a wallflower. I remember one unskilled dancer that shook his partner up and down and whirled her around, so that some of the cowboys nicknamed him "Bedsprings." One dance with him was enough for me, so I hid when I saw him coming.

Mr. Platt's place was the ranch at which people crossed over the Salmon on their way to Whitebird or their homesteads on the other side of the river. As a consequence, many stopped over night to be rowed across the next morning in a boat, swimming their horses behind. I experienced this only twice. Mr. Freeburn was across on the other side and called for someone to row him across. Della, two of the cowboys, several of the children, and myself went down to meet him. When his horse plunged into the water and those powerful legs began to thrash around and with the loud snorting sound from his nostrils, I wondered if we could make it across the river before one of the hooves capsized the boat. I don't think anyone could swim, and the water was very deep and swift. I rowed over another time, but no horses accompanied us. We tied our horses on our side of the river and there were horses waiting for us to use on the far side.

I had met so many men that stayed to be rowed across the river, I didn't think surely there could be any more in the country. So when Mr. Platt's brother Bill, Louis Jones, and their girl friends came one evening, after being introduced to Mr. Jones I said, "I thought I had met the limit in men before I met you." It gave the girls something to tease him about, as they had been trying all afternoon to find something to get even with him for some of his jokes. I was to hear about this at a later date.

Homesteader Sociability

There was a big dance in a cabin up the river late that fall and people from both sides of the Salmon attended. The horse I was supposed to ride this time, Mr. Kennedy had used to go up on the mountain to get his girl. It was tired out before I started because of the deep snow it had waded in on the trip. The horse gave out before we could reach the cabin. Mr. Freeburn threw the saddle aside and said I could ride his horse. I started to ride his powerful horse, but it kept wanting to turn back with me. I could really hear the Salmon River this time. I got off and told him I would follow, but it was dark and I ran into the horse's heels, which frightened me. So we tried to strike matches to see the trail. The wind would blow them out before we could advance very far. We were almost over the hill where we could see the light from the cabin, when Jimmy Moffit came along with a lantern to see what had happened. Some thought we wanted to be alone; Mr. Kennedy said maybe my horse had given out, so they sent Jimmy to light the way.

When we arrived I saw Louis Jones coming toward me and he said, "I may be the limit but I can find my way to a dance." Forgetting the misfortunes of the trail, we had a pleasant time, and when morning came and the dance was over, I rode behind the saddle on Mr. Freeburn's horse until we came to the one we had abandoned, eating grass. We caught and saddled it and I rode it the rest of the way back to Platt's.

Della and I had each made a cake for the dance, in the milk pan. Mine was half way between biscuit dough and cake; it clung to the pan even when it fell off my horse and rolled down a bank. There were so many cakes that were better looking than mine that I hid it. Della's was on a shelf under the lantern and kerosene dripped on it. We had my cake for breakfast next morning and the children said, "Teacher Platt can make good cake."

I discovered that dances were the main entertainment and chance for socializing for these isolated people. Dances were held at Bill Platt's and Louis Jones', who lived across the river; Mr. Platt's; several at Forest; and at Harry Weller's house warming. Mr.

Weller, whom I had met my first day at Forest, turned out to be a brother-in-law of Billy Freeburn.

One of the dances was at the Freeburn home. Della and I composed a notice to be tacked up at the post office in Forest to advertise it. It read as follows:

> Open your ears and you will learn
> There will be a dance at Billy Freeburn's.
> Next Saturday night half-past seven.
> We'll dance and dance way past eleven.
> There will be cookies and cake, the best
>   we can make.
> Bacon and beans, sour dough bread,
> Something substantial, won't go to your head.
> Now, bring your gal and swing her around.
> Even if she weighs two hundred pounds.
> The latch key hangs outside the door.
> Come kick the grease spots off the floor.

Blossom Time

When school was out in May, I spent a few days at the Freeburn home. It was while I was there that I became engaged to Billy Freeburn. At this time of the year the Salmon River country is at its loveliest, with fresh, balmy days; deep lush bunch grass; and carpets of wild flowers. It was a beautiful moonlit night when we sat on a rock and gayly planned the date of our marriage, which was to be July 2, 1913. There was to be a roundup the 4th and 5th of July, which we planned to attend on our honeymoon.

The afternoon that I was to go to my home 9 miles away from Genesee, Billy Freeburn, his sister Della, and a friend, Harry Clovis, and I drove over to Winchester. There were a few hours before they had to return to Forest, so we decided to take a boat ride on Winchester Lake. The boat leaked just enough to dampen the skirt of my tan linen suit. I tucked it up to prevent it getting wet, but some of the hem had dropped into the water and became more saturated than I was aware. When I got out of the boat you can imagine my embarrassment to find the back of my skirt had a large wet ring. I said, "I never did a trick like this before," meaning, of course, sitting in a leaking boat. I was not to escape an occasional reminder of this incident. We had to walk by the lake shore in the sun to allow the skirt to dry before venturing uptown.

Earlier when I went to arrange for a room at the Winchester Inn, the rooms were all taken, so I had to go to a loggers' hotel. There was no lock on the door, and that night I had just got into bed when I felt something crawling on me. I turned on the ceiling-hung single light, and to my horror saw several bedbugs waiting to feast on me. I never went to sleep, got up and dressed and spent the night killing every one that came in sight. I went over to the Winchester Inn for breakfast at an early hour. How weary I was, and equally anxious to catch the 8 o'clock train for home. My grandfather met me at Juliaetta.

The summer was spent helping with the usual work of women on a farm—cooking for haying hands, picking and canning fruit and vegetables, and sewing, cleaning and ironing. The day before my marriage I was helping face strawberries for market. I showed up late that morning and my grandfather said, "Where's Winnie? Is she afraid to soil her hands now that she has company?" Billy and Della had arrived the day before. Grandfather didn't know I was to be married at noon the next day. We didn't tell him because he would have gone to town and spread the news. We wanted only close relatives, as it was a busy season and I didn't want a big wedding.

I had gone to meet Billy and Della at Juliaetta when they arrived on the train the 30th of June. I hitched the horses to the buggy and started out early, as it was a warm day. When I had gone quite a distance across the Little Potlatch canyon, a band of sheep obstructed the road. If I had been left alone to drive through them all would have been well, but Charlie Frizzel, who had owned one of the horses, came out as I came by and offered to drive around the sheep. As we started to pass, the buggy tipped on its side because of the slope of the land, the slippery footing and his weight, which I think was over 200 pounds, sliding as it did to the lower side. We were thrown out; he first, and I on his lap. It didn't take me long to rush to the horses' heads, for Nellie, the horse he had owned, was a very nervous type and I knew if she started to run there wouldn't be any buggy left. The sheepherders came and helped to get the buggy and team back on the road, and I was on my way.

Naturally I was very happy to see Billy and Della, and also, somewhat shy and embarrassed. I couldn't help thinking it would have been a much more romantic meeting without the sister, especially when he placed a ring on my finger. I thought of an old poem:

> "Here's to the chaperone!
> May she be blinded by cupid
> To be sweetly stupid."

We were married at noon on July 2, 1913 by Rev. Orth, a Congregational minister. My brother, Rollin, and his wife brought him out. Grandpa and Ellis Lambert were our witnesses. I was getting my things packed to go, but Mother said, "Please stay with us until train time in the morning." We decided to please her by staying.

My brother got busy and rounded up some of the neighborhood boys to charivari us. Most of the family had retired when the noise began. We wanted to let them in, but

Mother said, "Don't pay any attention. It's just some hoodlums from across the canyon." Not to be denied, and aided by my brother Dave, they raised the window of our upstairs bedroom by standing on the roof, and turned the garden hose into our room. The water went into my suitcase and spoiled the shape of a very nice new white hat. However, ruining my hat wasn't as bad as the ugly water spots that appeared on the ceiling of the front room that we had just papered.

The boys came in and, after they had been offered the usual treats, gathered around the piano to sing while I played the accompaniment. One of the songs they wanted to sing was the following:

"Have you got another girl at home like Winnie?
Another little peach upon the family tree?
If you have another girl like Winnie - - -
Then that little girl will just suit me."

Then we heard my grandfather playing, "Oh we won't go home until morning," on his violin from his bedroom that adjoined the front room, and that broke up the party.

Ranch Wife Days

My brother Dave drove us to the train the next morning, and we spent two days at the roundup in Winchester. Next we took the stage to Forest, where Salmon River friends gave us another charivari at the hotel, so candy and cigars were in order once more. Billy went to get some horses for us to ride to his _K_ (K Bar) ranch. As we passed the Deer Creek mines, Mrs. Joe Lorang came out and took our picture. Another lady staying there said I reminded her of Ruth of Biblical times—"journeying to a far land." We had only been home about a week when they gave a dance at the mines. It was well attended and enjoyed by everyone.

Haying time came soon. Mr [Carson] Moffet and my husband exchanged work with each other since they were neighbors, so I went to cook while we were at his ranch. While we were there, moving pictures of the mines were being taken to send back east as promotional advertising to companies they were trying to interest in investing money in shares of stock. As a side highlight, they had a number of us dressed as cowboys and cowgirls ride horses down a steep slope at a gallop. I rode one of Mr. Moffet's white horses. The horse of one of the women, Sylvia McCoy, fell and she was thrown; although she was shaken up, no bones were broken.

A little later that fall Della Freeburn was asked to take a job in a cookhouse feeding harvest hands. This was on the prairie, where the grain was later in maturing for harvest

Newlyweds Billie Freeburn (L) and Winifred Spurbeck Freeburn (C), with Della Freeburn at right, at Deer Creek mine, enroute to K-Bar Ranch.

K-Bar Ranch cabin of Billie and Winnie Freeburn some time in the 1940s, after several years' abandonment.

than down on the Salmon River country. She asked me to help her. One place where we worked was called Icicle Flat. It was really cold. Our days began with breakfast at 6 a.m. Sandwiches and coffee were served at 10 a.m., noon meal at 12 o'clock, lunch again at 2 p.m., and, finally, supper at 6 p.m. It took lots of bread for all these meals. We made biscuits for breakfast, white bread the other meals. Sometimes we had to bake 20 loaves a day. I had two jars of yeast going all the time. Sometimes at night I dreamed I saw biscuits floating on the stubble where the grain had been cut.

That winter my husband and I pieced some quilts by hand. His stitches were very uniform and even as good as mine. I had a sewing machine the next fall. For amusement we had a phonograph, Melodian Organ, and harmonica. We did some visiting with my husband's folks and his married sisters, Mr. & Mrs. Harry Weller, Mr. and Mrs. Dan Critchfield, and Mr. and Mrs. Ralph Ross and their two children, Esther and Billy.

What I remember about little Billy Ross is the way he lifted his leg and pretended to strike a match on his little trousers. He wasn't more than 2½ years old. While I was at Platt's I had been invited up to stay all night with Mrs. Ross while her husband had gone out to pack in winter supplies. She was a very good cook and I enjoyed the meals as well as our visit. They had a part of beef hanging outside and the steak from it was, as the saying goes, "out of this world."

During the first winter we were married we also rode horseback to Genesee to see my folks. It was a long, tiring ride. When we came to the ferry at Spalding, the wind was blowing strongly and, as it turned out, from the wrong direction. The ferry stopped right in the middle of the Clearwater River and wouldn't move. The ferryman had a long pole that he tried to get it started with. By both he and my husband pushing, it began to move across. Their hands were numb with cold, as the end of the pole protruded just above the icy water. We were dressed warmly, but the wind seemed to cut right through our clothing.

When we arrived at Genesee my husband wanted to call it a day, but I wanted to go on to the ranch. My father and sister, Marguerite, were surprised to see us. My mother was in Salem, Oregon, visiting her mother.

In those days there was no plumbing in country homes, so everyone resorted to a chamber which was always to be found in the bedroom with a bowl and pitcher of water for washing up. Most bedrooms had a commode, a piece of furniture with a few drawers and a door enclosure that held a chamber, a washbowl, and a pitcher. These were used by guests and regular occupants to tidy up, as there were no restrooms. At the time of our visit there was only one chamber available, and that was in my father's room. I sneaked it out and upstairs that night. The next day Dad went to town and purchased three white ones. He told us that evening that Mr. Jackson, the clerk, called them "White Owls." I said, "There ought to be a lot of hooting tonight, then."

When spring arrived we put in a garden. The ground had black soil and was subirrigated, so everything we planted produced in abundance. I dried corn and my husband piled up bean vines around a stake and threshed them out when dry. We had potatoes, tomatoes, watermelons, squash, onions, lettuce, ground cherries, turnips, and peas. I canned a lot of vegetables that summer.

Our cellar was what was called a dirt cellar, as it was dug into a bank. It had a roof covered with soil to make it cool and frost-proof. Split shakes covered the inner walls, which made it neat and kept the soil in place. The shelves looked tempting and good with all the canned vegetables, fruit, and canned grouse gathered in the summer. We had two pigs which we fattened for our winter meat and cured in a smoke house.

One day while my husband was taking a nap I took his 12-gauge shotgun and went down the pasture to see if I could find a grouse. I hadn't gone far when I saw some in a tall pine tree. I had never shot anything but a .22 rifle, so the shotgun seemed awkward. The birds were so high in the tree that I had to point the barrel of the gun straight up. When I fired it kicked my shoulder a bruising blow, as I couldn't hold it steady at that angle. To my surprise I did shoot four, so had some to can the next day. We only canned the legs and breast, and stewed the bony pieces to make stew or a rich gravy to put on potatoes or biscuits. With a few staples like flour, sugar, and salt we were quite self-sufficient and there was always plenty to eat. My husband's father had two kinds of cherry trees, and a walnut tree, the harvest of which they shared with us.

I was up in the garden gathering some vegetables for dinner one day when a large black cloud appeared and it began to hail. The hail stones were enormous, almost as large as hen eggs, with ice centers coated with snow. I started for the house, putting my hands over my head for protection. I had a thin dress on, so my arms and back were black and blue as a result. I saw I couldn't make it to the house, so I ran into the chicken house. Most of the chickens were in, but the few turkeys that we had, unlike the chickens, had huddled in a corner of the chicken yard with no protection. One became crippled, but by splinting its leg it survived. Three others weren't so lucky, and were killed outright.

Rattlesnakes were quite a problem in the summer. When my husband mowed the alfalfa they would run toward the house and take shelter under the front step. We had a shepherd dog named Ned that killed them, but somehow one day, in spite of his skill, one bit him. His body swelled up stiff. I gave him milk and fat meat. He went down and lay in the mud below the spring, and the mud drew the poison out and he got well. Sometimes animals are smarter than humans when it comes to the struggle for survival.

One morning I took the hoe to the garden to get cabbage. I always used to cut the head off the root because it was too hard to pull up. There was a large rattlesnake curled around the one I had chosen to take. I cut off its head and then I heard one rattle

174

"A big one in the garden"

behind me. There was another one ready to strike. I turned and cut at it, but chopped near the tail this time, and the body attached to its head ran around and at me. About this time I was ready to abandon cabbage and snakes. I did take a head of cabbage, but one a distance from my struggle. That was the only time we ever found any in the garden. They must have been a pair going through the garden toward Gibbs Creek.

That day at noon Mr. Hall, a man my husband had hired to help him stretch a barbwire fence, and my husband were eating dinner and I was in the other room. When I came out I heard them talking about something with large spots. Naturally I thought they were talking about rattlesnakes, so I said, "I bet they weren't larger than the ones I killed this morning." Mr. Hall let me tell in great detail all about my experiences, but I noticed a smile on his face. Finally he said, "You're talking about snakes and we're talking about civet cats." He had seen some on his way up that morning. Civet cats are of the skunk family. They have a larger body and spots similar to those of the rattlesnake, rather than the distinct black stripe of the skunk.

175

When harvest time came the next summer I stayed home while my husband went out to work in the harvest fields. I was expecting my first baby in December of that year. There was a water problem that summer. It was so warm and rainless that the spring dried up and all I had was enough for cooking and the chickens. Bending to necessity I had to put the tub, washboard, and clothes on my saddlehorse and go over to Gibbs Creek to wash. The water where the sun reached it was warm enough without heating it over a fire, and I hung the clothes on the bushes until they dried.

Later Mary Platt, my former pupil, came to stay with me until school started, so I wouldn't be alone. Her parents then sent her and her brother Tom to stay with their grandma in Genesee for the school year.

That fall my husband chided me for the risk I took in saving a little calf from freezing. The mother had gone up a small hill, where it was born in the snow. I missed the mother, so went to see where she was. It was a bitter cold day and the calf lay stiff. Hurriedly I went to the house and returned with the sled we used to haul wood on, put the calf on my lap, and slid down the hill. The cow came bawling and charging after me. I had put some hay in a manger in a small shed, so I carried the calf in. I had quite a time getting the cow to follow. She was just a young heifer that had never been in an enclosure before. Finally she went in, licked the calf, and started to eat the hay. I slipped up and closed the stanchion shut. Then I picked up the calf and held it between my knees and milked some milk into its mouth. This revived it and in a short time I had it standing on its legs and helping itself to nurse.

First-Child Joys and Problems

My baby boy, Earl, arrived December 6, 1914. We were fortunate enough to have a telephone at the time. My husband called the doctor and when he arrived at Forest he called to check the progress, and found the baby had arrived. My husband's mother was a midwife, and had come to me at the first indication and had delivered the baby. He was a healthy little fellow, but I didn't have enough milk for him. We tried Mellon's Food and sweetened Borden's Evaporated Milk, but neither seemed to satisfy him, and we spent many hours walking the floor with him. When his Grandfather Freeburn said, "Are you going to try to raise him?" I was completely unnerved. Finally in desperation I took him out to my doctor, Dr. Toumy in Genesee. He put him on cow's milk and he grew very fast on that.

One of my husband's sisters, Emma Critchfield, made his clothes. She had always wanted a son of her own, and spent many long hours at her sewing maching fashioning garments for him. I appreciated this all the more because I didn't like to sew and as yet had no machine.

176

He crawled on his elbows, so the arms and the front of his rompers were the first to show wear. When he learned to walk, like most little boys he began his investigative career. There was a small opening in the cloth to which the wall paper was pasted. He had a little aluminum plate with ABC's around it. Somehow he had pulled a tack out and made an opening large enough to put the plate in. As he had other things to play with and I wasn't using it, I didn't miss the plate, but I did find the tack in his stool the next day. I would have been frantic if I had known he had swallowed that tack, and taken him to the doctor. When I noticed the crack in the wallpaper I took the hammer and drove a nail to close it. I noticed the nail was a little hard to drive, but thought it was probably a knot in the wood, as the cabin was built of rough boards. When I went to paper the next time, I discovered that I had driven through the rim of the plate.

One of his tricks was to pull aside the curtains that were on a lower shelf and splash his hands and arms right down into the bottom of the pan's cream and milk. I spanked his hands, but he didn't seem to understand. His daddy felt sorry for him, so put in some higher shelves that he couldn't reach. I had a screened cupboard in the cellar during the warm summer months, for the milk.

As I have mentioned previously, I raised some chickens, and Earl loved to watch them. He would follow the hen, sit down until she moved along in search of food, and then trot along again. He was so entranced with the first chicks he picked up one in delight and unknowingly squeezed it to death.

One time I took Earl up on the hill behind the house to see a little colt that my saddlehorse, Nellie, had given birth to. When we arrived up there he began to cry, and Nellie put back her ears and came for me. I shouted at her. She did turn back, but not until she had kicked up her heels at us. Luckily she was too far away to do us any harm.

Salmon River Medicare

One of my neighbors was an invalid lady, Mrs. Horseman. Sometimes when she was up in her wheelchair she phoned to me. I always stopped to see her on my trips into town taking milk, butter, or some vegetables, or stopping to make her some biscuits. I crocheted a rug to match her dressing robe, which was lavendar with black designs. As most of the women's stockings were black in those days, I was given some by relatives and friends to use, and I dyed underwear and flour sacks lavendar to provide the other color. She was very happy to have it by her bed. Her husband worked in an abandoned mine and was so busily occupied that the hours passed quickly and forgetfully, and she was left alone for long periods. Sometimes the cowboys bringing mail stopped and fixed a lunch for her, and took care of her bedpan.

One day Cora Ross Vallem and I went down to call on Mrs. Rudolph, at the mouth of Eagle Creek. While she smoked her corncob pipe, which she was reluctant to have me watch, we went up Eagle Creek to fish for trout. We had caught quite a number when Cora snagged a hook into her finger. It was necessary for someone to remove it immediately, as there were some dead grasshoppers at the base of the hook and she risked infection since the weather was warm. Mrs. Rudolph said, "I just can't bear to take the hook out," so it fell my lot to do it. I sterilized a straight edged razor and cut it out, and then soaked her finger in Epsom Salts, as no disinfectant was available. I wonder to this day how I was able to accomplish it, as I was most squeamish about such things. We spent the night there and by morning almost all the soreness had disappeared. On the way back home we met some cowboys we knew, and Cora's horse lay down in the trail, much to her embarrassment.

K Bar (K) Ranch Life

The next fall my father wanted to winter some of his cattle on our range. They were used to being in the barn or shed, so unlike our more hardy range cattle we lost some. He brought the calves over in a large wagon whose sides had water pipes for sideboards, placing them there especially for me so he could pipe water into the house. They were piled near the drag trail to be dragged in later. The drag trail was one that the miners used to drag supplies down to the mines. The terrain was too steep for a wagon road. They had two large excellently trained horses. They tied the lines to the side of the load and they would take the load down without anyone driving them. My husband took a mower and rake down the same way, only our team just seemed to sit down as they brought the equipment down.

I took a saddle horse up to meet my father, and my husband and several men drove the cattle and calves down to our _K_ Ranch. Soon the water pipes were brought down and a spring dug out, and the men set in furnishing my home with running water. One of the men of the mines made me a sink and drainboard with a shelf underneath. He still remained at the mine when it was closed down. I often gave him butter, cream, milk and vegetables. Several of my father's cows came fresh and gave a large quantity of milk, so I made some extra butter which the miners purchased from me.

One of the most unusual things I witnessed that year occurred when one of the cows became mired in the mud. With her head down hill, she was unable to get up. Our horse, Woodrow, took her by the neck and pulled her around to solid ground.

Another incident occurred that fall. My husband had spent many hours fashioning shakes, and built a sturdy roof over his hay. Shortly afterward we had a sudden powerful windstorm that lifted it right off, so the hay wasn't protected from the winter storms.

On March 17, 1916, we had a little girl. She was a very beautiful baby, with large brown eyes and dark curly hair. Unlike her brother, she was adjusted to her food and easy to care for, and a joy to us both. It wasn't long before the children were very attentive to each other, with a love that still exists. Her brother still calls her Babe. We had named her Marguerite Della for each of our youngest sisters.

She was reading some school books at the age of five. I had taught her some sounds. One day Amy Moffet called on me. She said, "Somebody is P R E T T Y." Marguerite spoke up and said "pretty," much to Amy's surprise. She and Earl always liked the story of Little Red Hen — the first one she had learned to read.

One of the things the children liked to do was to watch me make light bread dough. They would stand on a chair and to keep them occupied, so I could finish it, I played my hands were horses falling in the yeast starter water and flour, and pawing inside the pan as though trying to get up the bank-like sides.

They used to stand on the porch and watch their Daddy start out to Forest with the pack horses. Earl would call "rice" and Marguerite, "candy," for as long as they could see him.

They also liked to watch me dress a chicken. I would wash out the crop and blow it up like a balloon for them. By watching me, they could dress a chicken at an early age. Earl liked to make muffins, and Marguerite could cook a full meal when she was ten.

One day I saw my son, 3, and daughter, 2, laughing and having a lot of fun with a stick. Earl kept hitting up and down, so I went out to investigate and found they were playing with a small rattlesnake. Every time it curled up my son hit it down. I saw it had one button,[2] which would have made it just as poisonous as if it had been larger.

My husband came in one day for lunch after driving cattle, and left his horse with the bridle off to graze on the grass of a small hill near the side of the house, as he had to ride some more in the afternoon. I went out to call my Earl to come to lunch, and just then the horse came down the hill on a run with my son clinging to the pommel of the saddle. The horse ran until it came to one tied up to a tree, and stopped suddenly, pitching my son into some thorn bushes. We ran to pick him up, thankfully finding no broken bones, but we did have to comfort our frightened little boy and calm our own fears.

During World War I we were rationed. We had to use mixed flour with the white flour. I made some of it into steamed brown bread with raisins and molasses. It was hard to do much fruit canning because of the little amount of sugar received. I remember potatoes were very scarce that spring. My husband planted a hundred pounds of them. They were treated with something, and never came up. We had potatoes one meal a day, and turnips the other ones.

---

[2]The rattlesnake's rattle is made up of separate tail appendages of horny material loosely fitted, or "buttoned," together so that they make a sharp buzzing sound when the snake vibrates its tail. The snake produces one such section each time it sheds its skin, usually once a year. Hence, young rattlers with one "button" would be a year old, and capable of poison injection.

"starting off the mountain"

sheers

"Just Mention My Name"

A few years after my father's first visit, he and my sister, her husband, and their baby Bernice, came to the top of the ZigZag[3] trail by car, and walked down the rest of the way. They took turns carrying the baby. When they were just about there, father began to feel weak, looked up and saw a steep rocky projection ahead. He said to my sister, who thought it a joke to tease him, "Do we have to climb that too? If so, you go on and tell Winnie I died on the trail."

Mother heard so much about their trip that she thought she would like to come and see me, but they tried to discourage her. Although she hadn't been on a horse for 18 years, she was determined that she could make it. At the time we were at summer camp near Forest, so I hitched the team to the hack, put the saddles in it, and we started out. We rode horseback from the breaks on down to the ranch, and spent the night and returned the next day. She was a lover of flowers, so I gathered some rooted specimens that were new to her, to take home. Some of them wilted, but she was able to save a number of them.

[3]The trail referred to here was between the Weller place and Deer Creek Mine, rather than the one between the Lorang and Verzanni places, mentioned in Part I.

My sisters Marguerite and Pearl came over on horseback when the groundcherries were ripe. They each filled a flour sack of them to take home and tied them behind their saddles. Because of the husks around them, they arrived in good shape. Mother made her excellent preserves of them.

Another time my youngest sister, Marguerite Doyle, and her husband Joe, along with Jack Gehrke and his wife Ebba, decided to go down to see if they could find some grouse. They drove as far as Mr. Horseman's before they decided to camp. There wasn't any water available at that spot, so they went to ask Mr. Horseman about some. He said he had some in the house, but needed it for their own use. He asked them where they were from. They said, "Genesee." Then he asked if they knew me. When he learned that Marguerite was my sister he picked up his lantern and took them to the spring, and invited them to have breakfast as his guests the next morning. They did, and then packed up to start down the ZigZag[3] trail by foot. When they arrived at the mines they stopped again for drinking water. When the caretaker found out they were from Genesee, and that Marguerite was my sister, he asked them to make their headquarters there, as it was rather rugged to travel further on foot. He was overjoyed to see them, as he led a rather lonely life. Jack Gehrke said, "Now I can go down there any time—just say I'm a relative of the Freeburns."

A Sojourn in the "City"

Three years after our little girl arrived we were expecting our third child, so we decided to purchase a home in Forest [population 43] so that I would be nearer a doctor, Dr. McLaughlin, whose office was in Winchester. The only building available was a small hotel. We had a large room in the back that I used as a family room. I cooked the meals and had a girl help with the work and serving, Maggie Currier. Mildred Weller and Lillian Radley were hired to help. Then Cora Vallem, my husband's sister, came to take care of the baby and I. Mrs. Clovis came to dress the baby the first day.

My husband and children were eating breakfast when the baby arrived. Earl was so excited when he heard her cry, he jumped up from the table and said, "Coyotes, coyotes," and ran to peek through the keyhole, which was the rather large kind common to those days. When he saw Mrs. Clovis, who was bathing our new daughter, he ran back to his father shouting, "Two of them! Two of them!," which gave his father quite a start. We named her Mildred Esther. She had brown hair and hazel eyes. She was a very good baby. She learned to read at an early age. She finished school at Queen Anne in Seattle, and graduated from the University of Washington. She did this by helping earn her way. She and her father were real pals.

Real Life in Teaching

The spring when she was two years old, we moved back to Salmon River. As there were several families and children at that time, we applied for a school district to be located at a central point as near an equal distance from each family as possible. A board meeting was called to elect the trustees, and to take care of the building of the school, the fuel, and the teacher's salary. Mr. Mike Rudolph was made chairman of the school board, and Harry Weller the clerk. Every item was voted satisfactorily until it came time for the teacher's salary. I was asked if I knew the average teacher's wage. I said, "At least seventy-five dollars a month." One woman raised her hand and said, "Why, we only pay our sheepherders forty dollars!" Then I said, "That's fine, maybe I can get a job herding sheep when and if I don't get the school."

I was hired to teach, so I went down to Lewiston to renew my first certificate at the Lewiston Normal School, so as to be ready for school when it started in September. The school was finished and an addition added to it to be used as the teacher's cottage. The school board had a telephone installed, so the mothers might have an opportunity to call in and see if the children had arrived, during the cold winter months. Having it accessable made it handy for me, for if I needed additional milk or supplies my husband could bring them to me, or I could chat with him. We went home Friday nights and stayed until Monday mornings, if the weather was favorable. Sometimes we had to brave stormy weather, the brunt of which we had to bear, for we rode horseback. I always had some kind of warm food for the children as a supplement to their lunches during the winter months.

I had Marguerite and Earl, two Rudolph children, two Wellers, two Fountains, and Ted Woods. He was from Forest but was staying with his brother and sister-in-law. He wasn't getting along in school at Forest, so his mother called me back and asked if I could teach seventh grade "Arithmetic." I didn't have any trouble with him, for he was a real help with the children on the playground and applied himself well in school. With nine pupils in all, I had sufficient time to give them a thorough training in each subject.

Nature study seemed to be one of the subjects they enjoyed most. We studied live objects as much as possible. One morning on returning from my home I found a small owl had fallen down the stove pipe into the stove, so I rescued it and we had a lesson on owls. One child brought a duck, one a garter snake, and another a lizard. Pictures of each were drawn, and also wild flowers were gathered for models. Some excellent sketches resulted from these true-to-life examples

I had a first aid kit and tended minor injuries, and created considerable interest, I

Back row: (L to R) Forest "Bud" Rudolph, Louise Rudolph, Harold Weller, Edna Weller
Front row: Sarah Mae Fountain, Ogden "Pete" Fountain, Yvonne Fountain. At Eagle Creek School, 1922.

183

think, in health and hygiene. If they had a loose tooth they wouldn't let their parents pull it. It seemed to be a privilege to have me tend it. I put off extraction until the tooth was actually ready to be removed. It seemed to be a very healthy climate, for there were no occurrences of contagious diseases during the two terms I taught them.

Bigger School, Fringe Benefits, Etc.

The next year most of the families moved away or out to Forest, so the school was moved down the river to accommodate the Reeves children and others who wished to attend. I was going to southern Idaho to teach in a school near Weiser, where the John Lemons lived; she was my husband's sister. While I was debating whether to go or not, the trustees of Forest came to see me and wanted me to take the school at Forest.

They had hired a man teacher, but he had some grain to be threshed and could not take it at the fall term, so he wanted his wife to teach until he finished harvest. The trustees didn't like the plan, and told him to come and take the school right away or they were getting someone else.

His wife came down to our house and asked me to teach while she went to try to persuade her husband to come. I was busy, but helped her out that day. I liked the children but had no intention of trying to get the school. He refused to come, so they offered the job to me. There were 25 pupils and all the grades except the 6th. There was a teacher's cottage which I lived in, renting it for $25 per month, while my salary was $115 a month.

My husband had some stock to feed for a neighbor that winter. We had a large stock of hay at the _K_ which we sold to him. My days at Forest were full, as they started at six o'clock when I went over to a nearby barn; fed, watered, and milked the cow; returning to the house to strain the milk, put it away and start the fire. Then I got the children up to dress while I went to the school house to build a fire and return to prepare breakfast. After feeding the chickens I went back to the school, as some of the pupils came from quite a distance and I wanted it warm when they arrived. My children washed the dishes and then came to school with the lunches I had prepared as I made breakfast. After a day of classes I swept the school floors with an oil and sawdust mixture, and with my son's help carried in large chunks of wood for the next day's fire. I had hired a boy to do the janitorial work, but it didn't work out as he neglected it badly.

Next door to me lived a Miss Starr. She was rather elderly and seemed to have no source of income except what her brother contributed, so I used to send over some of our food. She was very saving on fuel. Many evenings she spent lying on my couch by the fire until I finished preparing my schoolwork for the next day.

School progressed very nicely, with a few exceptions. One of my brightest pupils

Forest School 1926
Back row: (L to R) Bill Howerton, Wm. Currier, Harold Weller, John Currier, Frank Newton, Isobel Truckiset, Anna Werhan, Agnes Truckiset, Billie Kemp, Edna Weller.
Front row: Lavern Howerton, Glen Howerton, unidentified boy, Steve Truckiset Katie Truckiset, Mary Currier, Walter Kemp, Lavetta Howerton.

was a girl named Helen Truckiset. Her father asked me not to let her read a lot of fiction. He was well versed in history and had always won the debates they had at "Literary" because of it. He emphasized that history was "his-story." I told him that history usually appealed more to boys, but I would supervise her reading. One day she had her geography standing on her desk. I asked her what she had hidden. She said, "A story book," and I had her bring it up to me. She went back to her desk and said frowningly, "Old fool." I told her when a pupil calls her teacher an old fool she has to stay after school. The next day when I went to get the mail I met her father. He said Helen had said, "Sometimes Mrs. Freeburn doesn't hear anything, but I called her an old fool today and she heard that."

I was pleased when my two eighth graders, Ellen Bedwell and Ralph Hosley, and four seventh graders, Tim Hosley, Beatrice Bedwell, Helen Truckiset, and Clara Currier, all passed the county examinations and received their diplomas. I gave several plays and was as well pleased with my pupils' acting as their parents were.

We sold my Dad's cattle for him, and my husband and Harry Weller farmed the Nelson place that summer, and punched cattle between times. They were required by law to work on roads with our neighbors. They were away some of the time and had to batch because of the distance. It fell to my lot to milk the cow at these times. She was a young cow not accustomed to women, and would run at me if I had a dress on. The only way I could milk her was to put on my husband's overalls, coat, and hat.

I had just joined the Rebekah Lodge before I went to Salmon River, so I transferred to the Forest Lodge. I was chosen Noble Grand while there. I rode 15 miles horseback to make my majority meetings. I was chosen as delegate the next fall to attend the Rebekah Assembly, which met at Caldwell, Idaho. A friend of mine, Etta Houghton Jump, of Winchester, whom I had known while going to school in Genesee, was chosen from Winchester. On the train we met the state Grand Noble and she asked us about our lodges. Etta said, "I don't have too much time for it, as I belong to several organizations and play piano for the theatre, but Winifred rode 15 miles for her majority meetings." She told her, "Better be one good Rebekah than have so many sidelines." She used this to illustrate her talk later at the Assembly. I brought back to our lodge a certificate of the unwritten work.

SALMON RIVER SAGA
A Reluctant Goodbye

My father had bought several adjoining farms during the war, so he offered us one to live on and farm in the Pine Grove School District, nine miles east of Genesee. I thought it was time for me to quit teaching and devote my time to my husband and children. Our fourth child, a little girl we named Marian Isabella, came to live with us the following February. She had curly dark hair and hazel eyes. She was the best, sweetest baby imaginable. My father said it was because I had experience taking care of the others. Marguerite loved to iron her clothes, and Mildred took great pride in teaching her to walk. I took her to Sunday School when she was 18 days old. Later she liked to play her violin and have her Daddy or me chord on the piano with her.

Thus ended the happiest days of my life. The memories of it are still in my mind.

Editor's Note:

The Freeburn family later moved to Seattle, Washington, where both Winnie and Billy died several years ago. It was there, as a disabled stroke victim in her advanced years, that Winnie Spurbeck Freeburn—one-time Genesee farm girl, frontier ranch wife, dedicated teacher, and boundless lover of life and people—recalled this account for her now urbanized children and grandchildren.

Now established with families of their own and scattered in Idaho, Oregon, and Washington, her four children still answer the lure of their Salmon River beginnings with nostalgic returns from time to time. It was on one of these pilgrimages, when they gathered at the home of sister Marian in Moscow, that I met them and obtained a copy of the account.

To facilitate reading, I have added the subheadings that here break the story into subject matter sections. Other than this, the story is just as she told it. With the warm personality of this hardy pioneer woman showing on every page, readers can readily see why she was so successful a teacher, and why the Platt "children," themselves now in their sunset years, still remember her fondly.

As with their own childhood Salmon River home, hers, too, now is attested by only a few scattered boards, on a wind-blown ridge above Eagle Creek. Hawks and magpies, skunks and coyotes—and, yes, rattlesnakes in abundance—have reclaimed their own. The ephemeral human occupants have moved on to other "conquests."

Looking down into Eagle Creek drainage from head of Fourth Gulch, 1917. Riders, L to R: Nora McCoy, Weldon Orr, Cora Orr Ashenfelter, Sylvia McCoy.

Some Eagle Creek settlers at Harry Weller - "Dosh" Freeburn wedding, May, 1912, L to R Billie Freeburn, Della Freeburn, Art Keane, Cora Freeburn (Mrs. Ralph) Ross, Ralph Ross, Emma Freeburn (Mrs. Dan) Critchfield, Emma (Mrs. John) Platt & baby Jack, Theodosia Freeburn (Mrs. Harry) Weller, Mildred Weller, Harry Weller, Nelson (Justice of Peace), Jacob Freeburn, Martha Bottorf (Mrs. J.) Freeburn, Children: Lorene, Mary, Frances, Kenneth, and "Tom" Platt.

Della Freeburn, near Freeburn home on Eagle Creek about 1914. Note mannish hat, gauntleted gloves and divided skirt, the fashion of the day. Ring stirrups shown were common for men but not for women. The decorations on bridle bit and headstall were used to dress up the "outfit."

Bringing lumber down Deer Creek drag trail for an addition to the Jake Freeburn homestead cabin. L to R Jake Freeburn, Emma Freeburn, Martha (Mrs. Jake) Freeburn

James "Little Jimmy" Moffett, an Eagle Creek homesteader mentioned in A Salmon River Teacher. A bachelor, he sometimes washed his clothes by dangling them in the creek from over-hanging boughs for several days. Also known as "Jimmy The Hard Case."

Winnie and Harry Weller, about 1910.

Cold Nerve or Hot Lead?

The Winchester rifle and Colt revolver of the post Civil War decades have been widely credited as the instruments that "won the West." The Winchester was the first rifle to bring repeat firing to mechanical efficiency in a convenient size, and served salutarily both in bringing outlaws to book and game to the table. The Colt revolver of frontier days was peerless in its function as the "great equalizer" of men disparate in physical prowess. Both guns were widely used in dealing out the frontier "justice" that honored summary decision and speed on the draw as the accepted expressions of legality where less violent and perhaps more equitable settlement of differences was not thought practical.

These two landmark accoutrements of the Western pioneer came to the fore about 100 years ago. As we look back at the 200 years since our 1776 founding, the prominent place of the Winchester and Colt at the mid-point of this span warrants analytic scrutiny. How much of the frontier violence was the product of these implements of violence? How much was it the product of the caliber and temper of men who peopled the frontier? In the final analysis, which dominated, man or gun?

The fact that individual "gun law" went out as settlement brought group law into control does not really answer the question. We need to look at it in the setting of the frontier itself. The following anecdote gives such a look. If it does not answer the question directly, at least it provides a provocative example.

Will Glenn was a robust and confident 19 years old when he and two other footloose young men decided to leave New York in 1861. The lure of the California gold fields had palled somewhat, but now word of fabulous new strikes in Idaho and Montana was coming in. Emigrant trains already had beat a highway of sorts across the Great Plains and the Rockies to fabled Oregon. Horace Greeley's "Go West, young man," merely stated the obvious for a second generation "Irisher" facing long odds for getting ahead in the crowded, hidebound and socially inhospitable East of that period. Off they went.

The route by train to Pittsburg, then by boat to St. Louis, was well established. Early March found them at this bustling, rowdy border town, thick with wagon makers, harness makers, saddlers, booters, blacksmiths, horse traders, gunsmiths, boatmen, hartenders, gamblers, prostitutes, soldiers, besotted Indians, aging mountain men, professional trail scouts, buffalo hunters, wagon train captains, and all the assorted renegades, scalawags, ruffians and adventurers that visions of riches, general confusion and indifferent law enforcement attracted to this hub of Western departure. This was the outfitting point for the great overland trek that would take them to the lands of opportunity. Here each westbound pilgrim made whatever changes he might still feel need of for suitable attire and travel equipment, and armed himself for encounter with the demands and hazards of untamed nature and unfriendly humanity.

It went without saying that the most critical items to be had from this point forward were the guns which would be depended on to stand off starvation, hostile Indians, claim jumpers, thieves and desperados. From here on it would be all rough company, and no quarter. The code of the West made no allowance for the weak or the unprepared. It was an all-or-nothing code. The gun was its arbiter.

There was still the human equation, of course. The same gun in different hands gave different results. Not just the gun, but also the man behind the gun, was to be reckoned with. How Will Glenn came out in this reckoning is the essence of our tale. So, let's hear his story.

★   ★   ★

Pattern For Life

The old man sat on the cabin steps, the illusory strength of early March sunshine faintly penetrating the worn buckskin jacket that hung loosely over his gaunt frame. His unhurried glance took in the crude dirt-banked cellar across the yard, and beyond it saddle shed, corral, beef hoist, stack butt and outlying meadow. It followed the trail threading across the willowed creek and up the long ridges toward Juniper Mountain. It probed the green shadows of the scattered juniper forest, noting the crafty darting of a jay from one refuge to the next through the opalescent sunlight. It bridged the deep gorge of the Owyhee River and came to rest on a gap in the rim beyond, where the trail passed out of sight. It sought diligently, but found not what it sought.

Winter was on its last legs. Snow still lay only where the deepest drifts had formed. The trail would be open any day now. Riders would be coming. Let them come, he thought. He would be ready. He had been ready always before.

A puff of wind rattled the bare white skeleton of the poplar by the spring. It swung the unlatched cellar door smartly on its boot-top hinges, and drew a squawk of momentary alarm from the red rooster busy with his small harem over the morning's kitchen scraps. It searched under the old man's loose jacket with chilling fingers.

He leaned away from its touch, pressing his back against the warmth of the weathered cabin wall. His gaze returned from the distant rim with schooled deliberateness. He slid his right hand to his belt, where it closed upon the gun that hung there.

He did not draw the gun at once. The closing of his hand upon it was a gesture of caress, like the meeting of old friends, equals.

They were in truth of long acquaintance. The gun had known that hand, that hand the gun, for more than fifty years. They had traveled the long trails and had known the lonely vigils of the frontier together. Ready to defend, ready to even the odds against justice, ready — — — .

Again he scanned the long juniper ridges, the distant thread of trail. And now there was movement. Through the gap in the far rimrock came two riders, tall in the saddle, dark against the horizon. For some minutes they rode in sight across the sloping sagebrush bench between the upper rim and the canyon wall, then dropped from view into the gorge of the Owyhee. Purpose was in their riding; purpose now came to Glenn.

The lead rider, on the big sorrel gelding, would be Charlie Manners. The one on the black would be his cousin, George Gunther. A long winter of lonely isolation on the distant Star Ranch behind them. A winter of brooding over last fall's man-handling of Charlie by Jud Winters at the Hallowe'en dance in Jordan Valley. Charlie had been out-of-hand, needed putting in place, but Jud had gone much further than the need. There would have been shooting then had not friends kept both men from their guns.

And now here was Charlie, heading back. Charlie Manners, twenty-three years old, full of pride and injury, dark of mood, looking for trouble and sure to find it. Charlie Manners, winner of every fall roundup pistol contest in the Malheur country the last two seasons. And with him in a loyalty both of youth and of blood, George Gunther, only slightly less efficient with his gun.

They must be stopped. He knew of but one way to stop them.

Glenn drew his gun slowly, examined it in detail. As ever, he found it in perfect working order. The bore was as clean today as on the day the weapon was bought. The trigger action was smooth, almost effortless. The bright, six-chambered cylinder brought up each new cartridge with faultless precision. There was a practiced fondness in his every touch and glance.

What he must do now, Glenn felt, was betrayal. Like abandoning a life-long friend. It was not a thing to be done lightly. Perhaps there existed some alternative which might yet occur to him. The riders would need at least half an hour to cross the gorge of the Owyhee. There was still time to think.

The gun now hung unnoticed from bony hand draped over bony knee. The old man's gaze roamed the yard speculatively, noting a pebble, a knot in a fence post, the jerking head of the red cock strutting beyond the cellar. The gun stirred and lifted, as if initiating the movement of the hand. And, as if thereby made aware, the old man looked at it.

It was not a large gun. In the large hand it seemed even smaller than its actual measure. In that hand it looked, in fact, almost effeminate. The bleached bone butt plates were delicately carved. The plated cylinder reflected more of grace than of force. The brief six-inch barrel seemed too slender to be the harsh carrier of death. The gun gave no sense of strength of its own. But as the hand closed upon it the strength of the hand and of the will behind the hand flowed into the gun, and the gun became spokesman for a force greater than its own, bidding beware the cruder forces embodied only in larger guns.

That force, in times past, had prevailed. Old Glenn relaxed his still powerful bulk against the cabin wall, his eyes half closed.

Effeminate. That was a word for his gun. Old Glenn did not think the word. It had passed long since from his conscious vocabulary, though once it had been there. But he thought its substance. No, not effeminate; that was too soft. Feminine, perhaps. No, female, and possessing the unsuspected strength of the female. The strength that overcame without direct assault, or brute force. There had been a day...His mind turned back over the years.

★   ★   ★

The month was March; the year, 1861. There was wine in the air, doubly potent — the wine of the first hint of spring along the middle reaches of the Mississippi, and the headier wine of adventure that overflowed the group of men crowding the forward deck of the sternwheeler *Allegheny*. The magic of the names "California" and "Oregon," was there, too.

Pittsburg, point of embarkation for most of the travelers, was forgotten. Louisville was a fast dimming memory; Cairo an already undefinable tang in the back of the mind, like the lingering taste of strange fruit. St. Louis lay ahead. A growing tenseness filled the group, breaking out from time to time in sudden brawls and fist fights. Wise in the ways of his human cargo, ham-fisted Captain Lister had, as a condition of passage, put under lock all manner of guns, knives and other weapons as they were brought aboard. He was capable of dealing barehandedly with anything short of armed insurrection. But the men were becoming daily more edgy.

Young Bill Glenn stood along the rail of the *Allegheny* near the bow, watching the Missouri side. The power of the river was blind and purposeless, he thought, an expression of mass without will. The power of the boat, though puny by comparison, was purposefully directed. It conquered not by overwhelming but by cutting through, deflecting, riding over and thereby voiding the power of the river against it. It used the substance of the river to make progress in the opposite direction.

Six months ago he had been drifting, like the flotsam on this river, his life bent to no particular end. Floating on the current of his time and place, he had been without volition. Now that inertia had been cast off; he was moving smartly against the current of his upbringing, directing his own destiny.

"Think we'll make St. Louis before dark?" A man near Glenn put his question at large.

"I hope so," said Glenn. "The sooner we get off this boat the better I'll like it."

"We'll get there, all right. We have to. There's no place to tie in the last ten miles, and not even Captain Lister could keep this channel in the dark."

Mather Herndon, slight and wiry, spoke with assurance. Though youngest of the three, his adventurer's instinct already had made him a veteran of two years at sea. Aboard the *Allegheny* he had quickly come to know the crew by their first names, visited every part of the boat, lent a hand here and there in the bad spots, and made himself liked by all. Whatever went on seemed to find him, if not at its center, at least well within the vortex of events.

It was so at this moment.

A warning yell turned all eyes forward. Over and between the heads of those in front of him Glenn glimpsed a huge drifting cottonwood, green and almost submerged, just as it rammed the prow. The boat lurched sharply. Glenn thrust a long leg forward to brace himself, felt someone trip over it and fall heavily. A chorus of yells and curses broke out all about the deck. The drifting tree scraped briefly along the side of the vessel, then swung clear. He turned from the rail.

Men had fallen at several places, and now were picking themselves up from a variety of sprawls. The man who had tripped over Glenn's leg was full length on the deck. Blood oozed slowly from his skinned knuckles. Someone had stepped on his hat, which he now pulled savagely onto his head, glowering furiously about him. About thirty-five, he was powerfully built, inches shorter than Glenn, but a good fifteen pounds heavier. Glenn remembered him as one who had been noticeable for turning up in more than his share of the various outbreaks of trouble.

"Sorry," said Glenn, and knew instantly he should not have spoken.

"You damn' dandy!" snarled the other, "why don't you watch where you stick them big feet?"

"Really I—it was an accident," Glenn stumbled over the words, feeling half guilty yet resenting the attack.

"Accident, hell! If you didn't think you was so much better'n everybody else you wouldn't be takin' up so much deck space. I got a good notion to trim you down to the space fittin' to you."

"Now wait, Kincaid," Herndon pushed forward. "It was an accident. Could have happened to anyone. Same thing happened to other guys."

195

"Sure, Kincaid, what's eatin' you? Think you're the only one got upset?" a man spoke from the circle forming around them.

"Naw, just the only one got sore about it," tossed in another.

"The hell with you guys," boiled Kincaid. "This kid needs manners, and I'm givin' him some right now."

The circle tightened expectantly. Glenn braced himself for Kincaid's rush, not welcoming it, not quite knowing how he would meet it, yet not afraid. Kincaid whipped off coat and hat, tossed them contemptuously into the faces behind him, and lunged forward. What might have been the outcome Glenn would never know, for a surge of the crowd threw Kincaid off balance, his blow went wild. And in that instant Captain Lister was upon them.

"What goes on here?" His bellow and momentum scattered the spectators. "You again, Kincaid!" With one hand he shoved the aggressor roughly back. "So help me, Kincaid, any more of this and I'm lockin' you up. Now get below and stay there till we dock."

Kincaid wrenched himself from the captain's hand, fuming but ineffectual.

"All right for you now kid," he gritted at Glenn." I'll see you ashore — when 'papa' ain't around." He stalked below. The crowd melted as quickly as it had formed.

"Well, glad that didn't go any further," admitted Glenn.

"He's mean, all right, but he's not as tough as he sounds," said Herndon. "Thinks because he's been out to California the last five years he can bluff everybody out just on his reputation. Ten to one he hatched up most of those big doings he's been bragging around. You find guys like him everywhere you go."

"Think he'll cause any trouble when we get off?" asked Glenn.

"Nah! He was just savin' his face," was Herndon's opinion. But Glenn was uneasy. The *Allegheny* made St. Louis just at dusk.

★　　★　　★

It was five days later that Glenn and Herndon boarded the freighter *Mandan*, first boat to attempt the opening spring run to Council Bluffs, shortly after sunrise and half an hour ahead of her scheduled departure from St. Joseph.

"Hey, kid, ain't you on the wrong boat? This trip might be tough," the sneering voice of Kincaid turned them around as he came up the gangway. "You wouldn't be tryin' to leave town ahead of me, now, would you? We never did have that little get-together ashore, you know."

Whether Kincaid had followed him, or their present meeting was only by chance, Glenn could not guess. From St. Louis he and Herndon had taken the first train north on the newly completed Hannibal & St. Joseph railroad, hoping to catch the party of trappers and fur traders that would be heading west from Council Bluffs well ahead of the first wagon train. As he watched the burly swaggart tossing aboard his heavy baggage he felt vaguely uneasy, but presently realized he was not afraid.

Kincaid viewed the deck, crowded with freight and boat gear, leaving little more than work space for the crew.

"Well, now, I can see things are goin' to be right chummy around here the next few days," he gloated.

"Sure, come on aboard. Guess I can stand it if the others can," Glenn returned evenly.

"You won't be so cocky before long," Kincaid growled. "The captain on this boat ain't so fussy. And what's more, he ain't so big as 'papa' Lister. He turned toward a stout middle-aged man now approaching. "Hey Captain! Heard you had room for one more, so I came aboard."

The captain viewed him with neither welcome nor distaste.

"Didn't figure on any more," he said, "but now you're aboard, stay aboard. I'll get you stowed later." He went on with the affairs of getting under way.

"See what I mean?" Kincaid queried pointedly.

The third afternoon out Glenn and Herndon, tired from the cramped quarters and lack of activity, decided to try shooting for sport at the countless waterfowl that thronged the river. They ought, Herndon said, to be getting some practice anyway, against the day when guns might be needed in earnest. Glenn agreed.

Since the first day Kincaid had been wearing a heavy revolver which he fired at targets large and small, near and far, with a success reflected in loud self-satisfaction. He had made no further move to intimidate Glenn. He was at the port rail now, as the two friends came from below and went to the opposite side.

The gun which Herndon carried was similar to Kincaid's—a long barreled, large-bore weapon designed to deliver power at considerable distance. He had bought it in St. Louis, on advice of an outfitter, as "the best friend a man could have" in the territory for which he was headed. Most of the other men had secured similar side arms.

Glenn's pistol was immediately conspicuous by its difference. Small in both size and bore, it was handsomely rather than heavily formed. As the two started shooting at their numerous floating targets its sound was unimpressive beside the loud report of the larger gun. It seemed plainly unsuited for the heavy duty generally expected of frontier firearms.

"You had that gun long?" Herndon asked presently.

"Father gave it to me just before I left home."

"Think it'll do?"

197

"I'm wondering."

"You could get one like mine at Council Bluffs."

"Maybe I will."

They continued to shoot, each slowly getting the feel of his gun.

"Who's got the popgun?" Kincaid's voice scoffed behind them. "Well, if it ain't Fauntleroy himself!"

He was followed by several other passengers, who grinned appreciatively at his gibe.

"Say," he mocked before Glenn could answer, "that thing looks dangerous for a boy. Maybe mama shouldn't of let you have it." He guffawed loudly.

Glenn felt resentment rising, and a hardening determination.

"Look, Kincaid," he said bluntly, "this gun suits me, and that's all I need of it. Let's leave it that way."

"Now, don't he say the cutest things?" Kincaid taunted. "Just forget it, he says. Might do that if 'twasn't for my natural instinct to pertect women and babies. It's your future I'm thinkin' of, kid. With that gun you ain't got a future in this country. Why, that lady killer wouldn't shoot through a good boot."

"My future is my worry, and I'll take care of it," Glenn's voice was cold. Then, rashly, "I'll match my gun against yours any time you like."

"That's a good one," Kincaid roared with derision. "Why, kid, I'll give you any odds you want I can knock off three ducks to your one, or shoot through three inches of wood to your one. How much you wanta bet?"

"I'm not betting, Kincaid. I'm not talking about shooting ducks, and I'm not talking about shooting through planks. I'm talking about you and me."

There was a sudden stillness in the group. Kincaid stared at Glenn incredulously. Glenn returned the stare, icily calm. Kincaid seemed struggling for words. His face reddened, his lips worked, but no sound issued.

"Son, don't you think you're carryin' this quite a bit too far?" an older man spoke from the group. "After all, a joke's only a joke, even if some folks is inclined to joke pretty rough. Mebbe you better think over what you said. And you, mister," taking Kincaid by the arm, "mebbe you better come on back t'other side while he's thinkin'."

Kincaid it was who finally pulled his eyes away from the deadly interchange. Still wordless, he turned and walked across the deck, around a mound of cargo and out of sight. Most of the spectators went with him. The rest made off to other parts of the boat. Herndon and Glenn were left alone, the latter still staring after Kincaid.

"Man alive! Did you ever stick your foot in deep," breathed Herndon. "He'll kill you sure if you go through with this."

"Probably. But I've made up my mind. It's like you say—there'll always be someone like him, wherever I go. If I take that stuff from him, I'll be taking it the rest of my life. I'd rather die. But if he does kill me, I'll kill him before I die. I think he knows it. And he's not ready to die."

"Man, you're talkin' like crazy! You may think you're willing to die, but you're not. Besides, if we play this right it will all blow over and no harm done. Let's go below and talk it out before he takes a notion to come back around here."

"Let him come," said Glenn, but he followed his friend below.

The *Mandan* tied that night on a deep eddy in the lee of a large island near midstream. A flurry of snow was in the air as dusk settled into darkness, plastering cargo and rigging with a thin white sheet. It matched, above decks, the chill tension that was felt by all below in the unresolved clash of the afternoon. The boat swung in beneath the overhanging trees as if to keep warm.

Glenn and Herndon were the first to reach the deck next morning. The crew was busy below. One of the paddle planks had splintered against an ice cake yesterday, and a replacement was being made. The boat would be an hour or more getting under way.

The squall of the preceding evening had left an inch of snow on the island.

"This is perfect," Herndon said softly. "Perfect."

Without a word Glenn walked to the rail, seized an overhanging limb, and swung ashore. He strode across a small opening and disappeared into a grove fifty yards away. Herndon watched until he was out of sight, then strolled to the offshore side of the boat. Here he drew his revolver and, after a casual survey of the many waterfowl that had spent the night on the eddy, aimed and fired.

At the roar of the shot the whole melange of birds rose fluttering and crying with a great noise. As if drawn by a magnet the remaining passengers gathered from below deck to the sound of the shot, the unsettled affair of yesterday in their minds and eyes.

"Get one?" someone ventured.

"No. Missed. Just shooting for fun anyway."

"Where's Glenn?"

"Went ashore."

"What for?"

"Going to get in some serious target practice, I guess."

The muffled crack of a shot from Glenn's pistol now drew all eyes toward the grove. There was a long pause, then another shot. Another pause, another shot. Again magnetized, the men moved toward the shoreward rail.

"I'm going to see," said someone.

"Me, too," said another.

By the time the sixth shot had sounded all were ashore, Herndon among the first, Kincaid among the last. As they entered the grove Herndon took the lead, following

Glenn's tracks on through to a small opening beyond. Stepping into this opening, he paused while the rest of the group came up.

Glenn was seated on a fallen tree some fifty feet beyond them, his back half turned, reloading his revolver. His tracks, plain in the fresh snow, led along the edge of the opening to the far side, then back to where he now sat.

"Where's your target?" Herndon called.

"Over there." Glenn pointed to a white barked aspen some thirty feet in front of him.

"How'd you do?"

"Don't know. Haven't been over to look." Glenn went on reloading.

With one accord the men moved toward the target tree. Chest high on the side toward Glenn was a four-inch circle with the bark peeled off, exposing the creamy sapwood beneath. There was no word as the group crowded in a semi-circle around the target. Bodies bent forward, necks craned, eyes squinted. Glenn, his reloading finished, came toward them.

"Damned if you didn't shoot a right neat target," said one, turning.

"Not bad," put in Herndon.

"Give a look," said another.

Glenn stepped to the tree and examined the target circle with care. The black-rimmed holes of five bullets stood out in it, three of them within an egg-sized area near the center. A sixth hole showed in the bark just below the circle.

"Fair," he admitted, "except for that low one. That was my second shot—I held too long."

"Going to shoot another?" asked Herndon.

"No, the gun seems to be shooting true enough. I don't think I need any more practice today," Glenn stated easily. "Let's go."

They turned toward the boat. In twos and threes, talking among themselves, the rest followed.

The company aboard the *Mandan* was a quiet one in the days that followed. Gradually the tension eased, the men sensing that the crisis had passed. There were no more clashes.

They disembarked at Council Bluffs on March 18, 1861. Glenn never saw Kincaid again.

The old man on the cabin steps stirred restlessly; past, present and future competing for his attention. The riders were nowhere in sight. The past held him. Old

Glenn again was young Glenn . . . .

Sioux, Cheyennes; gold camps, gambling rooms, dance halls. California, Oregon, Idaho; Placerville, Orofino, Boise Basin, Silver City. Excitement, adventure, danger, hardship, toil. Gain, loss, love, life—the bright panarama flitted desultorily across the screen of memory, its flashes and pauses only partly answerable to the will.

A wave had gone out before him from that incident on the *Mandan*; small, indefinable at times, but ever preceding. Its ripple he found registered on all the shores he touched. A word here, a sidelong glance there, a nodding of heads at his passing. Sometimes he was aware, sometimes not. Some things were easier because of it, some things harder. But that incident had been as the casting of a die within him; he could not have changed it if he would. There had been other incidents . . . .

1868. Silver City, high in the Owyhee Mountains of Idaho Territory, heart of a mushrooming frenzy of ten thousand gold seekers. Most took it the hard way, with pick and shovel; some the easy way, on the tilt of a glass, the lure of a soft bosom, the unseen turn of a card . . . . The Idaho Queen, brightest of the gambling spots . . . . Blackjack, fantan, roulette, poker . . . . Smoke, talk, laughter; curses, women, music—lights and shadows of sight, sound, smell, taste, touch . . . .

Glenn, seated with half a dozen other men at a large round table, the cards falling noiselessly among the stacks of chips and gold on the felted surface. "Silent" Jim Daniels, ace of gamblers, sitting opposite, dealing the hand. The opening, the raises, the freezing out, until only Daniels and Glenn remained in the pot. The final bet, the call, the turn of the cards. Glenn's cold challenge of misplay. Daniel's icy stare, probing, pushing, searching, calculating, finally capitulating.

The word drifted back to Glenn years later, as such things will:

"You pulling stakes, 'Silent?' I thought you liked it here. Anything wrong with the set-up?" Brady Mcpherson, owner of the Idaho Queen, was solicitous. Daniels had a reputation for high play that drew big money. He would be hard to replace.

No answer.

"Say, you're not pulling out on account of that slip with Glenn last week!" Mcpherson ventured. "Why, everybody knows you could've drilled him on the spot. Then or any other time. Snap out of it, man! Stick around!"

"In my business," Daniels was succinct, "men don't die for pulling the wrong card—they die for pulling it on the wrong man. Either you know men, or they plant you with a lily in your hand. I know men. I could have killed Glenn, sure. But he would have killed me, too. There's no future in that. I'll find another spot."

★　　★　　★　　★　　★

201

1872. Bill Glenn pressed his horse as swiftly along the stage road as the deepening dusk and need for caution would permit. Following down Jordan Creek from Silver City to Jordan Valley, the road turned southward across a succession of tributaries falling from the western flank of South Mountain. It was in the upper portion of this slope that Glenn now rode. The towering bulk of the mountain climbed steeply away in the left background, its outlines only faintly seen against the moonless sky. A mile ahead his homestead cabin stood beside a small stream born of springs at the mountain's base. The cabin itself would not come into sight until the last hundred yards. Only then would he know whether he was in time.

The Modocs were out again. They had been intermittently in open rebellion for six years, refusing to stay on the Klamath Reservation two hundred miles to the southwest. Warning of this latest outbreak had come three days ago. Cabins were being burned, livestock driven off, people killed wherever they did not get out of the way. Jordan Valley was next in line for attack.

No Indians had been sighted in the last three days, and no new reports had come in. In that time women, children and meager household goods had been rushed to the stockade in Silver City. Livestock were left behind for lack of time to gather and drive them. Glenn had taken his wife and two small sons to Silver City the day before yesterday. He thought of them now as he rode in the gathering darkness.

Timothy, a sturdy three years old, thrived on the rough fare of the frontier. George, the baby, unable to take his mother's milk, had been a problem from birth. Mare's milk had brought him through an early crisis, but now the mare was dry. The cow that had replaced her had been left behind in their flight to Silver City. If the Modocs were not here first, and if he could find the cow in the darkness, he could get far enough toward Silver to be safe by morning.

He thought of Miriam, his wife. Odd that he should think of her as strong—she who stood scarcely to his shoulder, and whose slender grace had held him almost in awe at their first meeting. Yet certainly it was strength that had enabled her, a year earlier when he was gone and roving Modocs had driven off half the cattle in the settlement, to face the grinning band as they swept up to the cabin door, and to tell the chief he must leave her livestock undisturbed. The savage leader had recognized that strength, and had respected it.

Glenn topped the last rise before the homestead and pulled up his horse. The small valley below was filled with shadow in which the willow grove sheltering the cabin was only a darker blur. A light wind blew from him toward it. No sounds but those of nature came to his ear. A desert owl hooted once softly from the hill behind him; its mate answered from the willows below.

He would go first to the cabin for a small keepsake Miriam had left, then start his

202

search for the cow.

The whispering of the willows in the wind around the cabin filled the night. In the half light of the stars he removed a small block of sulfur matches from the oilskin packet in his skirt. To get the keepsake would take but a moment. He slipped the wooden latch along its slot, swung the door and stepped in. There cold shock froze him to immobility.

Modoc warriors returned his glances from every direction, their war-painted faces wierd and chilling in the flickering light from the fireplace.

Though no one moved to seize him, Glenn sensed the futility of flight. No less than half of them had rifles trained on him. The hooting of the owls had been the sentries, warning of his coming. He had tied his horse securely; he could not hope to mount and ride before he would be dragged down. His heavy boots would make him easy prey in a flight on foot. He closed the door and latched it behind him.

Quickly appraising the faces about him, Glenn recognized none as belonging to men who had come to his cabin before for food or medicine. There was no hint of friendliness. That his cabin was not already in embers was only because it was serving as a needed shelter for the night. With blankets hung over windows and door, no light escaped to betray their presence as a campfire would have. That he was not already dead was only because they were waiting for any others who might be with him to step into the trap.

At a motion from their leader two braves slipped noiselessly into the outer black. Soon they would return to confirm that he was alone. He must make what he could of this brief respite. He raised his hand in a gesture of peace.

"Welcome to my cabin," Glenn knew enough of the Modoc tongue to manage the sense of the greeting.

"No more your cabin—our cabin," the leader jested grimly. "You welcome." A grunt of approval went round the room.

"My cabin always your cabin. Modoc always welcome," Glenn tried again.

"Modoc take cabin, take land. Always belong Modoc."

"Many sick papoose, sick squaw, sick brave come here; always help," Glenn avoided the bait.

"White man bring sickness. White man go, Modoc no need help. Only need land."

Glenn bit back the ready reply that the white men already outnumbered the red, that more were coming, and that they would never leave. It was an answer the Modocs could not grasp, and that would only infuriate them.

"Where white squaw, white papoose?" the chief cut in.

"Papoose sick, take to doctor," Glenn lied smoothly.

"All white papoose, white squaw, white brave, get sick, go to white doctor, when hear Modoc coming." Again the grim joke brought a ripple of appreciation.

Glenn pointed to himself. "Not go to doctor," he stated.

The chief rose suddenly, strode the short space that separated them.

"Bah! What is one man?" He spat contemptuously in Glenn's face.

His action was the ultimate insult, signaling an end to the brief barter of words and any hope of pacification. Glenn's reaction was instinctive, unreasoned. He grappled instantly, fiercely, with his powerful adversary.

For what seemed minutes they stood locked together, heads down, shoulders bulging; hands seeking, grasping, slipping; lungs heaving in short hard grunts; backs arched and straining; legs bracing and twining. By what quirk of pride or purpose the Modoc did not seek the deadly dagger on his belt Glenn did not know. Perhaps he thought to save his white victim for a more anguished death after he was first subdued. Glenn thought of his own gun, decided against trying to use it.

But as the struggle continued, now far beyond the first expectations of the confident chief, it took on a new nature. No longer was it a mere physical contest. It had become a contest for supremacy of will and of pride that each valued above life. Now, by a law instinctive alike to red man and to white, there could be no resort to weapons in deciding the outcome.

Slowly they began to sway, to rock forward and back as first one then the other found brief advantage. Then with a crash they were down, rolling and thrashing. The intent circle of painted faces closed and widened above them as the struggle moved about the room. There was no sound save that of the desperate effort of the two.

How long the contest might have lasted on the basis of sheer physical strength would have been hard to judge. They were evenly matched in almost every way. But now a cunning carried down from the past came to Glenn. Because they were evenly matched he could think as he strove. One by one he began trying for various wrestling holds he had learned as a boy in rough and tumble surroundings.

At last his moment came. Whether through ignorance or through fierce incaution, the Modoc exposed himself. Instantly Glenn seized the vulnerable wrist and forced it into a vicious hammerlock. Vainly his adversary strained and writhed. Inexorably Glenn drove home the bone wracking torture. For long minutes the chief struggled on, but at last he lay limp and gasping.

A burst of natural approval came from the wild circle, now laughing at the discomfiture of their chief. But Glenn raised a hand for silence. Releasing his hold, he lifted his fallen enemy.

"Welcome my cabin," he panted. "Modoc always welcome my cabin."

It was toward noon the following day that Glenn reached Silver City with the cow.

SALMON RIVER SAGA

Old Glenn's reverie drifted on across the kaleidoscope of years. Scenes changed, faces changed, time took its toll; but ever the master pattern remained fixed. Though the bits and pieces might shift in endless array, they could not escape the outer confines of the design within which they moved. For that design was itself the die cast in Glenn's mind and will long years before, and within which he found the limits of his world.

Many men had died in those earlier years—the years of "six-gun law." But out of the smoke of the guns gradually emerged a pattern: Merely to be fast on the draw was not enough. The man who was fast and right outlived the man who was fast and wrong. The difference was the force of right. Many times he had seen that force outweigh long odds in speed on the draw. They who lived by violence died by violence; they who lived by peace were left. This, then, was the pattern, ruling despite infinite variations and occasional individual exceptions. In the end the pattern prevailed.

And now, what of Charlie Manners and George Gunther, his thoughts coming back to the present? Could they escape the pattern? No, he did not see escape, but they could be made to understand it, he hoped, and to see a different place for themselves in it. But first there must be an unmasking, an abandonment of pretense. Time had run its course, and he his, and the purpose of the unmasking now outweighed any reason for its continuance.

In fact—the thought brightened and cleared in him—the act and purpose now before him was to be rather a fulfillment than the betrayal it had seemed half an hour ago when the two riders first showed on the horizon.

He cast back again over the years. The legend that was Glenn had served its purpose in its day. He thought how well he had nurtured it, telling no one. Not even Miriam, trusted partner through all their years together, had known. He had thought it better for her that she believe, as did all else, in his deadly efficiency. Only Herndon,, long since buried on windswept War Eagle Mountain above Silver City, had known.

He looked again up the trail. The riders had climbed out of the Owyhee gorge and were coming down the ridge. He watched as they rode out onto the meadow a quarter of a mile away, urging tired mounts to a trot.

Glenn now stood up on the cabin steps, stretched, raised his hat, settled it again on his head, making sure they saw him. Still in full view of the riders, he walked deliberately across the yard to the cellar door. At arm's length he stood and slowly emptied his gun into the weather-hardened leather of the top hinge, then studied the results. Satisfied, he returned to sit on the steps.

It would be hard to make them believe, those two headstrong young men, after all these years. Were it not for this last bit of evidence, how could he hope to convince them?

Would they believe him when he told them that the gun he carried never had been drawn against another man? Would they believe the truth—that on that distant day on an island in the Missouri River, employing a clever ruse drawn by Herndon out of his adventurous past, he had stood so, at arm's length from the target tree, and fired his six shots point blank into the target area, then quickly stripped off the bark to remove the tell-tale powder stains, before walking to the fallen tree on which he sat when the others from the *Mandan* came up? Would they believe that he had never so much as fired the gun since that day?

Most important, would they believe—could they understand—that it was the force of the man behind the gun, more than the force of the gun itself, which had fathered the legend that was Glenn?

He could only hope for the desired outcome, though somehow he felt an inner confidence. Charlie Manners and George Gunther were young, impetuous, strong willed. But they were also, he warmed pridefully, of better judgment than their years might indicate. There was a definite strain of Miriam's sound good sense in them both, he reflected as his two grandsons rode up to the gate.

"Howdy, Grandad!" they called in unison, dismounting.

"What you doing there? Driving nails in that hinge?" bantered George.

"Howdy yourselves," the old man called back. "Just wait till you see this target and you'll get an eye-opener."

Indeed, Glenn hoped it would open their eyes in a sense they had yet to learn. And there was a good chance it would. For Kincaid had been right in his judgment of Glenn's gun on that long ago day on the *Mandan* deck—not one of the bullets just fired had penetrated through the boot top.

Author's Note:

Although the names of the people in this story are fictional, the people themselves and the main incidents described are essentially factual, as recounted to me some 40 years ago by a son of the main character. Descendants of the family still live in the Jordan Valley and surrounding areas. They and others there may recognize their pioneer progenitor, and be honored in his memory.

SALMON RIVER SAGA

A CASE FOR THE INSPECTOR

Sepcial Agent Kane reined in his horse. Behind, the dim shades of towering pine and fir engulfed the last raucous screech of a pursuing jay. Kane silently cursed the jay and all its tribe. Before him the trail dropped away as though it had come to the jumping off place.

It might as well be dropping into hell, Kane thought sourly. Wiping brow and throat with a bandana already limp, he eyed the precipitous descent.

Sharp ridges fell away in long succession under the shimmering heat waves. His eye followed to where they plunged finally under the Salmon River, a silver ribbon tracing the gorge floor, to rise beyond in towering sweeps. Steep ravines below him grew into canyons reaching to the river.

If the sweat rolled off you in the shade of heavy timber, what could you expect boxed in with the sun in that canyon?

"Damn!"

Kane kicked his horse irritably into motion, jerked the animal again to a stop. #+ = ?#& the General Land Office for ever inventing special investigations. Anyone crazy enough to homestead in this Salmon River canyon ought to have a free claim. For all Kane cared at that moment, George Prout could have the whole Lower Salmon country if he wanted it.

It wasn't what Kane cared or what Prout wanted that counted just then, however. The disgruntled rider unbuttoned his left shirt pocket and took out a heavy manila envelope. Unfolding it, he removed and read the single crisp sheet:

Mr. A. T. Kane, Special Agent
U.S. Department of Interior
c/o Bollinger Hotel
Lewiston, Idaho

Sir:

You are hereby instructed to proceed at once to Forest, Idaho, to investigate Homestead Entry 417,963 held by George Prout.

Reason for investigation: Complaints charging Prout with locating his fence beyond the legal bounds of the above Homestead Entry.

Finding the above charges true, you will secure removal of said fences from their improper location. Said charges proving false, you will report for their dismissal.

Legal description is as follows:...

Kane skipped the rest.

Well, there were the orders, and here was the place. Rather, somewhere in that sizzling gorge was the place. Five miles south, his map showed, should be the nearest corner of the disputed land. Kane jammed the letter back into his pocket and swung his horse down the trail.

The first thing to do, he decided, was to go straight to Prout and get his side of the story. At least, let Prout know what was going on. It was a cinch, Kane ruminated, that he wasn't going to go prowling along any of Prout's fence lines without first making himself known. And as for removing any misplaced fences, well, that was a job that could wait.

"SPECIAL AGENT KANE"

Tampering with George Prout's fences, he had gathered was not exactly healthful. In fact, there was a notch in the stock of Prout's 30-30 Winchester right now marking the sudden demise of one man who hadn't seen eye to eye with him in the matter of fence locations. And that notch had come very near being twins.

The tall horseman gave himself over for some minutes to dodging the overhanging thornbrush that crowded the trail. Probably a gulch like that, he thought, emerging at last, down which Andy Hines had fled the avenging trigger finger of George Prout, leaving a dead companion behind.

Seven years ago, that was. But Hines still carried telling marks of the incident. He recalled the big man's nervous look.

"Something violent must have happened to that guy, the way his left arm is twisted," Kane had remarked to the nearest man, as he watched Hines dominating a poker table in the busy saloon last night.

"I'll say! He's the guy George Prout didn't quite get, seven years ago. Caught a 30-30 slug in that left arm from behind. Bullet took him acrost the side of the chest, too, but not deep enough to do much damage. Sure ruined that arm though. Thing that's makin' him nervous now is, Prout might take a notion to finish the job."

At mention of Prout's name, Kane took the cue.

"How come Prout let the finishing part go so long, if he's of a mind to do it?" Kane simulated casual interest.

"He wasn't in no position to do what he'd like for five-six year." The puncher leaned back against the bar, elbows propped up behind. "Been in the 'pen' down at Boise up to about a year ago. Been there another ten year, only they cut him loose on good behavior. It was Hines' testimony that sent him over the road."

"Must be a tough one."

"Mostly John Bull stubborn. But plenty hard, too, or he'd never of come back to this range. Reckon he's got more enemies than friends around here. Don't take up with nobody, and always squabblin' with his neighbors. More trouble brewin' right now over some fence locations. Funny part is, he's right most of the time."

"Sounds like an interesting character. By the way, Kane is my name. Harney? Glad to know you, Harney. What brand of poison do you take?" Kane motioned to the bartender.

Sipping slowly, he admired the puncher's careless draining of the fiery liquor.

"What did they send Prout up for, seeing he didn't kill Hines?" he asked.

Harney settled back.

"Well, as I was sayin', Hines is the guy Prout didn't quite get, seven year ago. Arch Boyer was with Andy that day, and Arch didn't get away. Prout cut loose on him first, and that give Andy a chance to duck into the brush. Miracle he got away even then, 'cause Prout could hit anything that Winchester could reach to. Only thing that saved him was the brush and some bluffs that stopped Prout's horse. When Andy come out the lower end of that thorn patch he didn't have much clothes left but his shoes an' some tatters. He hid out till dark an' then got to the sheriff. Sheriff went out with a posse next day to get Prout. They found Arch where Prout dropped him.

"Prout didn't make no attempt to run. He was home with his wife when the posse come. Figured they'd be along, he said. Had his horse saddled ready to go with them."

"About the last thing they expected, I suppose," Kane suggested, as Harney poured himself another drink.

"They was lookin' for trouble all right." Harney set down the empty glass. "Prout was a dead shot, an' afraid of nothin' nor nobody. The boys was none of them sorry when he came along peaceable.

"News of the killin' got all over the country that day, an' when the posse came in the town was full. All us waddies from down on the Circle Dot was in, havin' just finished the spring brandin' that morning. Hines' outfit had been busy talkin' up a necktie party, but they wasn't none too popular anyway, an' a lot of folks suspicioned that Arch an' Andy had got what was comin' to 'em. It was pretty well known that the Hines bunch had been tryin' to run Prout off by cuttin' his fences and strayin' his stock. So when the posse reported that they had found Prout's fence cut a lot of places, and two pair of wire clippers at the place of the shootin', most everyone sided with him, even though they hadn't much use for him personal.

"That's what saved his neck when it came time for the trial. Most of the jury was homesteaders that had wanted one time or another to do some shootin' of their own, what with having fences cut and stock scattered. So they put in for a light sentence and Prout got off with 5 to 15 years."

Kane looked again toward the poker table and Andy Hines. The group seemed to be talking a lot for poker players, he noted. Uninviting, too; other men gave them plenty of space.

"How did folks take it when Prout showed up so soon?"

Harney shifted to view the room. "They wasn't anybody overjoyed, so to speak. Andy, over there, has been scared of his shadow ever since. Him an' some more like him has been runnin' cattle down around Prout's homestead, eatin' up all the Old Lady's winter feed and tryin' to starve her out. But when Prout come back sooner'n Hines figured on, it kinda' took the show outa' him.

"Didn't take Prout long to put a crimp in that crowdin' business, either. First thing he did was to slap a fence around an additional homestead in just the right place to break that outfit's hoggin' operations in two. That's where the fight is comin' now."

"I take it you'd rather see Prout win, even if he *is* a trouble maker," Kane ventured.

"I got no love for Prout, but I'd admire to see him lick that Hines outfit. They're crooked as hell, but you can't hook 'em on anything. 'Fraid Prout don't stand much show, though. Too many against him."

Harney hooked a discreet thumb toward the poker table. "That's the outfit right there. An' I'll bet what they're talkin' about between deals ain't poker!"

Kane surveyed the group again. They were an unpromising lot, he agreed. Didn't look like one man would have much chance fighting them alone.

"No, sir," Harney concluded. "His only chance is to bluff 'em out. Think he's lookin' for them to make a move on him any day now. They're the kind that'll stoop to anything to get him out of the way, if they can get up enough nerve to go through with it."

★　★　★

The necessity for more brush ducking recalled Kane to his present surroundings. Crossing another gulch, the trail climbed to a rocky bench that ran for nearly a mile, then zigzagged steeply into a larger canyon. From far below came a faint undulating sound that marked the flow of a fair sized creek. Mopping his face and neck from time to time, the rider alternately cursed the heat and thought hopefully of shade and water below.

Couldn't be more than a couple of miles father he guessed. Harney had told him he would find Prout living in a stone cabin built into the side of the hill near the mouth of this creek. Mrs. Prout, Harney explained, was with the two sons on summer range in the timber country. Prout had stayed below to irrigate his hay patches and guard his fences. You couldn't miss the place, said Harney; it was the only habitation for miles and the trail passed right in front of it. Prout probably would be in, as the cabin was cool, and from it he could see most of the disputed fence.

That must be the upper end of the place now, Kane decided, viewing a fence line which cut across the canyon some distance down the creek. You had to hand it to Prout for the placing of that fence, he admitted. Running a quarter of a mile up each side of the steep canyon, it effectively cut off any natural movement of stock not privileged to pass through the gates. No wonder the Hines gang objected! Doubtless they had cooked up the complaints that had brought him here.

The sound of the creek grew louder. The sweating horse quickened its pace at the scent of water. Another half hour, thought Kane.

A languid breeze drifted up the canyon, carrying from far below the faint barking of a dog. The barking grew more insistent.

"Wonder what's ailing that lousy cur? Probably try to eat me alive when I get there.

211

The whole country looks dead as a mummy. Damn the heat!"

Kane slapped futilely at a fly seemingly created and sent solely to annoy him.

The barking ended in a sharp yelp, and simultaneously the echoing crack of a rifle bounced back and forth up the canyon. Kane pulled up his horse. What now—was that lunatic shooting at *him*? No Winchester would carry that far. He listened and peered intently. Another report cracked along the canyon walls. Then silence. Nothing stirred.

Minutes dragged by. Whatever was going on apparently did not stem from his presence. Still no sign of life below. The homesteader's hut, beyond a ridge top, was hidden from his view. Probably on this side of the creek, right across from those two converging gulches, judging by the sounds. Would that dog never bark again? Every sense intent, he eagerly sought the sound he had cursed in irritation a short time before. The continuing silence was ominous.

Kane tensed as a new volley burst from the cabin area, followed by sustained cracking of several rifles. Suddenly he understood. The Hines outfit, ganging up on Prout! Laying their plans at the saloon last night!

What chance had one man against half a dozen? Suicide to try to help, though, without a gun. Kane gritted his teeth and swore.

Maybe Prout could hold them off, at that, unless they got to him through the window or door. After all, even high-powered rifles couldn't do much to a stone house built into the side of a hill. Kane pictured the burly Englishman crouched against the wall, rifle gripped for swift retaliation should the chance come. Or perhaps there was a cellar opening from the hut into the hillside where he could take refuge.

More long minutes waiting for the firing to cease, followed by longer minutes of wishing for any kind of sound. Straining toward the hidden scene, Kane came erect at sight of a mass of rocks, debris and dust spouting high in the air, followed by a crashing roar that shook the canyon walls. His horse lunged, nearly unseating him. Dynamite!

The final echoes of the blast rumbled into distant silence. A mile away the cloud of yellow dust dispersed lazily in the breeze, belying the violence that had created it. Silence settled on the landscape like a pall.

In sharp reaction, Kane spurred down the steep trail. He'd face the whole murdering crew rather than wait longer! Anything but sit still.

He forced his thirsty horse across the creek, and vainly tried to put the animal to a gallop along the rough trail to the fence. The gate was wired securely shut. Tearing his hands on the barbed strands in a fever of haste, he realized despairingly the probable futility of his efforts. Could even a cellar have withstood that blast? Evidently the assassins had planned their work well, even to the warding off of such unexpected interference as his would have been. No doubt there had been a man posted to guard this gate, who had watched him as he sat his horse on the trail above. Nevertheless, he was driven to make such speed as he could. No longer any danger, he reasoned. The attackers would be leaving the scene of their crime even more urgently than he pressed toward it.

At last the final bend of the trail was rounded. Kane slowed his horse to a walk. Shattered rocks strewed the trail for a hundred yards from the gaping hole where the cabin had stood. Here and there a scrap of metal glinted in the sun, the remains of kitchen utensils.

The horse stiffened and snorted at the lingering odor of high explosives. Kane dismounted and approached the hole. Not one chance in a million, he thought. But he *might* find something, some hope of life. Would there be a cellar?

He found nothing.

Hat in hand, Kane gazed about, reconstructing the scene. The ambushers had hidden in the brush of those gulches across the creek—no need to look for evidence. From there they had fired through the door and window from two angles, keeping the doomed man in his fortress-tomb while comrades planted the dynamite from the up-hill side. Must have taken cases of the stuff to blow that hole! Kane shuddered.

A final look around. Nothing more to see. Nothing to do if he did find a—a scrap of—. The slipping of his foot on something soft, springy, brought sharp prickles to his scalp. He stepped back hastily, then forced himself to look down, his eyes involuntarily seeking what he hoped not to see.

Yes, there it was. He stooped quickly, bending double to peer closely, then straightened abruptly, his face twisted in a brief reflex of grimace.

"Part of the dog," he said loudly. Probably just part of the dog."

Staring at nothing, Special Agent A. T. Kane groped in his right shirt pocket, brought out a heavy manila envelope, counterpart of the one which two hours before he had taken from his left shirt pocket. Fumbling inside he pulled out several official looking sheets, the top one labeled: Special Investigation Report Form. From somewhere he found a pencil.

Spreading the sheet carefully on his right knee, the agent slowly printed across its face:

CASE CLOSED — NO APPEAL

IV
RANDOM TALES

The first two of these short bits recount early experiences of an old friend of mine, now famous as the author of many books on Pacific Northwest missionary history. The other two, though not from such impeccable sources, are based on factual incidents. Only because they seem so improbable as fact, they have been embroidered with enough invented dialogue and other details to put them in the "yarn" class for readers not prepared to accept them at face value. All four are on the humorous side, which is the element that made them seem worth saving.

KENNETH B. PLATT

White Man with a Red Face

Despite ample historical record showing that the American red man, continually maligned in his progressive defeat and subjugation during the 19th century, was generally a more honest and moral citizen than his white conqueror, the term "thieving Indians" for many years was a familiar one in the idiom of the West. I grew up with it, and not until manhood did I begin to learn that much of the pilfering laid at the wigwam flap of the hapless reservation resident really belonged at the door of some malicious white neighbor. It was all too easy for the guilty white man to raise the false cry, "thieving Indians," and have it accepted as genuine.

With better education and freer mixing with his white contemporaries in recent years, the Indian has lived down this unjust reputation. But he is still conscious of the injustice he has suffered under the ancient canard, and seldom misses an opportunity to set the record straight.

Such an occasion arose a good many years ago when a white Presbyterian minister was digging into the history of the Spalding missionary work among the Nez Perces in northern Idaho. This researcher had become well acquainted with a very able Nez Perce Indian Presbyterian minister who was assisting him in relocating historical sites and documents important to his study. The two traveled together to many points of interest, the Indian serving as guide, interpreter, and intermediary, as the need arose.

On one such trip the two men had driven in the researcher's car to a remote part of the Nez Perce reservation to view the site of some important early mission work. When they had driven to the end of the road it was necessary to leave the car and walk a considerable distance, being gone for some hours. As they were preparing to leave the car the white minister thought of the precious load of hard-earned historic items packed in the back seat, and a very unpleasant thought crossed his mind. Not wishing to offend his friend, he sought for some moments for the right words, and finally asked, "Do you suppose it is safe to leave the car unlocked while we are gone?"

"Perfectly safe," replied the Indian minister. "There isn't a white man for miles around here."

SALMON RIVER SAGA

The Preacher and the Bear

A minister I have known many years, now a national figure, during his seminary days spent a summer doing home missions work among the loggers on the Olympic Peninsula in northwestern Washington. Since recognized and set aside as a primitive area in the Olympic National Park, this region in those days immediately after World War I, was very primitive indeed. It was penetrated by only a few roads and trails, and these were mostly rudimentary. One of the most densely timbered regions in the world, it was almost void of habitation, save for the itinerant logging camps that followed the swath of axe and saw hacking at the fringes of the wilderness.

Notwithstanding his training and trust in divine providence, my friend was far from at ease in this environment. It was his first experience in timber country, out of an Iowa boyhood. Many a person raised in timber country, including yours truly, has often felt the somber pressure of a dense, almost skyless timber canopy, and can readily appreciate the depressing effect it had upon this boy from the Corn Belt. Add to this an unreasoning but very real fear of wild animals, and you can begin to appreciate the devotion to duty my friend displayed in carrying out his assignment. For there was then, and still is, a numerous population of bears and not a few cougar, as well as a wide range of smaller animals, in the Olympic Peninsula.

Of all the beasts that roamed these woods, my friend most feared bears. This fact did not pass unnoticed among his clientele, who gave him the benefit of many a magnified yarn not intended for his peace of mind so far as bears were concerned. His uneasiness was further heightened by the fact that the daytime feeding habits of the bears resulted in his seeing them rather frequently.

But, to get on with the story, our fledgling minister had equipped himself for the physical aspect of this work with a bicycle, with which he was enabled to cover a much wider area than walking would have permitted. Being of small means, he had been forced to content himself with a well-used machine, an old-timer of the pre-coaster-brake era. It had its advantages on the climbs, being light, but on the down grades the rider worked about as hard braking as he had worked climbing, keeping his feet on the fixed-drive pedals. To minimize this labor as far as possible, my friend would coast at every opportunity, simply sticking his feet out beyond the pedals and letting gravity take over.

This labor and time saving practice proved itself so worthy in his opinion that he applied it to ever steeper and longer slopes as he became more familiar with the roads and trails and more confident of his ability to overcome such obstacles as fallen limbs, open culverts, lethargic porcupines, etc., at brisk speeds. The technique held one element of risk that could not be overcome. Once under way at a rapid clip, the rider could not get his feet back onto the fast turning pedals to do a braking job of any sort—he was committed for the duration of that particular slope, come what might. He was the irresistable force, and he took his chances on the occurrence of the immovable object.

But all went well, and the summer neared its close without serious misadventure. All, that is, until one fine morning when Clifford set off on a trek that was to take him to one of the farthest camps. Armed with the Good Book and a plentiful supply of tracts, he had covered several miles and was in fine fettle when he topped the longest hill on the route. The trail was familiar from previous trips. The hill before him was long and steep, but the trail was smooth and hard, and perfectly straight save for the one bend which lay fifty yards below him. He had braked to his bend, then coasted the remaining distance, on several occasions. This morning, why not coast the whole distance? No sooner thought than dared. (Who says preachers aren't made of the same stuff as the rest of us.) He mounted, stuck out his feet, and was off. Half way to the bend the pedals were flying at a rate that permitted no retreat to a controlled speed; at the bend itself they were beginning to blur.

It was then that he saw the bear. Less than a hundred yards away, the huge creature was lumbering comfortably up the trail, all unaware of the terror bearing down upon it. Frozen with fear, the rider looked in panic for a turnout, a bank against which he could throw the speeding bike, a thicket into which he could plunge without being torn limb from limb. There was none. A yell of desperation burst from his lips as he bore down upon the unheeding bruin.

At his yell the startled bear half reared to its hind legs, preparing to do battle with this strange invader. But that reflex action was quickly superseded by an instinct for flight. Away went the bear, down the trail.

Now as everyone knows, who knows bears, a bear is not at his best running downhill. And the steeper the hill, the greater the bear's dislike for running it. This disinclination reaches a point where, on extremely steep slopes, the bear will turn around and back down, just as he always comes down a tree backward, since his claws are hooked to brake in only one direction.

The bear in this case was a normal bear. He was not inclined to run down hill any faster than absolutely necessary. And, notwithstanding his initial fright, he vastly underrated the speed of his pursuer. Under the circumstances the whizzing bicycle and its hapless rider swiftly narrowed the lead which, needless to say, both principals regarded as all too small in the first place. In a matter of seconds the gravel from the flying feet of the bear was peppering the face of the oncoming bikeman.

Now the hill here concerned was not so steep that a bear left to his own devices would back down it, let alone think of backing down it in the circumstances here described. But the bear didn't like this downhill charge any the more for being forced into it, and he was looking for an out. Unlike the Irishman who thought if he couldn't outrun the train on a perfectly level track he would certainly have no chance across country, the bear doubtless felt that if he could only get to going up hill he could do better. So every few jumps he would turn his head to look at the bank above the trail, hunting for a low spot or a hole in the brush. Every such survey brought a momentary slackening of speed, followed by a more urgent spurt when the bear saw that the demon behind him was ever closer.

This process of speeding the bear was by no means being left to chance during this time by my friend. Whether by design or by instinct, he was giving forth with a volume of yells that gave the bear about all the encouragement for speed that human lungs could devise. And as the gap between them rapidly narrowed, the efforts of both bear and man were pushed to limits which neither of them, probably, ever approached again.

Well, the bear never did find a hole in the brush or a low spot in the bank. In the end he reacted like a lot of us humans do when nothing else offers—he just made the best of what he had. When my friend was so close that the bear's hind paws were practically fanning the handlebars at every jump and he was ready to close his eyes for the moment of actually running under the bear's belly, old bruin gave one last mighty, desperate heave and betook himself up the almost perpendicular bank, scrabbling a shower of gravel, sticks and brush onto the flying bike as it zipped past.

The end of the hill by this time was not far away, and the rider made the distance in record time, having no other choice. But when the choice did come to him on the opposite slope he was in no mood to tarry. So thoroughly unnerved was he, and so sure that the bear would now be pursuing him, that he wheeled off on a side trail which soon ended at an abandoned log loading platform. There he took to his heels, and soon was lost. Still running, he came to a large swift stream into which he dashed unheeding and, halfway across, was swept off his feet. Since he couldn't swim a stroke he very well might have drowned had not unseen persons on the opposite shore come to his rescue. When he finally regained control of himself he found he had fallen in with a large-scale bootlegger's camp.

But that is a story in itself. This is just a bear story.

KENNETH B. PLATT

Incident at Black Bear Inn

I am not sure whether this should be called a "bear" story or a "bare" story—there are elements of both in it. But I shall content myself with the telling and let you put your own tag on the yarn. I'll give it to you as told to me by one of the two witnesses. There were a good many participants, too, but when you have read this you will see why it is not likely any of them have ever volunteered the account. They were probably too involved or too excited at the time to give a coherent account even at this late date. It is also just possible none of them saw the humor of the incident. Anyway, it's too good to keep and it's a good bet you've never heard it before. So be it, and here goes:

"Back in the middle 1930's," relates our witness, "I was traveling northern California as territory man for a large equipment firm. My route took me through a lot of scenic country, including a portion of the high Sierras much visited by summer tourists. Along this route was a wayside place known as Black Bear Inn which I had found to be a pretty good place to eat. It wasn't a swank establishment. I guess maybe some people would even say it was pretty rustic. The "plumbing" was still out in the open, and the guy who built the place had hacked out no more brush and timber to accommodate his whole enterprise than was necessary to encourage customers. The floor of the Inn itself was rough, there was no juke box, and the furniture was second hand. But the location was nice, the place had a friendly atmosphere, the food was good, and the prices were in my range, so I usually ate there whenever I went that way.

"One day as I approached Black Bear Inn, late in the afternoon and with my mind fixed on nothing else but a good meal, I drew up behind a large bus taking its own sweet time on the narrow winding road. Before I got a chance to pass it I had plenty of time to notice that it was licensed in Missouri and that it was loaded with women.

"I've got nothing against either Missouri or women—I just mention these items because they come into the story.

"Well, I wasn't far from the Black Bear when I passed them, and I hadn't much more than got parked and dusted off when the bus pulled in, too. The driver parked it right in front of where I was standing on the Inn porch. He opened the passenger door and women began piling out. That was when I began to take notice.

"They were about as odd a bunch as a guy would ever see. There must have been twenty-five or thirty of them, and they were of all ages and sizes. But the thing that had me gawking was the clothes some of them had on. Honest, I saw just about everything in the book, back to and including button shoes. They went to the other extreme, too, but I was used to that, being in and out of California resort towns all the time. They all just kind of milled around for a few minutes, looking the place over, like any bunch of tourists will. I guess I just stood there with my eyes hanging out.

220

"By that time the bus driver had made the rounds, thumping all the tires with a lug wrench to check the air pressure, and headed up the steps by me. Some of the passengers were beginning to drift inside, some heading for the Chic Sales facility across the yard marked "LADIES," and some were still busy getting the cramps out of their muscles and the wrinkles out of their clothes. Me, I was still gawking.

"Well, being naturally inquisitive and not too bashful, I tagged the driver as he came up, to get the inside dope.

" 'School teachers,' " he gave out, " 'on a vacation tour.' "

"That still didn't explain it to me. Where I came from school teachers had always been a pretty up and coming grade of chicks, regardless of age.

" 'Some parts of Missouri are pretty backwoods yet,' " the driver admitted. " 'Most of the teachers who take tours like this are the ones from out-of-the-way places. First time away from home, for a lot of them, since they went to school themselves. That's been quite a while for some. It takes a trip like this to show them how things has changed.

" 'You'd be su'prised,' " he went on, " 'how much a lot of them has changed just since we started. Specially the young ones. They's six, seven girls there that I bet hain't got a stitch of the stuff today they left home with a month ago. All new clothes. Some, I guess, won't ever change.' "

"You could see which ones he meant, both ways. A few of them were right up to the minute, and there were some that looked about as changeable as the Rock of Gibralter. One of these was just about big enough to remind you of Gibralter, too. She was one of them that had on button shoes.

"Well, while we were talking they had all got lined out, with about a dozen heading down 'that well worn trail' and the rest going inside. The driver and I were just ready to go in, when a black bear came around the corner of the Inn.

"He kind of startled me. I had been in and out of there all summer and hadn't ever seen any bear, or knew they had one around. My first idea was that he was one of those garbage bears that get to hanging around summer resorts. But about then I noticed he had a collar on, and my hair settled back into place.

"He was a big one. Somebody ought to do something about him, I thought. Even if he is tame, he hadn't ought to be running loose around a place like this. I hadn't any more than thought it when he started down the trail. Oh, oh, I thought, here comes trouble. He kept on going.

"Well, as I said to start with, the Black Bear Inn was what some people would call on the rustic side. The 'LADIES' place was definitely designed for the wide open spaces. The place for the men was just like it, for that matter, but that's beside the point. Anyway, it was shaped like a real wide capital U, with the open side toward the Inn, and

221

a sort of false front standing out away from it about four—five feet. There was a nice lattice work around each end of this false front, extending past the ends of the building and giving the patrons complete privacy from the outside world, even though the building didn't have any door. I guess that must be a kind of a basic design, because you see them like that all over the West even yet.

"Well, the bear went on down the trail, like I saying. He went right up to the end of the lattice where the main traffic went in. I didn't know whether to yell, or what to do. Then he turned off and started around back, and I sort of relaxed. But I hadn't taken two breaths when back he came and in he went.

"Things happened after that, and they happened fast.

"First, there was the most blood curdling scream I ever heard, followed by a lot of shrieks and commotion. The first one out was the bear. He came out the way he went in, only he didn't make the corner around the lattice. He came right through it. He was a traveling bear in more ways than one. He was making about the best time of any bear I ever saw, and he had a lady's handbag hung over his left ear. In spite of his hurry he was only running on three legs. Every jump he would fan his right ear with his right front paw. I thought at first that he was confused, and that he was trying to get rid of the handbag but hadn't got it figured out yet, but after while I concluded he knew what he was doing all right. The gal who screamed must have screamed right into that ear, because the bear sat down and went right on fanning it for a while after he got rid of the handbag.

"Well, so much for the bear.

"However fast he got out of that place it wasn't fast enough for some of those women. They stampeded, and when they came out they knocked that false front down like it was cardboard. You know how it is with a doll house, with one side off so you can look into all the rooms and see all the details. That's how it was from then on. You could see then that even though the building was of simple design it had been equipped with enough wash bowls, mirrors, and other essential fixtures to accommodate a lot of people at once. And when the false front came down all the fixtures were in use.

"I don't know what I'd have done in their place, so I don't blame those women for not seeming to know what to do next. The ones that had stampeded seemed to be in a worse fix some ways than the ones that had stayed. Two or three of them had their dresses half torn off in the scramble, and every one of them had lost her handbag, and you know how helpless a woman is without a handbag. They just stood around in bunches about half hysterical, some looking for the bear, some trying to pin up their clothes, some looking back down the trail, and all of them jabbering like mad.

"I guess most of them that had stayed maybe hadn't even seen the bear, and didn't know what had happened. There was one young chick that was down to panties and bra, scrubbing her face at a wash bowl. Another, not so slender, was bravely sacrificing the comfort of the day for an evening of allure by putting on a very tight girdle. She was just half through this ritual when the wall came down. She had been wearing slacks and she grabbed them and tried to put them back on, but they wouldn't go on over the girdle. She put on quite a show before she finally found the right bag and got into a dress. The other one might as well have been performing before footlights, for all it bothered her.

"There were a couple of lucky ones who were just tidying up their hair, but I guess they thought they were in an earthquake, the way they took for the open.

"Of course the ones worst off were the three 'queens.' Two of them 'dethroned' so fast they were just a kind of a blur, but the third one was 'Gibralter,' and she was in a bad way. Not only was her size against a fast getaway, but her old fashioned black 'Bloomers' took a lot of tugging to get in place.

"Well, you know how it is at a fire or some other big excitement—you see a lot of things just in flashes, without intending to see them. I mean, they're there, and you see them, and you don't have time to think till afterward. That's how it was with all those things. The bus driver and I were standing there on the porch facing all the action, and we saw all I've told you about, I suppose, in less than a minute. It all happened so fast we didn't have time to think. We could see the bear hadn't hurt anyone—he was worse scared than the women, at least at the start. Of course, everyone inside the Inn had rushed out to see what was going on, and they were milling around asking us, and that didn't make us any calmer. Right after the stampede we noticed that one of the women had fainted just outside the lattice, and you couldn't tell how many might have run over her. The driver started to run down to pick her up, but the ones that were left down there screeched so loud that he decided against it and came back.

"About that time I noticed a girl right down in front of me with nothing on but her scanties, so I grabbed the blanket off the seat of my coupe and went to put it around her. My dad told me when I was a kid never to come up on a strange filly from behind, but I wasn't thinking about that just then, and it sure was a mistake. She didn't even see me coming till I was just ready to drape the blanket over her, and when she did see me she must have thought I was part of the act because she screamed and took out of there, heading for the woods. There was a lot of poison oak out there that sure wasn't going to do her any good, so I yelled at her to stop and took out after her.

"It was a short race, because the clearing wasn't more than a hundred feet across, but I was up to her before she hit the woods. I've wondered ever since just what I would have done with her if I had got that blanket around her—probably would have got my eyes scratched out. Anyway, just as I was reaching for her again I stepped on one edge of

223

the blanket and down I went and rolled myself up in the darn thing like a cocoon. By the time I got untangled she was out of sight.

"With that the driver and I gave up trying to help and took to laughing. Not that we hadn't laughed plenty already, but now we were able to give it full time. The more we laughed the madder the women got, but we couldn't stop. They'd found out by then that the bear was tame, and that made them all the madder. It took them about twenty minutes to coax that one back out of the woods. I don't remember what they did about the poison oak on her, if I ever knew. I couldn't tell you what they did with the one that fainted, either, but she was all right after a bit.

"By the time they found all their things and got each other pinned up they were so mad they cancelled their dinner reservation and ordered the driver to take them on to the next place. How he ever kept that bus in the road the next few miles I don't know, because he was too weak from laughing to get into it by himself—I had to help him."

SALMON RIVER SAGA

Charley and the Swede

An Irishman ot my acquaintance, now a responsible federal official, was in his youth a person of no mean ability in the "manly art of self defense." Charley was far more than just "handy with his dukes," to use the idiom of that day. Tough as rawhide from a hard youth on a pioneer cattle ranch, he had shown more than ordinary aptitude in applying a year of capable boxing instruction received in a term of prep school attendance. With some hundred eight-five pounds of raw-boned weight to put into his blows, Charley had little difficulty in winning an undisputed crown in his local territory.

In all fairness to Charley, I hasten to point out that this crown was almost wholly unsought. Charley was not the bellicose or belligerent type. He was, and still is, naturally reserved, and most of his fistic encounters arose out of the desire of others to topple the invisible crown from Charley's curly head. From such engagements Charley was never known to retreat. So far as that category of prowess is concerned, we may truly say that Charley retired an undefeated champion.

But there was one notable exception in the record of Charley's fistic glory. That exception was his encounter with the Swede.

The Swede must remain a nameless character, noble though he was. Our only knowledge of him is through the incident here related. And, important as this incident is in the life of our hero, it came and went without disclosing, further than his stalwart race, the identity of the man who deflected Charley's career definitely and permanetly into peaceful pursuits.

But let us get on with the story.

In the rip-roarin' railroad town of Murphy, Idaho, in its 1914 heyday, a wide assortment of stalwart men of many arduous pursuits commonly foregathered for relief from the strain and boredom of such occupations as hardrock mining in the nearby Owyhee Mountains; wagon freighting to the mines through one of the roughest pieces of country ever conceived by nature; raising cattle and horses on a profitable basis despite the efforts of some rather able rustlers; and various associated trades. These various activities had two things in common: they produced men of outstanding physical capacities and they produced ill-tasting dusts which only alcohol in various dilutions was deemed capable of washing from parched throats. It was only natural, therefore, that the dispensary of these dilutions, the frontier saloon, was sanctuary to all the sons of toil in their hours of need.

Into Murphy on a certain hot afternoon rode our Charley, together with a friend named Joe. The dust of the long trail from Meadow Creek Ranch, thirty miles away, was sifting down their necks and gritting in their throats. With relief now only blocks away, they dismounted smartly at the livery barn watering trough and stood none too patiently while thirsty mounts gulped its alkaline contents. Unsaddling and "cuffing down" were done in jig time. Five minutes later the sweaty horses were rolling luxuriously in the dust of the corral and Charley and Joe were making expectantly toward the one emporium to manly thirst which the town boasted.

Even the uninitiate of this later, softer generation will have no difficulty, I am sure, in appreciating the shock felt by our friends upon being hailed by the first responsible citizen on their route and urgently warned to keep out of the Red Stallion.

"Why?" chimed Charley and Joe in simultaneous disbelief.

"Has 'Shorty' got the smallpox, or something?" Joe followed hopefully. Not waiting for an answer, "I've had smallpox," he said.

"Me, too," said Charley.

"No," their informant replied, "it ain't smallpox, but it's a mighty violent form of plague."

"Yeah?" queried Charley.

"There's a Swede in there about four axe handles high," said the R. C., "and he's throwed out every man that's went in there this afternoon."

"Such as?" leads Charley.

"Buck Tingle, Lefty Murdock and Big Mike," says the R. C. significantly, ticking off three recognized barroom greats, "to name a few. The last two in one bust. Of course, It's you fellows' necks if you want to try it."

"How does this 'Swenski' operate?" Charley wants to know.

"He calls you every name in the book and then invites you up to drink."

"Then what?"

"Nobody's got that far—nobody would take the rawhidin'."

"What you think, Joe?" Charley asks.

"I'm pretty thirsty," Joe says, thinking how handy Charley is with his dukes.

"Let's go," says Charley.

"Well, don't say I didn't warn you," encourages the responsible citizen, looking regretfully after them. "Sorry I can't go with you, but I got business to tend to."

"We'll be seeing you," says Charley, "after we get a drink. Thanks for the tip."

With that they headed on down toward the Red Stallion.

"He's probably not so tough," Joe spoke in the next block, still thinking of how Charley packed a mule kick in each hand.

"Ought to be mellowed up pretty well by now," was Charley's thought.

"And if he ain't, maybe we can soften him up a bit," Joe judged, giving Charley a full step lead at the Red Stallion door.

Well, there was the Swede, all right, with his right foot on the rail and his right elbow on the bar and an empty glass in his left hand that he was just shoving over to Shorty for a refill. As Charley and Joe stepped into the room he faced around and set both elbows on the rail behind him.

"What the --- /***@@@¢"& ---., ##--? you think you doin' har," he took off on a blistering tirade that displayed full mastery of all the choicer revilements known to mule skinners, straw bosses and others used to dealing with recalcitrant animal and human flesh.

"You going to take that off him," asks Joe, halfway through the Swede's review of their nefarious ancestry. "If I was as handy with my dukes as you are, I don't think I would."

It was in that moment that vainglory, for one time, and one time only, found our Charley vulnerable. What a feather—what a glorious feather—for his cap to add the Swede to his list of conquests! No crude rough-and-tumble brawler he, like Buck and Lefty and Big Mike. No, he would simply walk up to the Swede, explode one swift, unexpected keg of dynamite on his jaw, and then step out of the way while his victim crashed out at full length.

By the time the Swede had exhausted his vocabulary and was reaching for his glass, Charley was standing squarely in front of him, his distance measured, his muscles cocked and primed for the kill. As the unsuspecting Swede faced back around, the refilled glass in his left hand, his giant frame relaxed against the bar, Charley hoisted his very best haymaker. It came with such dazzling swiftness that the Swede didn't even see it coming, So swiftly it came that it crossed in front of the Swede's left arm as he swung back around before that arm had time to get in the way. It landed on the exposed jaw with all the power of Charley's eager hundred eighty-five pounds solidly behind it. It jarred Charley's arm so hard it hurt all the way down to his hips.

And what did the Swede do?

He looked annoyed—very annoyed.

"You looka har, now, kid," he set his glass down hard on the bar, "You do that again and I wipe up this place with you!"

And with that he downed his glass, still looking annoyed, and shoved it back at Shorty.

Charley looked at Joe; Joe looked at Charley.

"Let's go," said Charley.

They went.

KENNETH B. PLATT

Salmon River Saga
ABOUT THE AUTHOR

Kenneth B. Platt was born in 1907 at the bottom of the Salmon River canyon, some 25 miles south of Winchester, in the panhandle of Idaho. His parents, John A. and Emma C. Platt, were the first permanent settlers in the area. Remains of their pioneer log cabin still stand near the mouth of Deer Creek, ten miles up the Salmon from its confluence with the Snake River at the mouth of Hells Canyon.

The family lived at this isolated ranch site until the fall of 1917, when they moved to a stock ranch near Genesee, 60 miles to the north, on the edge of the fabled Palouse Country wheat farming area. In high school at Genesee the author found his first writing interest as the initiator and editor of the school newspaper in 1924. Again an editor in his senior year at the University of Idaho in 1930, Platt wrote "E-da-ho" as his first poem, to grace the frontispiece photo in the agricultural college annual. It started a flow of verse that surged through the 1930s and 1940s, and has continued at varying pace ever since, to be collected in his book, *Underneath The Bough*, brought out in 1976.

As an employee of the federal Grazing Service (now the Bureau of Land Management), and later in foreign aid work of the State Department, Platt wrote both professional and popular articles. His published works, ranging from land management subjects to national defense, have appeared in such diverse outlets as *The American Cattle Producer, The Idaho Farmer, The Pacific Northwesterner, The Scientific Monthly, The Oregonian* newspaper of Portland, *The Idaho Statesman* of Boise, and many smaller newspapers. Notable in career channels are his "Land Reform In Iran," and "Land Reform In United Arab Republic," the country histories prepared for a 1970 world review of land reform experience.

Now retired at Moscow, Idaho, with his wife, Jeanette, Platt looks back on kaleidoscopic memories. "In 32 years I was stationed at 15 different places. The longest we ever lived at one place was six years, and that was at Tehran," he recalls. B.L.M. duties took him to or through more than 40 states from 1936 to 1958. Foreign aid assignments in Egypt, Iran and Korea brought travel through most countries of Europe and Asia in the 1959-70 period.

"In a way, most of my adult life has been spent in pioneering," Platt says. "My first permanent full time job, titled 'Assistant In Extension,' University of Idaho, was a writing and editing job created to sort out and localize the informational materials spewed broadside to the state agricultural colleges by the Agricultural Adjustment Administration, the Soil Conservation Service, and other new federal agencies of the early 1930s. As a second duty I ran the new one-man farm and home news program of the College.

229

"After four years of that I stepped into the new and burgeoning field of range conservation, in the brand new role of range examiner, where I was responsible to say how many livestock for how many months each ranch or range area would feed. This was virgin territory for all concerned, and a lot of the results were in the "guesstimate" class until we gained experience. Going up the ranks in this field opened fresh territory at each level, with new demands for initiative and ingenuity to deal with new situations. I must have gained some reputation in this regard, for I drew such special jobs as superintendent of the Squaw Butte Range Station at Burns, Ore., the only such station operated by the Grazing Service; writing a history of grazing on the western range lands; and determining the navigability of the Green River in Utah, a once-only report used to adjudicate oil and uranium rights in the bed of the river.

"I went to Egypt in the beginning of the Point IV program as one of the first two Grazing Service men to go into foreign aid. One of the projects I worked on there located the site for the now famous High Aswan Dam. Later, in Iran, I worked on the revolutionary front of land reform, and on food relief programs to bridge the gap between local production and national food requirements. In Korea my assignment was to construct a national agricultural economics research organization that could show the farm level profit or loss outcome of farm enterprise changes promoted by the Korean government. There were no precedents in any of those jobs—each was a pioneering venture in which I had to find my own way."

What next? A book of recollections and history on ranch life in the Genesee area during the closing years of horse farming (1917-1935) is planned as a sequel to the present volume. As editor of the *Quarterly Bulletin* of the Latah County Museum Society, Platt plans to continue developing the rich field of pioneer history subjects lying neglected in Latah and surrounding counties. Poetry writing also is an abiding interest.

Closing The Gate

Their work completed, horse and rider paused —
    Herd newly pastured, fences all secure —
To close the gate, the final act of care;
    Then home to cabin, comfort and corral.

So went their days when yet the land was young;
    So went the years, till now the land is old;
And fences are but ghosts along the rims,
    Where spectral riders check that all is well.

When wafts the breeze adown the breaks at dawn,
    When sigh the pines of days no longer known,
Then stir the forms of past forever gone
    Across closed gates to memories now flown.

Kenneth B. Platt
February 12, 1978

Index

A

Alberta, 142, 145
Alforja, 51
Allegheny, 194-196
Allentown, Dakota, 16
Amundson, Roald, 103
Androcles, 68
Arabs, 51; United Arab Kingdom, 229
Aram family, 20
Arizona, 34
Arrowheads, 74
Ashenfelter, Cora Orr, 188
Aswan Dam, Egypt, 230
Aytch place, 81

B

Balboa, 103
Barefooted, 71
Bassano trail, 143
Batdorf, Jesse, 18, 136, 146, 160; Jessnie, 18, 145-159; Chas., 18; Bertha, 18; Emma Caroline, 135, 136; Martha, 188; Mary Gaumer, 18; Sam, 18
Bean, Mabel E., 150; Isabella M., 150
Bear, Grizzly, 142, 217-219, 220-224
Beaver Creek, 18, 19, 145
Bedwell family, 81; Beatrice, 97, 186; Ellen, 97, 186; Jack, 97; Kenneth, 97
Belle, 54
Big Eddy, 27
Big House, 34-41
Big Trees, 88
Big Sandbar, 27
Bitterroot Mts., 7
Black, Charlie, 141
Black Bear Inn, 220-224
Blackfoot Indians, 143
Blue Mts., 19, 146
Boise, Fort, 7; City, 88; Basin, 19, 145
Boles family, 20
Boots, cowboy, 55-57
Bottorf, Martin, 58-60, 78, 108, 129; Raymond 60, 78
Brace family, 20

Branderberg, Mary, 141
Branding cattle, 133-134
British Columbia, 7
Bronc busters, 57
Brown family 20; Helen, 20, 34, 41; Paul, 34; Frank, 34
Brownie, 54
Buck, 54
Buffalo Hump, 17, 72, 80
Bull Durham, 67
Bull fights, 91-92, 134
Burns, Ore., 230
Burton place, 83, 92
Byrd, Richard, 103

C

Cairo, Ill., 194
Caldwell, Ida., 186
California, 7, 19, 145, 146, 147, 191, 194, 196
Campell, John, 142
Canada, 144
Canadian border, 7
Charley and the Swede, 225-227
Charivari, 170-171
China Rapids, 33, 94
Civet cats, 175
Clark, Mrs. Lucille, 142; George, 142-145
Clark's Fork, 7
Clarkston, WA., 141
Clearwater River, 7, 9, 17, 99, 173; Valley, 97
Clovis, Harry & Mrs., 59, 94, 97, 169, 181; Spence, 94, 96; Nettie, 97
Coal oil, 81
Codfish, 38
Colt revolver, 191
Columbia River, 7, 16
Columbus, Christopher, 103
Cook, Capt., 103
Cortez, Hernando, 103
Cottonwood, Ida., 33, 80, 108, 143, 145; Butte, 79; Creek, 131
Council Bluffs, 7, 196, 197, 198, 200
Country Gentleman, 34

Coyote grade, 99

Coyotes, 60-63

Craig Mountain, 16, 28, 34, 63, 64, 72, 79-88, 92, 94, 99, 100, 132

Craig, Wm., 79

Craigmont, Ida., 10

Critchfield, Dan, 38, 40, 108, 173; Emma, 176, 188

Currier, Aaron, 97; Margaret, 97, 181; Wm., 185; John, 185; Mary, 185; Clara, 186

D

Dakota, 16

Dances, 38-39, 167-169

Daniels, Silent Jim, 201

"Day money," 58

Deer Creek, 15, 16, 17, 19, 20, 22, 25, 26, 27, 28, 29, 33, 35, 49, 53, 56, 61, 63-71, 72, 77, 79, 80, 81, 86, 94, 96, 100, 104, 132, 136, 189, 229; Irrigation system, 19, 20-23, 31, 49; Falls, 64, 79; Mines, 81, 87, 88, 133, 165, 171, 172, 180

DeLeon, Ponce, 103

DeSoto, Hernando, 103

Dorchester, Wesley, 20, 78; Laura, 20, 78; Leonard, 20, 78; Caroline, 20, 78

Doyle, Joe, 181; Marguerite, 181

Drake, Francis, 103

Drury, Dr. C.M., 6, 215

E

Eagle Creek, 34, 56, 78, 100, 108, 178, 187, 188, 189, 190; School, 182-183

Edison, 40

Egypt, 229, 230

Emerick, Chauney, 56; Herscel, 56, 58; Esther Taylor, 130

England, King of, 15

F

Farr, Mr., 165

Ferington, Frank, 141

Fisher, Mrs., 164; Archie, 164; Marjory, 164

Florence, Ida., 17

Footlogs, 28

Ford Model T, 99

Forest, Ida., 34, 54, 60, 72, 80, 81, 94, 95, 96, 98, 99, 108, 164, 165, 168, 169, 171, 179, 180, 182, 184; Hotel, 96, 164; Lodge, 186

Fort (cf. proper names)

Fountain, Ogden, 183; Sarah Mae, 183; Yvonne, 183

Fourth Gulch, 188

Freeburn, Billy, 34, 59, 95, 108, 166, 169, 170, 172, 181, 187, 188; Theodosia, 94, 95, 188; Emma, 188; Jacob, 95, 188, 189; Martha, 184; Cora, 95, 188; Della, 95, 166, 167, 168, 170, 171-172, 188, 189; Earl, 176-177, 181, 182; Mildred Esther, 181, 187; cf. Winifred Spurbeck

Frizzel, Charlie, 170

G

Gehrke, Jack, 181; Ebba, 181

General Land Office, (U.S.), 10

Genesee, Ida., 5, 14, 16, 17, 20, 34, 99, 145, 163, 169, 173, 176, 181, 186, 187, 229, 230

Genesee News, 81

Gibbs Creek, 175, 176

Gilson, Mrs. Stanley, 37; Mrs. Dale Gilson, 37

Glenn, Will, 191-206; George, 202; Miriam, 202, 205, 206; Timothy, 202

Grangeville, Ida., 164

Gray, Zane, 34

Greeley, Horace, 191

Green River, Utah, 230

Ground cherries, 181

Grouse, 92

Gun law, 191, 205

Gunther, Geo., 193, 205-206

Guthrie, Dorothy, 97; Wilder, 97

H

Hall, Fort, 7

Hall, Mr., 175

Hannibal & St. Joseph R.R., 197

Harney Lake, Ore., 19

Harris, Carrie, 16, 30

Hartenges, Mrs., 141

Hatrack, 54, 93, 167

Hawthorn, wild, 67
Hell's Canyon, 9, 15, 86, 229
Herndon, Mather, 195-200
Hiawatha, 34
Hickman, Will, 99, Carrie Mae, 99; Esther, 99; Harriet, 99; John, 99; Marvin, 99; Ormond, 99; Susie, 99
High Desert, Ore., 146
Hines, Duncan, 38
Holden, Tom, 95
Hollingsworth, Scotty, 72
Hollister, Cal., 19, 146, 151
Holly, Chris, 94; Ed, 95
Holy City, The, 40
Homestead Law, 1862, 107, 108
Horseman, Mrs., 177, 181
Horses, 49-60
Horse wrangling, 90
Hosley, Bob, 97; Ellen, 186; Eva, 97; Harvey, 97; Ralph, 97, 186; Timothy, 97, 186
Howerton, Bill, 185; Glen, 185; Lavern, 185; Lavetta, 185
Hudson, Henry, 103
Huett, Albert, 141

I

Icicle Flat, 173
Idaho (State), 6, 8, 9, 15, 31, 72, 86, 87, 104, 142, 145, 187, 190, 229; Miners, 7; Territory, 16, 164, 201; University, 5, 141, 229
Idaho Extension Service, 5
Idaho Queen, 201
Indian, Blackfoot, 143; relics, 74-75; war, 142
Iowa, 16
Iran, 5; land reform, 229

J

Jackman & Long, 19
Jacks, Mrs. B.F., 140, 141; Henry, 141; Jack, 140; Jess, 140, 141; Orrin, 140, 141; Perlie, 140, 141
Jacobson, Kemmie, 95
Jackson family, 20; Lena, 20
Jeeps, 100
Jones, Ada, 40; Louis, 168; Vivian, 20

Jordan Valley, 193, 202, 206
Joseph Plain, 28, 136
Judith Basin, 18
Juliaetta, Ida., 164, 170
Jump, Etta Houghton, 186
Juniper Mt., 192

K

Kane, Inspector, 207-213
Kansas, 19
Kay Bar, 54, 93, 171, 172, 178-179, 184
Keane, Art, 96, 188
Kelly, Alice, 150
Kemp, Billie, 185; Walter, 185
Kennedy, Jim, 72, 166, 168
Kenrick, Ida., 141
Kenyon, Agnes, 97; Jack, 97
Kettenbach, Frank, 143
Kincaid, 195-200
Kincaid, Garret D., 161-162
Kinnikinic, 80
Klamath Reservation, 202
Kootsie (cf. Frances Platt), 25-31
Korea, South, 5, 13, 229

L

LaFollett, Mr., 18
Lambert, Jim, 142; Ellis, 170
Land Claims, Patented, 108-117; names of recipients, 119-128
Landing, C., 141
Land Office, 104
Lapwai Creek, 7; Lapwai, Ida., 79
Latah County Museum, 5, 230
Lawrence, Kansas, 18, 145
Legends, 139-162
Lemars, Iowa, 16
Lemon, Ernest, 58; John, 184; Walter, 56
Lewis & Clark, 7, 103
Lewis, Charlotte, 151; Mrs. Will (Jennie), 19, 145, 147, 148, 161; Jesse, 145, 146; J. Lewis, 151
Lewiston, Ida., 8, 73, 79, 88, 141, 142, 145, 182; Normal School, 34, 182
Lewistown, Mont., 145, 154
Lister, Capt., 194-197
Little Potlatch Canyon, 170
Lloyd Bros., 143
Lolo Trail, 7

Lorang, Mrs. Joe, 171; Julia, 97; Olivia, 97; Ray, 97; Vincent, 63, 81, 97, 180
Louisville, Kentucky, 194

M

McCormack, Jack, 40, 143
McCoy, Sylvia, 171, 188; Nora, 188
McLaughlin, Dr., 181
McMahon, Bill, 20, 66, 108; Jesse, Katherine, Willie, 20, 66
McPherson, Brady, 201
Magellan, Ferdinand, 103
Magpies, 24, 69
Maine, 103
Malheur country, 193
Mandan, 196, 199, 200, 206
Mange mite, 62
Manners, Charlie, 193, 205-206
Mason Butte, 79
Maud, 54
Maynard, Thad, 94, 96
Medicare, 177-178
Merrill, Fred, 56
Mexico, 51
Miller, Frank, 58; John, 95
Mineral Point, Wis., 16
Miners, 33
Minnesota, University of, 5
Mississippi Valley, 108, 194
Missouri River, 194, 206
Modoc Indians, 202-204
Moffett, Amy, 179; Carson, 56, 86, 133, 165, 171; James, 190
Moffit, Jimmy, 167, 168
Molasses, blackstrap, 33
Montana, 7, 18, 147, 191
Moscow, Ida., 5, 141, 187, 229
Mounce, Lafe, 142, 143; Junior, 143
Murdick, Roy, 73; Eva, 73

N

Nails, rusty, 68
Nash family, 20
Nelson, Alice, 34; Eddie, 59; Horace, 143; J.P., 188
New Meadows, 72
Newton, Frank, 185
New York, 191

Nez Perce country, 142; Indians, 7, 32, 145, 216; language, 79; reservation, 9, 16, 216; wars, 16, 72
Northern Pacific R.R., 72

O

Oakland auto, 97
Oddfellows Lodge, 97
Olympic Peninsula, 217; National Park, 217
Omaha, Neb., 16
Oregon, 7, 19, 142, 187, 191, 194
Oregon Desert, The, 19
Oregon Trail, 7, 19, 191
Organ, 41, 173
Orofino Creek, 7, 17
Orr, Weldon, 188; Cora, 188
Orth, Rev., 170
Owyhee River, 192, 193, 205; mountains, 201

P

Pacific Ocean, 79
Packing, 51-53, 81; packstring, 52, 96
Palouse Country, 8, 16, 161, 162, 229
Patton, "Red" Walter, 56, 58, 59
Peary, Robert, 103
Pendleton, Ore., 19, 58
Persians, 51
Phonograph (Edison), 40
Pierce, Capt. Elias, 7
Pine Grove School District, 187
Pittsburg, Pa., 191, 194
Platt brand, 133
Platt family, Edw. Jesse (Tom), 25, 34, 54, 63, 64, 78, 83, 90, 92, 99, 133, 136, 165, 166, 176, 188; Edw. T., 16, 25, 108, 130; Emma Batdorf, 18, 19, 30, 34, 66, 96, 151, 188; Frances (Kootsie), 25, 30, 34, 61, 62, 63, 78, 83, 93, 96, 136, 166, 188; Jack, 25, 30, 62, 93; Kenneth B., 5-6, 8 ftn., 10, 14, 96, 108, 161, 188, 229-230; Jeanette, 229; John A., 14, 16-18, 19, 22, 65, 96, 108, 132, 135, 136, 137, 142, 145, 146, 163, 229; Lorene, 25, 30, 37, 62, 83, 96, 166, 188; Mary, 25, 30, 34, 62, 78, 83, 96, 136, 176, 188; William T., 129, 168

Portland, Ore., 15, 72
Potlatch River, 17
Pruitt, "Red," 58

Q

Queen Anne school, 181

R

Radley, Dewitt, 97; Donald, 97; Mrs. Doug, 97; Lillian, 97, 181; Lionell, 97
Raeder, Cody, 133
Railroad, Idaho, 72
Range, kitchen, 76
Rattlesnakes, 73, 75-76, 174, 179
Rebekah Lodge, 186; assembly, 186
Reed, Jimmy, 95
Reeves, Alice, 34, 184; Mrs. Ben, 34; Lorene, 34, 184
Rencehousen, Clyde, 23, 72
Reo auto, 99
Rice, Mrs., 140
Riggins, Ida., 9
Ringer, Len, 56, 58
River of no Return, 8, 9, 31
Robinson Crusoe, 73
Robinson, Yank, 133
Rock rolling, 73-74
Rocky Mountains, 191
Rodeos, 58
Ross, Billy, 173; Esther, 173; Mrs. Ralph, 62, 81, 86, 173, 188; Tommy, 62
Roundups, 58-59
Rudolph, Forest Bud, 183; Louise, 183; Mike, 78; Mrs., 177, 182
Rural Women's History Project, 141

S

Sacramento Valley, 151
St. Joseph, Mo., 196
St. Louis, Mo., 191, 194, 195, 196, 197
Salem, Ore., 173
Salmon River Country, 6, 7, 14, 15, 16, 17, 49, 52, 55, 56, 60, 71-80, 81, 86, 96, 103, 104, 108, 162, 163, 169, 172, 182, 186, 187, 229; River, 7, 8 ftn., 9, 14, 15, 18, 19, 20, 22, 24, 25, 26, 28, 31-33, 63, 79, 92, 99, 100, 132, 146, 167, 168; Little Salmon River, 72

Salt Lake City, Ut., 72
Sands, Jim, 95
San Francisco, Cal., 16
San Jose, Cal., 151, 152
Santa Monica, Cal., 142
Satan, 54
Scovel, Grace, 150
Seattle, WA., 181, 187
Seven Devils Mountains, 86-87
Shasta, Mount, 19
Shears, Carl, 10; Duane, 6, 10; Mrs. Edna Weller, 10
"Shorty," 68
Silver City, Ida., 201, 202, 205
Skeleton Gulch, 19, 78, 130, 136
Skunks, 69
Slate Creek, 63
Smoking, 67
Snakes, 75, 145
Snake River, 9, 15, 16, 17, 24, 63, 71, 79, 143, 145, 146, 229; Indians, 7; Plains, 7
Solomon, King, 14
Sorrel, 54
Sotherland, Jack, 141
Southern Pacific RR., 16
Southwick, Ida., 140
Spalding city, 99, 173; park, 137
Spalding, Rev. H.H., 7, 79
Spanish, 51
Spencer, Len, 40
Spokane, WA., 8, 72
Spurbeck, "Winnie," 34, 162-187, 172, 180, 187; Dave, 171; Earl, 176, 179; Marguerite, 173, 181; Marguerite Della, 179, 182, 183; Marian Isabella, 187; Pearl, 181; Rollin, 170
Squaw Butte Ranger Station, 230
Stackpole, Frank, 133
Stareout Mountain, 15, 27, 33
Star Ranch, 193
Starr family, 81, 184
Stevens Brothers, 94
Stock salting, 91
Sundown, Jackson, 58

T

Taylor, Elmer, 20, 39, 56, 72, 73; Esther, 130; Stillman, 131; Mrs. T., 131; B.F. Taylor, 131; Zachary, 73

Tammany country, 142
Tehran, Iran, 229
Toledo Blade, 81
Toumy, Dr., 176
Township patterns, 106-107
Truckiset, Agnes, 185; Helen, 186; Isobel, 185; Katie, 185; Steve, 185

U

Uncle Josh, 40
U.S. Agency for International Development, 13; Bureau of Land Management, 5, 229; State Department, 5, 229
U.S. Highway 95, 9
Union District, 163
Union Pacific R.R., 72

V

Vallem, Cora Ross, 177, 181; Robt., 56, 108
Van Pool family, 20; Herman, 58
Verzanni, Ernest, 86, 180
Vespucci, Amerigo, 103
Von Humboldt, 103

W

Wapshela Point, 22, 49
War Eagle Mt., 205
Washington State, 187, 217; University, 181
Wayne, Gilbert, 58
Weiners, brined, 38
Weiser River, 72; City, 72, 184
Weller, Harry, 56, 59, 81, 88, 94, 96, 165, 168, 173, 180, 182, 186, 188, 190; Edna, 183, 185; Harold, 183, 185; Mildred, 181, 188
Werhan, Anna, 185
West, American, 58, 139, 191, 216; Code of, 192
Wetaskin, Alberta, 20
Whiffenpoof Song, 14
"Whistling Rufus,", 40
Whitebird Creek, 9, 63, 73, 103, 108, 167
"White Owls," 173
Wickham, Hawley, 142
Wickiup camp, 137
Wildfire, 34
Wilkes, Willie, 59
Willamette Valley, 7
Winchester, Ida., 54, 80, 97, 164, 169, 171, 181, 186, 229; Inn, 164, 169; Lake, 169; rifle, 191-192
Winter of 1914-15, 24
Winters, Jud, 193
Wisconsin, 16
Wohlen, Paul, 59
Wood supplies, 78-79, 92
Woods, Frank, 58; May, 97; Ted, 97
Wolf, Billy, 95
Worhan family, 81
Wyeth family, 81; Beulah, 97

Y

Yellow Rose School District, 163
Yellowstone Park, 19, 145

Z

Zig Zag Trail, 180, 181